In the Hegemon's Shadow

A VOLUME IN THE SERIES

Cornell Studies in Security Affairs

edited by Robert J. Art, Robert Jervis, and Stephen M. Walt

A list of titles in this series is available at www.cornellpress.cornell.edu.

In the Hegemon's Shadow

Leading States and the Rise of Regional Powers

EVAN BRADEN MONTGOMERY

Cornell University Press

Ithaca and London

First published 2016 by Cornell University Press

Printed in the United States of America

Library of Congress Cataloging-in-Publication Data
Montgomery, Evan Braden, author.
   In the Hegemon's shadow : leading states and the rise of regional powers / Evan Braden Montgomery.
        pages cm
   Includes bibliographical references and index.
   ISBN 978-1-5017-0234-1 (cloth : alk. paper)   1. Hegemony.
2. Great powers—Foreign relations.   3. Great powers—History—
19th century.   4. Great powers—History—20th century.   I. Title.
   JZ1312.M66 2016
   327.1'14—dc23

                                                    2015034158

Cornell University Press strives to use environmentally responsible suppliers and materials to the fullest extent possible in the publishing of its books. Such materials include vegetable-based, low-VOC inks and acid-free papers that are recycled, totally chlorine-free, or partly composed of nonwood fibers. For further information, visit our website at www.cornellpress.cornell.edu.

Cloth printing   10 9 8 7 6 5 4 3 2 1

To Lillian

Contents

Acknowledgments

I suspect that I might have fewer debts than many other authors. Nevertheless, those that I have incurred over the years run incredibly deep. Although I am undoubtedly biased, in my view the University of Virginia has no rival when it comes to studying international relations theory, diplomatic history, and the intersection between the two. That is thanks to faculty members such as Dale Copeland, Melvyn Leffler, Jeffrey Legro, Allen Lynch, and William Quandt. Each of them had a significant influence on this book, even though not all of them were directly involved. John Owen deserves special mention for his help along the way. He has always been generous with his time and advice, not only when I first tried to get this project off the ground but also later as I worked to bring it to a close.

The Center for Strategic and Budgetary Assessments has been my home for close to a decade and embodies the best characteristics of a think tank: it is a place to ponder big issues, challenge the status quo, conduct in-depth research, and constantly learn from colleagues. My thanks to all of them, past and present, for making it a stimulating place to work, but most of all to Eric Edelman, Andrew Krepinevich, and Jim Thomas for their guidance, and to Brendan Cooley and Zack Cooper for sharing their thoughts on the theory chapter as I worked my way through revisions. At Cornell University Press, Robert Jervis and an anonymous reviewer provided detailed and constructive comments on the manuscript. When both of them zeroed in on the same issue, it was clear that there was still work to be done, but the end result was worth the effort. The manuscript would have never received their careful attention if not for Roger Haydon, and I truly appreciate his enthusiasm for the project. I also benefited from the expert work of Ange Romeo-Hall, Kathryn Moyer, and Mary Ribesky, who guided the book through the production process, as well as Kay Banning, who compiled the index. Of course, financial support makes the difficult task of writing a book much easier, and I am grateful to the Smith Richardson Foundation for a Strategy and Policy Fellowship that allowed me to complete the first draft.

Not surprisingly, my deepest debts are on the home front. My parents, Braden and Helen Montgomery, have been a constant source of encouragement and a reliable pair of proofreaders, while my father-in-law, Steve Pettyjohn, tolerated many questions about the American Civil War with good humor. No one deserves a bigger thank-you than Stacie, however, for her moral support as well as her substantive feedback. She is a wonderful spouse, an extraordinary colleague, and the benevolent hegemon of our household.

Introduction

The Puzzle of Regional Power Shifts

In January 2015, President Barack Obama traveled to India. This was his second trip to the world's largest democracy, which none of his predecessors had visited more than once and some had never visited at all. He was also the guest of honor at the annual parade celebrating its constitution, which no U.S. head of state had ever attended. "I realize that the sight of an American President as your chief guest on Republic Day would have once seemed unimaginable," he remarked. "But my visit reflects the possibilities of a new moment." Although Washington and New Delhi had often found themselves at odds in the past, recent U.S. administrations had taken a number of steps to overcome this antagonistic legacy, most notably spearheading a unique arrangement that legitimized India's status as a nuclear-weapons state even though it was not a signatory to the Non-Proliferation Treaty. Obama's historic trip was the perfect opportunity to build on this foundation and forge closer ties. During a joint press conference with his counterpart, Prime Minister Narendra Modi, the president declared that "a strong relationship with India is critical for America's success in the 21st century." In his view, the two countries were "natural partners."[1]

Not long after Obama returned from the subcontinent, U.S. relations with Iran were capturing headlines around the globe. As part of the "P5+1" group (the five permanent members of the United Nations Security Council plus Germany), the United States was trying to reach an agreement with its long-time adversary to impose strict limits on the Iranian nuclear program in exchange for relief from crippling economic sanctions, which had brought Tehran to the bargaining table. Most U.S. policymakers, including the president, believed that allowing Iran to join the nuclear club would have disastrous consequences and therefore that force might be necessary to avoid this outcome. "A nuclear-armed Iran would raise the risk of nuclear terrorism," Obama had explained two years earlier. "It would undermine the non-proliferation regime. It would spark an arms race in a volatile region. And

1

it would embolden a government that has shown no respect for the rights of its own people or the responsibilities of nations."[2] Negotiations finally appeared to be making progress, however, and by July the parties settled on the terms of an accord. As he rallied support for a diplomatic solution and responded to critics who believed that the deal was too lenient, the president repeated his previous warnings and reaffirmed the need to prevent Iran from acquiring nuclear weapons. He also cautioned that although the agreement could achieve this goal, it would not resolve the underlying sources of tension between the two nations. "We have no illusions about the Iranian government," he argued, which was still a threat to American interests and a source of instability across the Middle East.[3]

U.S. efforts to court India and counter Iran have little in common at first glance, aside from being prominent items on Washington's foreign policy agenda. Yet they do highlight an important issue, namely, how the leading state in the international system responds to rising regional powers (RRPs): actors that are not yet and might never become great powers but that are increasing their strength, extending their influence, and potentially reordering their corner of the world. To date, this issue has been almost entirely overlooked in the scholarly literature, even though the relationship between established powers and emerging powers is one of the most important topics in international politics and despite the fact that U.S. policymakers now face rising powers in multiple regions.[4]

In general, leading states—great powers that occupy a unique position thanks to the sources of their wealth, the types of armed forces they build, and the responsibilities they assume—have a straightforward decision to make when a capable and ambitious actor appears on the scene. On the one hand, they can opt for accommodation and accept the redistribution of power that is taking place. On the other hand, they can choose opposition and resist any significant changes to the status quo. Although there is a large body of work that tries to explain how a leading state weighs these alternatives when it confronts a new peer competitor, particularly an aspiring hegemon on the European continent, few studies consider how it reacts when a rising power in the periphery challenges the prevailing regional order. A quick glance at the historical record reveals that this situation is not uncommon, however, and that leading states have adopted a variety of policies toward RRPs in the past.[5]

Great Britain, for example, was preoccupied with shifting distributions of power outside Europe during the nineteenth century, when it dominated global commerce while its navy ruled the waves. In the 1830s, the entire Middle East was in turmoil as the Ottoman province of Egypt defeated its nominal sovereign on the battlefield and carved out an empire stretching from the Sudan to the Levant. Then, in the 1860s, North America reached a turning point as the Confederacy broke away from the United States and divided the continent between two bitter rivals. Finally, in the 1890s, Japan

launched a successful war against the much larger Chinese Empire, upend-
ing the traditional order in East Asia. As these events unfolded, Great Britain
sought to check Egypt's expansion and reverse its territorial gains; it
maintained a policy of neutrality in the American Civil War that enabled the
Union to subdue the Confederacy; and it pursued a more benevolent form
of neutrality during the Sino-Japanese War, one that favored Japan and fore-
shadowed a military alliance between London and Tokyo.

Like its predecessor across the Atlantic, the United States has navigated a
number of power shifts in peripheral regions since it emerged from the Second World War with unprecedented economic and military advantages.
In South Asia, for instance, India fought a pair of conflicts against Pakistan
that had the potential to reorder the subcontinent. When these two neighbors clashed in 1965, the United States withheld military aid to both sides,
notwithstanding its recent efforts to make India a strategic partner against
communist China. When India and Pakistan went to war again in 1971, however, Washington sided with Islamabad, especially after New Delhi launched
a military intervention that divided its opponent in two. The distribution of
power was even more unsettled in Southwest Asia between 1979 and 1991
due to a series of developments, including the Iranian revolution, the Iran-
Iraq War, and the Iraqi invasion of Kuwait. Moreover, U.S. policy toward
the main actors in the region varied sharply during this long period of upheaval. Although the United States supported Baghdad during its confrontation with Tehran, it later conducted a massive military operation that restored Kuwait's sovereignty and decimated Iraq's armed forces.

All of these conflicts prompted high-level debates within the leading state
over its core interests in the area, the chief threats to those interests, and the
role of regional powers in its grand strategy. Many led to diplomatic or military intervention. Some even influenced patterns of cooperation and competition among the great powers. To date, however, no study has examined these
cases collectively or explored the issues that they raise. This book attempts
to fill that gap. In the chapters that follow, I develop and test an argument
that explains why leading states have accommodated some RRPs and opposed others, especially when local power shifts have led to war.[6] This argument emphasizes the interaction between two key factors—the type of regional
order that a leading state prefers and the type of power shift that it believes
is taking place—to shed light on an interesting historical puzzle. It also provides insights into problems that are likely to become more important over
time, especially as the United States enters an era characterized by "the rise
of the rest."[7]

The Relevance of Rising Regional Powers

From Thucydides's historic account of the Peloponnesian War to contemporary debates over the consequences of China's rise, managing the emergence of new powers has always been a central issue in the study of international relations. That seems unlikely to change anytime soon. According to a report by the National Intelligence Council, shifting distributions of power will shape the world of 2030 in a variety of ways. The United States, it predicted, will lose ground relative to nations such as China, even though it will remain in a class by itself compared with aspiring peers. At the same time, India will begin to shrink the capability gap with its neighbor to the north, especially if China's economic growth continues to slow down. In Europe, both Germany and Russia are likely to experience decline thanks to unfavorable demographic trends. Meanwhile, Brazil will cement its dominant position in Latin America just as power transitions are reordering Africa and Southeast Asia.[8]

Given the significance of power shifts, not just globally but locally as well, why has the reaction of leading states to RRPs received so little attention?[9] This empirical and theoretical gap has deep roots. Over the past five centuries, international politics has been nearly synonymous with great power politics: the rise and decline of the world's strongest nations, the recurring bids for world dominance by expansionist empires, and the Cold War competition between the United States and the Soviet Union. For realist scholars in particular, nations that have not achieved great power status cannot alter the underlying structure of the international system and therefore merit only passing attention. In the words of Kenneth Waltz, "the story" of international relations "is written in terms of the great powers of an era."[10] Yet this perspective underestimates the importance of regional powers, as well as the significance of great power–regional power interactions.

For example, some regional powers can become great powers over time.[11] Consider the gradual evolution of the United States into a global hegemon or the comparatively rapid transformation of Japan into a massive empire that dominated almost all of Asia. More recently, China has overcome decades of domestic turmoil to surpass its neighbors in most indicators of material power and is now on pace to overtake the United States as the world's largest economy sometime in the near future. Looking further ahead, India also has the potential to become a great power one day, especially if it can harness its resources, manage its internal challenges, and play a larger role on the international stage.

The rise of regional powers does not occur in a vacuum, however, because great powers often hold the fate of weaker actors in their hands. Until the twentieth century, when the United States became a key player in the continental distribution of power, Europe was an "autonomous" region. That is, local nations could not look to outside parties for meaningful support and did not need to worry that extraregional powers might obstruct their rise. As one study notes, however, "the same cannot be said of most regional systems operating in the shadows of external great powers."[12] Over and over again, the world's strongest nations have influenced distributions of power in North America, East Asia, the Middle East, and elsewhere, sometimes through their actions (for example, by intervening in local conflicts) and sometimes through their inaction (namely, by allowing events to unfold without interference). These decisions can have enormous ramifications over the long run, even if policymakers do not always appreciate it at the time. For instance, imagine the impact on international politics if Great Britain had sided with the Confederacy during the American Civil War, potentially leading to the permanent dissolution of the United States.

Of course, not all regional powers have what it takes to become a pole in the global order. Even still, they are often "pivotal states" that determine the stability and security of their own neighborhoods.[13] Thus, they can find themselves in the crosshairs of great powers that are looking to protect their interests, preserve their influence, or improve their position relative to other outside actors.[14] This is especially true when the local distribution of power is in flux and a conflict breaks out. If a rising power in a peripheral region challenges the status quo, then great powers in general and the leading state in particular must decide how to respond—a choice that can determine the future of that region and, in some cases, the international system as a whole.

Realist Theories and the Rise of Regional Powers

Although only a handful of studies try to explain why established great powers accommodate or oppose emerging regional powers, there is no shortage of research looking at how they manage the rise of peer competitors, most of which can be found within the realist camp.[15] Notwithstanding their many similarities, different versions of realism stake out contrasting positions on a number of core issues, such as whether the ordering principle of international politics is anarchy or hierarchy and whether parity between nations is a deterrent to conflict or a necessary condition for war. Thus, the two main schools of realist theory—balance-of-power realism and preponderance-of-power realism—highlight a number of factors that influence how great powers react when global power shifts occur. While some of these factors can be identified during regional power shifts as well, at best they offer only partial explanations for how leading states respond.[16]

For instance, many balance-of-power realists emphasize perceptions of intent because they can influence the severity of the security dilemma: the situation in which one side's defensive measures frighten others, heighten tensions, and increase the likelihood of war.[17] From this perspective, established powers should accommodate emerging powers unless and until the latter demonstrate their hostility, in the hope of avoiding unnecessary spirals of conflict and starting virtuous cycles of cooperation.[18] This argument encounters a pair of problems, however, and not simply because intentions are hard to discern and can change over time.[19] First, although a leading state should obviously oppose an RRP that represents an unambiguous danger to its interests, this situation is likely to be rare. The single greatest constraint on the emergence of any new power is the possibility that its actions will trigger counterbalancing behavior or perhaps a preventive attack. This concern looms even larger for regional powers than great powers because the former are much more vulnerable than the latter. Thus, they have significant incentives to reassure stronger actors regardless of their true aims. As a result, these efforts will not be very credible and are unlikely to have a significant influence on the calculations of leading states, at least on their own.[20] Second, even if an RRP is clearly an aggressive actor, a leading state could still choose to accommodate it for a number of reasons. For instance, an aggressive RRP might be the best available partner against an even bigger threat, such as a hostile great power that is bent on expansion. Alternatively, a leading state might not like the status quo that an RRP is trying to change. In short, its tolerance for revisionist behavior in the periphery can vary.

By contrast, preponderance-of-power realists stress that relative power trends shape foreign policy. Consequently, they suggest that decline vis-à-vis new challengers can drive leading states to accommodate RRPs. According to Robert Gilpin, the preferred strategy for a dominant nation that is watching its position erode "is to eliminate the source of the problem" by fighting a war while it still retains an advantage. Yet he and others have noted that relative decline can result in retrenchment instead, as a leading state tries to reduce its extensive commitments and conserve its dwindling resources.[21] If so, this suggests that leading states should be inclined to engage RRPs, not only to avoid the costs of keeping them down, but hopefully to share the burdens of managing international order as well. There are two limitations with this line of argument, however. First, while relative decline might provide an added incentive for leading states to rely on local actors in some cases, the former often depend on the latter to help protect their interests, even when their relative power advantage is not in jeopardy. Simply put, burden sharing is not restricted to periods of sharp decline because even the strongest nations cannot be everywhere at once or do everything on their own. Second, if a leading state does require the help of a local actor, there is no guarantee it will choose a rising power over a declining one, especially if it wants to keep the local status quo intact. Although the former might be more capable, the latter might be more likely to enforce that status quo than to overturn it.

Finally, both versions of realism hint that an emerging power's impact on the existing regional order is the key to understanding how a leading state will respond, although they hold opposing points of view.[22] For instance, balance-of-power realism suggests that leading states should favor parity in peripheral regions and therefore should oppose any nations that try to achieve primacy. Local hegemons represent a direct threat from this perspective because the absence of nearby counterweights leaves them free to cause trouble abroad.[23] Alternatively, preponderance-of-power realism suggests that leading states should favor primacy in peripheral regions and therefore should oppose any nations that try to establish parity. Just as a global hegemon is uniquely capable of contributing to international stability, a local hegemon can play a similar and complementary role within its own neighborhood.[24] Yet both of these arguments are incomplete because leading states have supported regional parity in some cases and regional primacy in others.[25] Moreover, neither version of realism explains the competing incentives that leading states face or the conditions under which they will prefer one form of order to the other. For balance-of-power realists, a local hegemon represents a future competitor. But it could also be a useful frontline ally against great power rivals that are attempting to expand. For preponderance-of-power realists, a local hegemon represents a barrier to disruptive conflicts. Yet it also has the potential to withhold valuable resources, impede transit through its region, and restrict the flow of commerce.

To extend these arguments and address their limitations, I develop a new theory that borrows insights from both schools of realism and brings them together in a logically consistent framework. This theory is built on two core observations. First, leading states do not view all peripheral regions in the same way. Rather, they can have different preferences over local distributions of power based on the risks that concern them most. Second, leading states do not view all power shifts in the same way, either. Instead, they often focus their attention on certain characteristics of a power shift to forecast the likely outcome, assess the impact on their interests, and decide what strategy to adopt toward an RRP. The characteristics they emphasize, however, will depend on the regional order they prefer.

Theory and Evidence in the Study of Rising Regional Powers

Established powers can respond to emerging powers in a number of ways. According to Randall Schweller, the former have adopted at least six distinct approaches toward the latter in the past. At one end of the spectrum, they have embraced engagement to try to avoid any conflict. At the other end of the spectrum, they have launched preventive wars to try to stop looming threats in their tracks. Between these extremes, established powers have also attempted to bind emerging powers to international norms and institutions; they have bandwagoned in the hope of profiting from any changes to the status quo; they have resorted to internal and external balancing to keep the

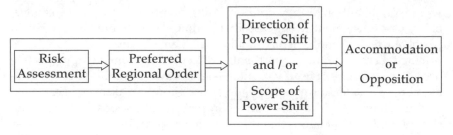

Figure 1. The causal argument

status quo intact; and they have passed the buck so that others might balance for them.[26] Nevertheless, all of the measures available to established powers can be placed in two broad categories: strategies of accommodation and strategies of opposition. This distinction simplifies a complex phenomenon and captures the fact that almost any option, even neutrality, usually helps or hinders an emerging power's rise, depending on the circumstances.[27] It also has another virtue when it comes to addressing the empirical puzzle at the center of this book: using a binary dependent variable allows me to show how the same causal factors account for leading state responses to RRPs across a diverse set of cases, even if accommodation and opposition took a variety of forms.[28]

To explain how leading states choose between these strategies, I develop a two-step argument, the basic outlines of which are summarized in figure 1. The first step is to establish whether policymakers have a preferred regional order and, if so, whether they favor local parity or local primacy. I argue that these preferences can be traced back to their assessment of certain risks, in particular the risk that local actors might withhold valuable resources or keep outside powers away, which I refer to as *access denial*, along with the risk that outside powers could gain control of the area, which I refer to as *containment failure*. When both of these risks are low, a leading state should be impartial between parity and primacy because its only major interest will be avoiding instability, and either distribution of power can deter regional conflicts, at least in principle. When access denial is a leading state's overriding concern, however, it should prefer parity because a preponderant local power is the most significant threat to access, and the presence of two or more relatively equal actors can prevent regional domination. Finally, when containment failure is a leading state's main fear, it should prefer primacy instead because military conquest is the worst form of failure, and a dominant local actor is a better obstacle to regional intervention than a handful of weaker nations.

A leading state's preferred regional order provides a baseline for its evaluation of local power shifts. The second step, therefore, is to understand what outcome policymakers expect when a change in the distribution of power occurs and, just as important, whether that outcome is compatible with their preferences. How do they make these judgments and decide on a strategy? I argue that policymakers will focus on different aspects of a power shift at different times. When they are impartial between parity and primacy, they will want to know whether an RRP can create a durable local order, irrespective of which order it is striving to create. In this case, therefore, they will look at the *scope* of a power shift. When they prefer parity, however, they will want to determine whether an RRP is trying to prevent its rival from dominating the area or is attempting to become a local hegemon itself, regardless of whether it ultimately succeeds. In this instance, then, they will look at the *direction* of a power shift. Finally, when they prefer primacy, they will want to assess whether an RRP can surpass its neighbors and sustain that advantage. As a result, they will take both of these dimensions into account.

To illustrate and test these arguments, I employ qualitative case studies that track how leading states in different historical eras have responded to RRPs across the globe. In each of the cases examined in this book, I draw on evidence from the relevant secondary literature as well as primary sources such as media reports, memoir accounts, oral histories, government documents, and the private correspondence of senior officials, all of which are used to recreate the decision-making process and see if my theoretical expectations are confirmed. This type of approach is warranted for a number of reasons. First, although significant shifts in local distributions of power are more common than major changes in the global distribution of power, which are especially rare, they do not occur frequently. Hence, the universe of cases is quite small and not well suited for quantitative analysis. Second, while my arguments would be undermined if there were a mismatch between expected and observed outcomes, even accurate predictions would yield only partial support for the theory. Ultimately, process tracing is still required to determine whether the causal factors I emphasize were present and had the effects that I hypothesize.[29] Third, because similar policies can be interpreted in different ways depending on the specific context, case studies are needed to overcome any ambiguities surrounding the dependent variable. In particular, they can be used to determine what the absence of intervention truly means. Finally, understanding how individual policymakers assess risks, form preferences, and evaluate changes in the distribution of power requires examining their perceptions—and that calls for a close look at the historical record. For instance, some policymakers might interpret events differently from their colleagues, not because they are irrational, but because they bring different prior beliefs to the table. They might even reach conclusions that appear off the mark in retrospect, not because they are prone to misperceptions, but rather because they do not have the luxury of concentrating on a single issue, are often expected to reach decisions quickly, and must act under conditions of imperfect information. A qualitative research strategy is particularly useful for capturing and contextualizing these dynamics.[30]

How Leading States Respond to Rising Regional Powers

The rise of regional powers can have significant consequences, not just locally but globally as well, because great powers often have a stake in the outcome. This is especially true for leading states: great powers that stand apart in a number of respects, from their emphasis on overseas commerce to their unparalleled military reach, and use these advantages to provide collective goods that others cannot and shape the international system in lasting ways.[1] During the nineteenth century, for example, Great Britain enjoyed the status of first among equals in a multipolar world. Not only did it organize coalitions against aspiring hegemons, but it also patrolled the high seas and promoted open markets abroad. The United States has played a similar role during the bipolar and unipolar eras of the past seven decades, albeit on a much larger scale. In addition to preventing a hostile actor from dominating Eurasia, it has guaranteed freedom of the commons, extended deterrence to dozens of nations, provided a stable reserve currency, and helped build a network of economic and security institutions.[2] With such extensive interests and diverse responsibilities, leading states rarely turn a blind eye to power shifts in peripheral regions. In fact, they often become involved in some form or another, and even when they do not, the absence of their involvement can still impact the course of events. Yet they have adopted very different strategies when these changes have occurred. The purpose of this chapter is to explain this puzzle.

At its core, the theory developed below comes down to a pair of issues, namely, the type of regional order that a leading state prefers and the type of power shift that appears to be taking place. The first reflects a leading state's overarching interest in a peripheral region and serves as the baseline for its evaluation of any changes in the status quo. Would it like to see a balance of power rather than a preponderance of power? Does it actually favor primacy over parity? Or is it impartial between these two alternatives?[3] The second indicates how a local power shift is likely to unfold. In particular, which regional order is an emerging power trying to create, and does a leading state believe that it will succeed? Ultimately, I show how the interaction between a leading state's preferences and its expectations can account for the decision to accommodate or oppose RRPs across a range of cases.

The main arguments can be summarized briefly. If a leading state has little reason to fear the takeover of a peripheral region by a local actor or an outside power, then it should not have a strong preference when it comes to the type of order that exists there. In principle, both parity and primacy can prevent disruptive conflicts, the avoidance of which will be its chief objective in these circumstances. Therefore, a leading state should accommodate RRPs that can achieve either one because they will enhance local stability over the long run. Conversely, it should oppose RRPs that fall short of this threshold because their rise will contribute to persistent unrest. If a leading state is worried mainly that a local actor might dominate a peripheral region, however, then it will prefer parity to ensure that its own access to the area is not jeopardized. In this case, it should accommodate RRPs that are attempting to weaken local hegemons and oppose RRPs that are trying to gain control over their neighborhoods. Finally, if a leading state is more concerned about an outside power conquering a peripheral region, then it will prefer primacy instead because the strongest local actors are the best barriers to intervention. Thus, it should accommodate RRPs that fully overtake their rivals and oppose RRPs that fail to do so.

Leading States and Regional Orders

As John Ikenberry has argued, "The central problem of international relations is the problem of order—how it is devised, how it breaks down, and how it is recreated."[4] International order refers to the underlying norms and rules that govern relations between states and has traditionally been reducible to certain distributions of material power, namely, a balance of power or a preponderance of power.[5] At the global level, the world's strongest nations can establish equilibrium as they try to prevent each other from overwhelming the rest, or a single actor can achieve a position of dominance, particularly if it is able to win a major war against its rivals or exhaust its opponents in peacetime competitions. At the local level, geographic subsystems can be characterized by parity or primacy as well.[6] The difference, though, is that these subsystems are rarely free from outside interference. Instead, great powers can promote regional powers through various forms of assistance or undermine them through various forms of coercion. As a result, they often have a say in the type of order that exists. Moreover, thanks to their considerable wealth and military reach, leading states arguably have the biggest say of all.[7] How, then, do they wield their influence over local actors? The first step toward answering this question is to recognize that leading states can have very different preferences over regional distributions of power, which will frame their options when RRPs challenge the status quo and local conflicts break out. Specifically, a leading state might favor parity in some situations and primacy in others. It could also be willing to accept them both. I argue that these preferences will depend on how leading states assess the two main risks they face in peripheral regions: the risk of access denial and the risk of containment failure.

ACCESS DENIAL AND CONTAINMENT FAILURE IN THE PERIPHERY

Just like their competitors, leading states want to avoid any decrement in their relative power, which underpins their advantageous position in the international system. They also want to keep their reputations for responsibility and resolve intact. These objectives require preserving their ability to use overseas assets and preventing them from falling into the hands of their rivals. Given their global interests, leading states depend on economic markets and military bases located throughout the world. They also need the freedom to navigate distant lines of communication without interference and often have obligations to ensure that others can as well. At the same time, leading states worry about expansion on the part of their adversaries, especially their major power adversaries, because it could provide them with raw materials that will fuel their growth, give them control over strategically important territory, or create fears of a domino effect by demonstrating that they cannot be deterred.[8] The risk of access denial, therefore, refers to a local actor withholding indigenous resources or restricting the presence of outside powers within its neighborhood, in particular by refusing to export commodities, impeding passage through the area, charging higher rents to host foreign troops, or evicting those forces and barring their return. By contrast, the risk of containment failure refers to an outside power subjugating a peripheral region, either in whole or in part.

Both of these risks can come in a variety of forms, some of which are more extensive and more enduring than others and therefore will have an outsized impact on a leading state's calculations. For instance, because certain nations happen to own critical resources or control valuable terrain, they can always attempt to withhold what they already possess. In other words, some risk of access denial is almost inevitable in many situations. If a local actor were able to monopolize key resources in its vicinity, increase its relative power, and eclipse its neighbors, however, then it could potentially limit access to the entire region and might even be capable of keeping stronger nations at bay. Likewise, an outside power can extend its grasp in different ways, such as establishing spheres of influence through bribery or subversion, creating client states by providing security guarantees, and launching invasions to conquer foreign territory. Unless they want to cede an advantage to their rivals, leading states cannot afford to ignore any of these possibilities in regions that matter. The prospect of an invasion is much more serious than the alternatives, though, because it could lead to direct control over local assets and a permanent presence in the area.

In sum, as they gauge the risks of access denial and containment failure in a peripheral region, leading states will emphasize scenarios that could have the most detrimental impact on their interests, namely, local domination and external military intervention. Thus, they will take into account several factors, including the overall significance of a subsystem, the inherent vulnerability of any assets located there, and, perhaps most important in many cases, the level of threat from revisionist actors. For example, the risk of access denial should be highest when a leading state relies on indigenous resources to sustain its economic or military power, those resources are relatively easy to capture because of their character or location, and there is a local actor that appears willing and able to expand. It should be lower if a leading state is much less dependent on a region's resources, prized assets are safe from seizure, or local actors seem unlikely to pursue aggrandizement. Similarly, the risk of containment failure should be highest when a peripheral region contains valuable resources, those resources are tempting targets for potential aggressors, and there is an outside actor that poses a genuine danger to them. It should be lower if a peripheral region is far less important to a leading state, any assets are secure from external threats, or there are no hostile powers capable of engaging in conquest.

Although these factors are fairly broad, it is difficult to forecast the specific indicators that a leading state will look at or to project which components of risk will matter most, especially across a diverse set of cases, because the significance of local assets, the extent of their vulnerability, and the gravity of potential threats are all dynamic and context dependent. For example, a peripheral region can quickly become more important if valuable resources are discovered there or changing patterns of great power rivalry make it the ideal location for military bases. The importance of a peripheral region can decline just as suddenly, though, if a leading state finds alternate sources of supply or the development of new weapons systems makes existing bases obsolete. At the same time, asset vulnerability is not always generalizable, making its impact on risk assessments difficult to predict. For instance, controlling lines of communication might require holding large swaths of territory in some cases or a single geographic choke point in others, while valuable commodities could be widely dispersed in one region and clustered together elsewhere. Finally, although the level of threat to a subsystem will hinge mainly on the existence of a revisionist power, it will also depend on the difficulty of local expansion or external intervention. That, in turn, could be influenced by a host of factors, such as the logistical challenges of military operations and the availability of forces to conduct an assault. Despite this complexity, the general framework outlined above can be applied to individual cases to understand how leading states calculate risk in peripheral regions—namely, whether they believe that access denial and containment failure are nothing to fear, that one of these risks outweighs the other, or that both are a cause for serious concern. It can also provide insights into how these risks evolve over time.

REGIONAL PARITY AND REGIONAL PRIMACY IN THE PERIPHERY

What are the implications of a leading state's risk assessment for its preferred regional order? In general, the distribution of power within a peripheral region can either exacerbate or mitigate concerns about access denial and containment failure. For instance, it can influence the likelihood that a local actor will be able to extend its control over the area or impact the barriers that an outside actor will have to overcome if it attempts to intervene. Therefore, as summarized in table 1 and discussed in greater detail below, the presence, absence, or combination of these risks will determine whether a leading state actually has a preferred local order and, if it does, whether it prefers regional parity or regional primacy.

Regional Order in Low-Risk Areas In some cases, both the risk of access denial and the risk of containment failure could be low. For instance, a peripheral region might not have much value from the perspective of the leading state, its allies, or its adversaries.[9] Even if it does contain important resources or its location has intrinsic geopolitical significance, local actors might not be in a position to expand throughout the area, while outside powers might not have the capacity for conquest. Under any of these conditions, a leading state need not worry that a hostile party will gain control of critical territory. Nevertheless, it should have an enduring interest in preserving stability. In other words, it will want to prevent regional conflicts or bring them to an end. Although a war might not result in the seizure of key assets by a local actor or an outside power, the conflict itself could still interrupt commerce and inflict heavy casualties. It could also create opportunities for an adversary to extend its influence or enhance its prestige, namely, by providing the combatants

Table 1. Risk assessments and preferred regional orders

Risk of containment failure	Risk of access denial	
	Low	High
Low	Regional parity or regional primacy	Regional parity
High	Regional primacy	

with assistance or by trying to broker a settlement between them. As a result, policymakers could face domestic or international pressure to become involved. They might even be moved to act on normative grounds. At the very least, they could be distracted from higher priority issues that demand their attention. When it comes to avoiding these consequences, however, a leading state is unlikely to have a strong preference between regional parity and regional primacy because either one has the potential to keep the peace. Simply put, the existence of local order will be much more important than the specific form that it takes.[10]

Regional Order and the Risk of Access Denial In other cases, the risk of containment failure could be low but the risk of access denial could be high. For instance, a peripheral region of some importance might be safe from outside powers, perhaps because it is too isolated to be conquered easily or because potential threats are occupied elsewhere. At the same time, there might be a much greater chance of a local actor extending its hold over the area, bringing additional resources under its control, and gaining greater leverage over the countries that depend on them. This type of challenge has received considerable attention in recent years, especially with nations such as China and Iran pursuing a variety of military capabilities— including ballistic and cruise missiles, submarines, and naval mines—that could increase their clout over neighbors and inhibit the United States from defending its allies.[11] The general problem is hardly a new one, however, because the possession of raw materials, lines of communication, and other valuable assets has long been a source of power and influence.[12] Leading states have therefore played a central role in preserving access to and through vital regions, both for themselves and for others. During the nineteenth century, for example, Great Britain continuously worked to secure the land and sea routes to India, the centerpiece of its overseas empire. As for the United States, it has de facto responsibility for guaranteeing the uninterrupted flow of petroleum from the Middle East to markets throughout the world. When the risk of access denial is a leading state's greatest concern the implication for its preferred order is clear: it should favor regional parity instead of regional primacy so that no local actor can dominate the entire area.

Regional Order and the Risk of Containment Failure These conditions could also be reversed. That is, the risk of access denial could be low while the risk of containment failure could be high. If so, a leading state should favor regional primacy instead of regional parity. The rationale for this argument is straightforward. Because they have commitments in so many areas, leading states often spread their forces too thin to deter aggression and might not be able to concentrate those forces quickly enough when new threats arise. Their strategic challenges usually go deeper than just resource constraints, though,

15

and create pressing demands for strong local partners, even in the periphery. Specifically, for at least the past two centuries, leading states have been maritime powers: insular nations with secure borders and easy access to the sea. By contrast, their chief adversaries have been continental powers: interior nations with insecure borders and limited access to the sea.[13] Given their geographic isolation, maritime powers need to overcome enormous logistical hurdles when they conduct military operations abroad, from "the tyranny of distance" to "the stopping power of water."[14] Compounding these obstacles, they can also find themselves at a significant disadvantage in direct clashes with their rivals, for two reasons. First, while maritime powers emphasize air and naval forces to defend their far-flung interests, continental powers emphasize land forces to protect their frontiers and pursue expansion. That means the former might not have enough troops to directly contest aggression by the latter. Second, air and naval forces might not be effective coercive instruments unless continental powers have significant overseas assets that can be held at risk. As Halford Mackinder famously argued, the Eurasian heartland where past continental powers have emerged is "the greatest natural fortress on earth."[15]

At times, therefore, leading states can be ill equipped to deter or counter expansion on their own, which means they must find allies that are willing to help them.[16] For example, even when Great Britain was the world's dominant naval power, defeating potential hegemons in Europe required land power partners. And even though the United States emerged from the Second World War with undisputed supremacy in the air and on the seas, it still relied on Western European armies to offset the Soviet Union's quantitative military edge on the ground.[17] Moreover, this dynamic has been evident in peripheral regions as well, which have frequently been the main battlegrounds for maritime–continental rivalries.[18] Just as Great Britain depended on a number of minor powers to prevent the Russian Empire from expanding throughout Asia during the nineteenth-century "Great Game," the United States partnered with a host of nations outside Europe to prevent the Soviets from gaining control over many of the same areas during the Cold War. For leading states, however, the remote location of peripheral regions and their secondary importance relative to other theaters can exacerbate the limitations described above. Under these conditions, local actors can serve as a critical first line of defense, and the strongest local actors are often the best candidates to play this role. In fact, when the risk of containment failure is high, a preponderant local power that is not distracted or weakened by its neighbors might be the only potential ally that can prevent external intervention, especially by a more capable great power. By contrast, a handful of weaker nations would be vulnerable to divide-and-conquer tactics and could be picked off one by one. A preponderant local power should also be more capable of resisting indirect forms of aggression, including efforts to establish a sphere of influence, because it is less dependent on outside actors for economic or military support and therefore less susceptible to inducements that come with strings attached.[19]

In some situations, of course, the risk of containment failure and the risk of access denial could both be high. Leading states will face conflicting incentives when the two go hand in hand because the same conditions that mitigate one are likely to heighten the other. To be more precise, nations that are too weak to dominate their regions might also be too weak to stop external intervention, while a local actor that is strong enough to help contain outside powers could also be strong enough to restrict access to the area. In these circumstances, I argue that a leading state will place greater emphasis on avoiding containment failure than on preventing access denial and therefore will still prefer primacy over parity, for one simple reason: if an outside power gained control of the region due to the absence of an effective local counterweight, it would almost certainly prevent a leading state from freely using the area's resources, transiting its lines of communication, or maintaining a forward military presence there. In other words, even though regional primacy could heighten the risk of access denial, containment failure would almost certainly result in a loss of access as well, in addition to its other negative consequences.

Regional Power Shifts and Leading State Strategies

Understanding the relationship between a leading state's risk assessment and its preferred regional order is a crucial first step in developing the theory. Preferences alone cannot explain why a leading state would accommodate some RRPs and oppose others, however, because a change in the status quo could be compatible with its objectives or incompatible with its aims, depending on the circumstances. The second step, therefore, is to determine whether an RRP seems poised to reinforce, establish, undermine, or overturn the type of local order that a leading state prefers. In other words, policymakers will try to forecast the outcome of a power shift to gauge the impact on their interests. Only then will they have enough information to decide on a course of action. How do policymakers arrive at these projections? They do so by looking at certain aspects of the power shift that is taking place, namely, its direction or its scope and in some cases both. I argue that these attributes provide a window into the long-term consequences for a region that concern policymakers most: its susceptibility to destabilizing conflicts, the accessibility of its resources, or its vulnerability to external intervention.

THE DIRECTION AND SCOPE OF POWER SHIFTS

An intuitive but important observation in the literature on power shifts is that not all changes in the distribution of power are alike.[20] Instead, they can unfold in a number of ways based on the quantity and quality of resources that nations possess, their ability to extract those resources from society, and their effectiveness at translating them into economic and military strength, among other factors. For example, power shifts can vary in terms of their size: a rising nation might reduce a declining nation's relative advantage or overtake it by a large margin. Power shifts can also vary in terms of their speed: a rising nation could narrow the capability gap with a declining nation in a short period of time or embark on a much more gradual ascent. To date, these characteristics have typically been used to explain why some changes in the distribution of power lead to war while others do not rather than to explain how third parties react when power shifts take place. They have also generated widely divergent predictions. According to one study, large power shifts should lower the probability of conflict because declining nations that know they will be overtaken have little incentive to resist the inevitable. According to another study, though, large power shifts should raise the probability of conflict because nations in deep decline are more willing to attack possible challengers in the hope of preserving their position.[21] Likewise, the speed of a power shift can cut both ways. On the one hand, rapid power shifts might be extremely dangerous because declining nations are caught off guard and unprepared. On the other hand, rapid power shifts might be much less hazardous because rising nations can improve their position before anyone tries to stop them.[22]

Although the basic insight that changes in the distribution of power can have different characteristics is a significant one, these arguments do not shed much light on how leading states evaluate the implications of regional power shifts, which is not surprising given their empirical focus and theoretical disagreements. For instance, the size of a power shift could have very different implications for a leading state depending on its core interest in an area. In some cases, a relatively small change in the distribution of power might be viewed as a positive development, especially if it weakens a local hegemon that represents a threat to access, while a larger change might be considered a serious challenge, particularly if it creates a local hegemon that poses an access threat. In other cases, however, the opposite could be true. That is, a relatively small change in the distribution of power might cause concern because it weakens an ally against outside expansion, while a larger change might be acceptable because it creates a more capable partner. In addition, the historical record suggests that the speed of a power shift does not have much bearing on how leading states respond to RRPs. To cite one piece of evidence, the rise of Egypt and Japan in the nineteenth century followed similar timelines, as both actors enhanced their strength over roughly two-and-a-half decades and then fought a pair of wars during the following ten years that revealed their capabilities to the world. Yet Great Britain opposed the former and accommodated the latter.[23]

Table 2. Different types of regional power shifts

	Direction of a power shift	
Scope of a power shift	Counterhegemonic	Hegemonic
Complete	A rising regional power (RRP) pursues local parity and establishes a balance of power.	An RRP pursues local primacy and becomes a preponderant power.
Incomplete	An RRP pursues local parity but fails to establish a balance of power.	An RRP pursues local primacy but fails to become a preponderant power.

Despite the limitations of these arguments, I argue that power shifts can be categorized in other ways, which are based on many of the same underlying factors but better capture how outside observers judge the potential implications of any changes in the distribution of power. First, a power shift can vary according to its direction: whether a rising nation appears to be pursuing parity or primacy, irrespective of its ability to establish a new order in its neighborhood. For instance, some RRPs are not plausible candidates for local hegemony. Rather, due to their limited wealth, insufficient mobilization capacity, or relatively modest ambitions, they are attempting only to establish equilibrium with a preponderant power in decline. Other RRPs have the resources and the drive to make a realistic bid for regional dominance, though, either by surpassing a peer competitor or supplanting a local hegemon. A power shift can also vary according to its scope: whether a rising nation appears capable of attaining parity or primacy, regardless of which type of order it is attempting to create. Put simply, while some RRPs are strong enough to achieve their aims and sustain their new positions over time, others are not.

In general, any change in the distribution of power will vary along both of these dimensions. As summarized in table 2, the direction of a power shift can be counterhegemonic or hegemonic, while the scope of a power shift can be complete or incomplete. More important, these attributes can have a significant impact on a leading state's calculations when an RRP challenges the status quo and a local conflict breaks out.

ACCOMMODATION, OPPOSITION, AND REGIONAL POWER SHIFTS

The direction and scope of a power shift can each provide a useful lens for assessing the changes that are taking place when a local distribution of power is in flux, especially for outside observers who want to determine what the likely result will be and how it will impact their interests in the area. Nevertheless, a leading state will not always care about both characteristics when it is trying to decide between accommodating and opposing an RRP. Instead, as summarized in figure 2, the particular aspect of a power shift that concerns it most will depend on its risk assessment and preferred regional order. Specifically, if a leading state does not have a preference over the type of order that exists because its main objective is preserving local stability, then it will only need to look at the scope of the power shift, which can indicate whether the new status quo will be relatively durable or extremely fragile. What matters in these cases, therefore, is whether a change in the distribution of power is complete or incomplete. If a leading state prefers regional parity to reduce the risk of access denial, however, then it will only need to look at the direction of the power shift, which can reveal whether a dominant local actor is receding or on the rise. Thus, the relevant distinction in these situations is whether a change in the distribution of power is counterhegemonic or hegemonic. Finally, if a leading state prefers regional primacy to mitigate the risk of containment failure, then it will need to take both of these characteristics into account because the direction and scope of a power shift will influence whether a viable local ally is likely to emerge.

Power Shifts and the Sources of Local Stability As described above, if the risk of access denial and the risk of containment failure are both low, then a leading state should be willing to tolerate a balance of power or a preponderance of power in a peripheral region since either form of order can deter local conflicts. What does that mean when the distribution of power is changing? The most important question for a leading state in this situation is not whether an RRP is attempting to counterbalance its local rival or control its entire neighborhood. Rather, the most important question is whether it can actually succeed. A complete power shift, therefore, occurs when an RRP clearly establishes local parity or local primacy. In general, these outcomes are likely to be resilient over time. For instance, a rising nation that manages to create a balance of power should be strong enough to convince a declining nation that its lost primacy cannot be restored. Likewise, a rising nation that becomes a preponderant power should be capable of deterring or defeating any future challenges from its former peers. Alternatively, an incomplete power shift occurs when an RRP gains ground on a dominant nation yet fails to form a balance of power or when it surpasses its nearest competitors but falls short of becoming a preponderant power. Because the previous order is no longer quite intact but has not been overturned, either outcome could be contested in the region and therefore an enduring source of conflict, particularly as nations in decline fight to avoid further losses and regain their previous positions.[24] Thus, a leading state that simply wants to preserve local stability will accommodate an RRP when a complete shift is under way and oppose an RRP when an incomplete shift is taking place, regardless of its direction.[25]

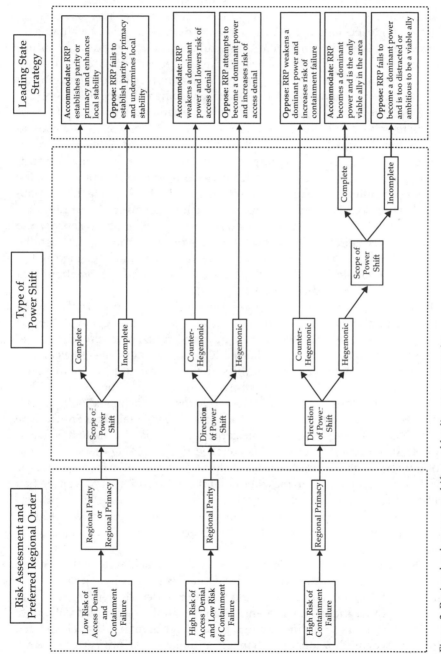

Figure 2. Regional orders, power shifts, and leading state strategies

Consider American foreign policy in the Middle East during the 1950s and 1960s. Given its petroleum reserves in particular, the region was hardly insignificant for officials in Washington. Nevertheless, the risk of access denial was not especially high. Although local nations possessed valuable resources that they could withhold, something that was a persistent concern for U.S. policymakers who worried about the dependence of American allies on Middle Eastern oil, there was no local nation capable of bringing all of these resources under its control. Meanwhile, the risk of containment failure was even lower. Of course, U.S. policymakers did worry about Soviet efforts to enhance its influence in the region. Yet there was little reason to believe that Moscow would launch a military invasion. Thus, the United States was preoccupied with preserving regional stability, which was threatened by fragile economies, domestic unrest, and, most worrisome of all, the ongoing dispute between Israel and its Arab neighbors.[26] In fact, U.S. policymakers feared that increased instability could have significant ramifications, particularly if the cause were an Arab–Israeli war. For instance, Arab nations might temporarily restrict supplies of oil to the West unless the United States came to their aid, while the Soviet Union might engage in diplomatic maneuvers to erode Washington's standing with Arab nations that were desperate for outside support.[27]

In these circumstances, policymakers were essentially impartial between a balance of power and a preponderance of power in the region. Although they generally preferred the former until the mid-1960s, this simply reflected conditions on the ground. That is, while Israel enjoyed a clear military edge, the Arab nations had offsetting advantages in territory and population size.[28] This assessment even survived the Suez War in 1956. Despite Israel's lopsided victory (albeit one that was achieved only against a single adversary and with the assistance of Great Britain and France), the United States forced it to return the captured Sinai Peninsula to a defeated Egypt. At the time, senior officials believed that retaining the Sinai would not only be a barrier to peace but would also trigger an arms race that the Israelis could not win.[29] To the extent that the distribution of power seemed to be shifting in the direction of Israeli primacy, therefore, that shift appeared to be incomplete, and Washington remained determined to preserve local parity. Yet it adopted a very different approach during the next Middle East war.

After Israel's even bigger victory in 1967 (which it achieved on its own and against a coalition of Arab nations), the United States did not attempt to restore the status quo ante. Unlike the situation a decade earlier, there was little doubt that the tenuous balance of power in the region had collapsed, perhaps for good. According to one U.S. intelligence report, "Israel emerged from the war with a greatly enhanced military superiority over its Arab neighbors."[30] For McGeorge Bundy, the previous national security advisor to President Lyndon Johnson who returned to help coordinate the American response, Washington's existing approach to the region was now obsolete. In his view, "the old mold of Middle Eastern policy is broken forever, and I think we need new guidance."[31] That ultimately meant refusing to pressure Israel into returning the territory it had acquired without a comprehensive peace agreement. It also led the United States to embrace Israel as a close ally, now that a complete power shift had occurred and it was undoubtedly the strongest actor in the area.

Power Shifts and the Dangers of Access Denial When a leading state is concerned only with preserving local stability, the scope of a power shift is the critical factor that will shape its strategy toward the region. When it is worried mainly about access denial, however, the direction of a power shift will matter most. Specifically, a change in the distribution of power can be counterhegemonic or hegemonic, regardless of whether it actually produces a new regional order. In the case of a counterhegemonic shift, an RRP attempts to weaken a dominant actor or divide control over valuable territory, but it is not on track to rule the area itself, and it might not even be able to establish a durable balance of power. In the case of a hegemonic shift, an RRP attempts to defeat its rivals and extend its control over critical resources, although it might not emerge as the uncontested preponderant power. These scenarios have very clear but very different implications for a leading state, which should accommodate an RRP when a counterhegemonic shift is taking place and oppose an RRP when a hegemonic shift is under way, regardless of its scope. Whereas the former reduces the risk of access denial because it contributes to local parity, the latter heightens this risk by raising the specter of local primacy. Under these conditions, then, a leading state should align with the weaker side in a regional competition to ensure that the area does not fall under the sway of a single actor.

A classic illustration of this logic involves Dutch and English policy in Scandinavia shortly after the Thirty Years' War. Between 1655 and 1660, as the Netherlands and England competed with one another to be the dominant maritime power of the day, both nations faced a shifting distribution of power in northern Europe. Although Denmark had previously been the strongest actor in the region, by the second half of the seventeenth-century Sweden had surpassed its local rival. Nevertheless, Danish territory still included the island of Zealand and the southern Scandinavian coast, which gave Copenhagen control over the Sound—the narrow waterway bridging the Baltic Sea and the North Sea. As a result, this contest was closely monitored in the Hague and in London. Over the preceding decades, the Dutch had become the main beneficiaries of Baltic trade, while England relied on imported resources to build and maintain its fleet. Thus, both maritime powers feared being cut off from eastern Europe.[32]

These concerns became acute in 1655 when Charles X Gustavus, the new king of Sweden, embarked on the first of several military campaigns that nearly eliminated Denmark as a rival power. That year, Swedish forces launched an invasion of the Poland-Lithuania Commonwealth in an attempt to gain control over the entire southeastern coast of the Baltic Sea. Despite early successes, Charles X became bogged down in a costly conflict, one that opened the door for King Frederick III of Denmark to launch an ill-conceived war in the hope of checking Sweden's rise. Thanks to a bold counteroffensive, Charles X captured the Jutland Peninsula and advanced on Copenhagen. Clearly defeated, Frederick III was compelled to sue for peace and sign the Treaty of Roskilde in 1658, which ceded Denmark's Scandinavian provinces to Sweden. Then, less than six months later, Charles X broke the peace and launched a siege of Copenhagen, this time with the goal of completely defeating his local rival and gaining full control of the Sound.[33]

The hegemonic shift that was taking place in the north during this five-year period drew the maritime powers together and brought them into action against Sweden. In 1656, the United Provinces dispatched several dozen ships and approximately six thousand troops to stymie Charles X's campaign in West Prussia.[34] For its part, England helped to negotiate the Treaty of Roskilde, which saved Denmark from total defeat and divided the Sound between the two northern kingdoms.[35] Then, after Charles X resumed his war against Frederick III, the United Provinces and England adopted similar measures to manage the conflict. While the Dutch sent a fleet to break the Swedish siege of Copenhagen, the English deployed their own naval forces to encourage and, if necessary, compel both sides to negotiate a peace treaty based on the previous agreement.[36] In sum, while the two maritime powers were "mutually antagonistic," they were also "resolved that no single janitor should again possess the keys of the Baltic."[37]

Power Shifts and the Dynamics of Containment If a leading state does not have a preferred regional order and simply wants to maintain local stability or if it prefers regional parity to mitigate the risk of access denial, then it will focus on just one aspect of the power shift that is taking place. If it prefers regional primacy to reduce the risk of containment failure, though, then it will focus on both of the attributes described above. The key issue here is whether the new status quo is expected to include a dominant nation that is strong enough to serve as a barrier against intervention. Consequently, a leading state should accommodate an RRP only when it believes that a hegemonic and complete shift is taking place, one that concentrates power in the hands of a single actor, establishes a clear hierarchy with that nation at the apex, and cannot be overturned without significant outside interference. In this situation, a leading state will have little choice but to embrace an RRP; not only will it be the most capable ally in the region, but it might also be the only potential ally left standing. In any other scenario, however, the drawbacks of accommodation are likely to outweigh the benefits.

Why must a change in the distribution of power meet both criteria for a strategy of accommodation to be the better option? The answer to this question reveals how the direction and scope of a power shift can impact a leading state's calculations when it is worried about external threats to peripheral regions. Specifically, a leading state should oppose an RRP if a counterhegemonic shift is under way because any actor that is pursuing local parity will only make its neighborhood more vulnerable to outside intervention. In other words, a hegemonic shift is a necessary condition for accommodation. It is not sufficient, though, because a leading state should also oppose an RRP that is pursuing local primacy if the power shift appears to be incomplete. This point might seem counterintuitive. After all, an RRP that aims for dominance but falls short of achieving it could still be the strongest actor in the area. Yet it might not be a very useful ally unless the power shift is complete as well, for two possible reasons.[38]

First, an RRP could appear too distracted to be a worthwhile partner, particularly if it fails to eclipse a peer competitor in a balance-of-power subsystem. With both sides locked in an ongoing struggle, an RRP might be more focused on countering a local adversary than on containing an external threat. Meanwhile, unsuccessful efforts to achieve primacy could sap its strength and erode the barriers to expansion by an outside actor. Thus, a leading state is unlikely to side with an RRP or provide it with much assistance since these efforts could fuel a regional rivalry and increase the odds of containment failure. In the early 1960s, for example, India seemed poised to leave Pakistan behind and become the dominant actor in South Asia. As a result, it was viewed by policymakers in the United States as the best candidate in the region to stand up to Communist China, and many of those policymakers were ready to pursue closer ties between Washington and New Delhi. Nevertheless, India's failure to achieve a decisive victory over Pakistan during the Second Kashmir War in 1965 poured cold water on these nascent plans. Rather than demonstrate that a hegemonic and complete power shift was taking place, the conflict seemed to confirm that India could not achieve local primacy without paying a very steep price and might not achieve it at all. The war also raised the possibility that both sides would wear each other down and leave the region more susceptible to intervention.

Second, an RRP might seem too ambitious to be a useful ally, especially if it fails to replace a preponderant power in decline. In this situation, a leading state could decide that an RRP is weakening a local actor that still has the ability to be an effective partner, albeit one that requires some assistance. Moreover, while a rising power might have military advantages that a declining power lacks, it could also be a source of problems that its neighbor would not pose. Emerging powers usually see their interests expand with their capabilities; that is, revisionist aims often correlate with increases in relative power.[39] Thus, an RRP might be prone to a variety of aggressive behaviors, such as instigating conflicts that could entrap its patron or band-wagoning with other major powers to enhance its position.[40] It might even be tempted to withhold local resources that a leading state depends on or limit the presence of outside powers in its neighborhood. By comparison, a preponderant power in decline should be much less risk acceptant, much less opportunistic, and much less likely to restrict outside access to the region. For instance, during the 1830s, Egypt's growing power brought it to the cusp of achieving local hegemony in the Middle East at the expense of the Ottoman Empire, which was a British ally against Russia. Although the rising Egyptians were a tempting replacement for the declining Ottomans, policymakers in London concluded that the latter had not been permanently weakened and could restore much of their strength with only modest reforms. In short, they did not believe that Egypt had fully overtaken the Ottoman Empire. They were also reluctant to support an expansionist and unpredictable rising power, at least while another capable partner was still available. If given a choice, then, a leading state will align with a local actor that is capable of defending the area but that does not represent a serious threat to its other interests there. When a preponderant power is experiencing deep and irreversible decline, however, and cannot resist intervention without substantial external aid and significant internal reform, opposing an RRP that aims for primacy—even an extremely ambitious one—will no longer be an option.

Why have leading states accommodated some emerging powers in peripheral regions but opposed others? This chapter has provided an explanation for this overlooked empirical puzzle, one that focuses on the interaction between two main factors: the type of regional order that a leading state prefers and the type of power shift that it believes is taking place. The next five chapters present evidence for this argument by examining how Great Britain responded to RRPs throughout the nineteenth century and how the United States responded to RRPs during the Cold War.

Egypt's Bid for Mastery of the Middle East, 1831–1841

Following more than two decades of conflict, Great Britain emerged from its final victory over France in 1815 as the leading state in the international system. London's economic and military strength, along with the concert system of diplomatic consultation that was established at the Congress of Vienna, contributed to almost four decades of great power peace.[1] Yet the relative tranquility that existed during this period was nearly shattered on a number of occasions. Moreover, when great power crises did occur the proximate cause was often clashing interests in peripheral regions. The Ottoman, Persian, and Chinese Empires that once dominated most of Asia were each experiencing relative decline throughout the nineteenth century. In their weakened state, they lost the ability to control territory they ostensibly ruled and to resist aggrandizement by stronger nations. This trend was the catalyst for a protracted competition among major powers such as Great Britain and Russia for political influence and economic advantage, one that eventually stretched from the Near East to the Far East.

During the first half of the nineteenth century, the emerging rivalry between London and St. Petersburg centered on one issue in particular: the future of the Ottoman Empire. Simply put, the so-called Eastern Question, which eventually led to the Crimean War and the demise of the Concert of Europe, was how to manage the decline of Turkey.[2] Under the sultan, Constantinople managed an expansive empire that included Anatolia, the Balkans, the Levant, the Arabian Peninsula, Mesopotamia, and North Africa. Over time, however, the central government (often referred to as the Sublime Porte) found it increasingly difficult to govern these far-flung provinces and began to confront territories in open rebellion. For example, the most significant aspect of the Eastern Question prior to the Crimean War was the rise of Egypt under its Albanian governor, Mehmet Ali. Although it was formally part of the Ottoman Empire, by the 1820s Egypt had not only achieved de facto independence, but it had also carved out its own empire extending from the Sudan to the Hijaz—an area that included both coasts of the Red Sea and the Islamic holy cities of Mecca and Medina. Mehmet Ali even managed to defeat the Ottomans on the battlefield during the 1830s, which gave him control over the province of Syria, raised fears that he would depose the sultan, and demonstrated to the world that the Egyptian governor could field a stronger military than his sovereign.

This shifting geopolitical landscape presented challenges for some great powers and opportunities for others. Great Britain, however, was affected more than most. Two of its core strategic interests, which went hand in hand, were preserving its naval dominance in the Mediterranean Sea and protecting its empire in India. For policymakers in London, Turkey played a critical role in achieving both of these aims. Not only did the Porte control access to the Mediterranean from the Black Sea via the Bosporus and Dardanelles Straits, but its empire also included overland routes to India that ran through the Middle East. As the dominant local power, therefore, Constantinople was a critical barrier to Russian expansion and a key element in Great Britain's strategy of containment. With Turkey in decline and under assault, however, the risk of containment failure loomed large, and London had to decide whether the Porte would remain a useful partner or whether Egypt could be a potential replacement.

After an extended internal debate and a period of indecision, Great Britain eventually chose to support the Ottoman Empire and oppose the rise of Egypt. For much of the 1830s and 1840s, London's foreign policy was in the hands of Henry John Temple, better known as Viscount Palmerston. Despite his occasional doubts, Palmerston consistently maintained that the Ottomans were not as weak as most observers feared, while the Egyptians were not as strong as many of his contemporaries believed. Although it was undeniable that Mehmet Ali hoped to supplant the sultan and dominate the region, Palmerston was never convinced that Egypt could completely displace the Ottoman Empire. Of course, the foreign secretary was not blind to the fact that Turkey was under duress and would need outside assistance to counter threats from predatory great powers and rogue provinces alike, but he did not see these problems as insurmountable. Instead, Palmerston repeatedly argued that with modest fiscal, administrative, and military improvements, as well as a period of undisturbed peace to enact necessary changes, the Ottoman Empire was capable of reasserting its authority and resuming its role as a barrier to Russia—and could do so largely on its own. From his perspective, therefore, a hegemonic power shift was clearly taking place in the Middle East. Nevertheless, that shift was incomplete and could be easily reversed.

Palmerston's position on the Eastern Question thus "depended on the supposition that the Ottoman Empire could be reformed."[3] As one historian notes, this was "the *idée fixe* which was never to leave him."[4] Given this assessment, supporting Egypt would have represented an enormous gamble. Whereas the Ottoman Empire was unlikely to challenge Great Britain's interests in the Middle East, for instance, by denying access to transportation routes that ran through its provinces, Mehmet Ali was much more ambitious and, as a result, much less reliable. Palmerston feared that the viceroy or one of his successors might eventually threaten the lines of communication to India, something that the Porte could not and almost certainly would not do. So long as the Ottomans appeared capable of fending off Russia on their own, therefore, abetting Egypt's rise was an unnecessary and undesirable course of action.

Ultimately, the decision to oppose Egypt as well as the reasons behind it offer strong support for the theory. Not only did Great Britain prefer regional primacy given the high risk of containment failure, but it also monitored both the direction and scope of the power shift that was taking place in the Middle East as it determined how to respond to Egypt's rise. Furthermore, although it was unwilling to support Mehmet Ali while his bid for local hegemony appeared incomplete, Palmerston strongly implied that Egyptian domination of the region was preferable to Russian control over Constantinople. That is, the foreign secretary very likely would have accepted a greater risk of access denial to contain St. Petersburg, if the power shift had been complete and there was no other alternative.

The Rise of Anglo-Russian Antagonism and the Decline of Ottoman Power

Although the Ottoman Empire became an important strategic partner for Great Britain during the early nineteenth century, the relationship between the two powers was not always so friendly. In prior decades, Turkey had played a distinctly marginal role in British foreign affairs.[5] For instance, London's economic interests in the sultan's domains were minimal, especially in comparison to those of France. When London did pay close attention to the Ottoman Empire, its policies toward it were shaped in large part by the demands of the Anglo-French rivalry, in particular the desire to secure Russia as a continental ally against France. Because Paris enjoyed close ties with Constantinople and because St. Petersburg and Constantinople were long-standing opponents, Great Britain often treated the Ottoman Empire as an adversary by association, although not a very consequential one. London's outlook began to change in the closing years of the eighteenth century, however, when Turkey first emerged as a useful shield against expansion by Great Britain's competitors.[6]

London's shifting calculus on the strategic value of the Ottoman Empire can be traced back to 1791, when the Russo-Turkish war that had been taking place for several years raised the specter of worrisome territorial losses for Constantinople. During past conflicts between these two rivals, the British government had generally ignored or abetted Russian offensives, mainly in the hope of preserving friendly ties with St. Petersburg. It had even turned a blind eye when Catherine the Great annexed Crimea several years earlier and left Turkey extremely vulnerable to coercion by its neighbor to the north.[7] This time, however, the situation was different. The cabinet, led by Prime Minister William Pitt the Younger, concluded that Russian expansion along the northern coast of the Black Sea represented a potential threat to British interests and nearly instigated a war with Russia before backing down in the face of domestic political opposition. Pitt's decision to challenge St. Petersburg stemmed from concerns that its actions might upset the European balance of power by further weakening the Ottoman Empire, which could in turn harm the security of Prussia, Great Britain's ally at the time in the Triple Alliance. He was also worried that Russian expansion would give it control over both the Baltic Sea and Black Sea maritime trade routes, enabling St. Petersburg to restrict British access to raw materials such as hemp and timber, which were needed for shipbuilding.[8]

This crisis is often cited as the origin of Great Britain's interest in preserving the Ottoman Empire against internal and external threats.[9] An even more important catalyst, though, was the invasion and occupation of Egypt by Napoleon Bonaparte in 1798, which radically altered perceptions of Turkey throughout England. Until this point, the idea of aiding the Ottoman Empire was not a popular one. That quickly changed once France seemed poised to use Ottoman territory as a staging ground for a military expedition against India, the crown jewel of Great Britain's overseas empire. Soon afterward, Pitt signed a secret treaty that guaranteed the Ottoman Empire's territorial integrity for the next eight years.[10]

Despite Constantinople's emerging role as a barrier to expansion by Great Britain's rivals, London actually went to war with Turkey in 1807. After yet another Russo-Turkish conflict had broken out the previous year, the Porte had turned to Paris for support and agreed to open the Turkish Straits—the Dardanelles and the Bosporus—to its naval forces. Russia was a British ally against Napoleon, however, and now faced the threat of French warships entering the Black Sea from the Mediterranean Sea. In response, London dispatched a fleet to the Sea of Marmara and deployed several thousand troops to Alexandria in an attempt to coerce the Porte into withdrawing its support for France. Although these efforts did not succeed, the British and Ottoman governments signed a treaty in 1809 that ended the war between them and, notably, obligated the Porte to close the Straits to all foreign warships during peacetime. This provision would become a key issue in the Anglo-Russian rivalry that was on the horizon because it helped to ensure Great Britain's day-to-day naval supremacy by preventing a Russian fleet from entering the Mediterranean Sea from the Black Sea. If St. Petersburg planned to threaten Great Britain's forces, it would have to sail its navy from the Baltic Sea to the Atlantic Ocean and then pass through the Strait of Gibraltar, a key maritime chokepoint under British control. Moreover, so long as

Constantinople could be counted on to side with London in any future Anglo-Russian war (a safe bet given its long-standing rivalry with St. Petersburg and its geographic position between the two powers), the sultan could still allow a British fleet to enter the Straits and strike at Russia's Black Sea coast, since the treaty would no longer apply once hostilities had broken out.[11]

At the conclusion of the Napoleonic wars, Great Britain had therefore come to accept Turkey—the dominant local power—as a critical bulwark against Russian expansion. Moreover, key policymakers such as Lord Castlereagh (foreign secretary from 1812 to 1822) and George Canning (who succeeded Castlereagh and led the Foreign Office for a second time from 1822 to 1827) would continue to hold that opinion in the years ahead.[12] As Kenneth Bourne explains, "Britain's main interests in the Near East were clear enough: to check the expansion of Russia, to protect the Mediterranean and its communications with the Near and Middle East against the intrusion of Russian naval power, and to preserve the security of a large area susceptible to British economic penetration. The maintenance of the Turkish Empire, with its axis at Constantinople and the Straits, was therefore of vital importance to England."[13]

London's dependence on the Porte would only increase over time. By 1818, its conquest of India was nearly complete.[14] Although the possible emergence of a European hegemon remained the gravest danger to British security, a large colonial empire on the subcontinent—one that could be reinforced only over lengthy supply lines—was a potential weak point that an adversary might exploit. Consequently, policymakers in London grew increasingly concerned that a rival might invade India or, more likely, expand its influence in nearby Central Asia and incite a rebellion against British rule. Moreover, while France no longer posed a serious threat to the subcontinent, the challenge from Russia seemed to be growing. In 1828, for example, the czar was concluding one war against the Persian Empire and beginning another against the Ottoman Empire. These conflicts extended his reach to the south, demonstrated his apparent desire to expand even farther, and convinced many British policymakers that the subcontinent was his real target.[15] Thus, the multidimensional Russian threat and the inherent vulnerability of India transformed the Porte into an especially valuable military ally.

Just as the Ottoman Empire was becoming a more important partner from London's perspective, however, it also became less and less capable of playing the role that British policymakers envisioned for it. Although Turkey's decline is dated to various points and attributed to a host of factors, the end result is clear in retrospect: economic backwardness and institutional stagnation contributed to growing military weakness; military weakness resulted in a string of defeats at the hands of rivals such as Russia; those defeats undermined the central government's ability to control its far-flung territories and facilitated the emergence of autonomous or semiautonomous provinces; and this devolution of authority further weakened the empire from within.

By the middle of the eighteenth century, if not sooner, the distribution of power between the Ottoman Empire and Europe's strongest nations was heavily tilted in favor of the latter, and Turkey no longer ranked among the great powers, at least according to its former peers. Nevertheless, it was not until the first several decades of the nineteenth century that it truly came to be seen as the "Sick Man of Europe," especially within Great Britain, due to a series of developments.[16]

The first critical event that crystalized perceptions of Ottoman fragility in foreign capitals was the Greek War of Independence, which began in 1821 and eventually involved most of the great powers. Far more than previous indicators of the Porte's weakness, the rebellion in Greece "exposed the decline and enfeeblement of the Ottoman Empire with all that that implied for the stability of Europe."[17] By 1825, British Foreign Secretary George Canning was attempting to cooperate with Russia in order to secure autonomy for the beleaguered Ottoman province, not only from an inherent desire to help the Greeks, whose cause had become a popular one in England and throughout Europe, but also in the hope of containing Russian expansion and preserving what remained of the Ottoman Empire. In particular, he wanted to discourage unilateral Russian intervention in the conflict and prevent a Russo-Turkish clash that would not only settle the Greek question for good but could also seriously weaken Turkey and allow Russia to expand its frontiers.[18]

Despite British efforts, the two rivals fought again in 1828–1829. This conflict was the next major piece of evidence that the Ottoman Empire was in sharp decline. The Porte's eventual defeat had a jarring impact on British policymakers, who not only became more concerned about Russia's long-term intentions but also began to fear that Constantinople would soon fall into its sphere of influence. As a result, they grew extremely skeptical of the Porte's ability to block Russian expansion and became hesitant to provide assistance that might increase its strength.[19] "It would be absurd to think of bolstering up the Turkish power in Europe," concluded the Duke of Wellington, Great Britain's prime minister at the time. "It is gone in fact and the tranquility of the world . . . along with it."[20] As he reflected on the initial terms of the Treaty of Adrianople that ended the conflict, Wellington argued that all of Europe's powers should view the agreement "as the death blow to the independence of the Ottoman Porte and the forerunner of the dissolution and extinction of its power."[21] Great Britain's foreign secretary, the Earl of Aberdeen, concurred. The continuing survival of the Turkish Empire, he declared, "may be said at this moment to depend upon the absolute will and pleasure of the Emperor Nicholas." Thus, British officials "ought not to occupy ourselves in vain efforts to restore its existence."[22] Moreover, the implications of the Russo-Turkish conflict were magnified by its timing; the war began shortly after St. Petersburg ended a successful campaign against the Persian Empire, which extended its influence into the

Caucuses and undermined London's sway over another buffer state along the approaches to India.[23] Thanks to its recent victories, Aberdeen lamented, "Russia holds the keys both of the Persian and the Turkish provinces; and whether she may be disposed to extend her conquests to the East or to the West, to Tehran or to Constantinople, no serious obstacles can arrest her progress."[24]

Perhaps the most important development that highlighted the frailty of the Ottoman Empire, however, was the rise of Egypt, which demonstrated that Constantinople was not even the strongest power in the region. By the outbreak of the first Ottoman-Egyptian war in 1831, Egypt was "a prosperous and a powerful State, vassal only in name to the Porte."[25] This transformation was accomplished by Mehmet Ali, a merchant and soldier who arrived in Egypt in 1801 as second in command of an Albanian troop contingent, which had been dispatched by the sultan to enforce his authority over Egypt following the withdrawal of French forces. Mehmet Ali soon took charge of his fellow soldiers and used them to establish control over Cairo at the expense of warring Mameluk factions that had once ruled the area. In 1805, the Porte recognized Mehmet Ali as governor of Egypt, and by 1810 he had secured most of the province.

Over time, the new governor took a number of steps to strengthen his regime and safeguard his position, such as establishing a system of direct taxation; instituting mass conscription; employing European advisors to train his armed forces; and creating a patrimonial system of rule whereby family members, trusted lieutenants, and a Turkish-speaking elite were placed in key positions throughout the burgeoning civil and military bureaucracy. Meanwhile, Mehmet Ali's external policies were even more disruptive to the regional distribution of power. At the Porte's request, he sent military expeditions to Arabia in 1811 (to counter the growing influence of the Wahhabi movement) and to Greece in 1825 (to help put down the revolt against Ottoman rule). Both campaigns allowed Mehmet Ali to expand his territory, which soon included a large portion of the Arabian Peninsula as well as the island of Crete.[26] In the interim between these two campaigns, Egypt also occupied the Sudan in an independent but largely unsuccessful quest to find slaves for its growing army and gold for its treasury. [27]

As one study explains, "The Pasha's stormy expansion . . . should be viewed within a grand design of independence and regional hegemony."[28] Mehmet Ali himself indicated that he had even more ambitious notions of his place in the world. "I want nothing but Egypt," he claimed during the conflict in Greece. If the European powers did not interfere with its rise, "this country will be so transformed that besides the four great world powers, England, Russia, Austria and France, Egypt by its money will be the fifth."[29] Beginning in 1831, however, the viceroy courted the prospect of European intervention when he launched a military campaign in Syria to secure timber for Egypt's navy, manpower for its army, a new market for its goods, tax revenue for its coffers, and a geographic buffer in case the sultan ever attempted to remove his nominal vassal from power.

The Causes and Consequences of the First Syrian War

In November 1830, the Wellington government fell from power. A new cabinet was soon formed with Earl Grey as prime minister and Viscount Palmerston as foreign secretary. Except for a brief interruption in 1834–1835, the latter would remain in this position for more than a decade (and would occupy the Foreign Office for a third time between 1846 and 1851). Early in his tenure, Palmerston was responsible for navigating a major crisis over the fate of the Ottoman Empire. On October 31, 1831, Mehmet Ali sent an expedition into Syria under the command of his son and chief general, Ibrahim, with the goal of expanding Egypt's territory and perhaps even overthrowing the sultan. Because the threat of a powerful but rebellious vassal was not unusual, the Porte waited until the following April to formally declare war against Mehmet Ali and depose him. That response proved much too little and much too late.

The conflict demonstrated just how much the regional distribution of power had shifted in a very short period of time. Egypt's army clearly outmatched the Ottoman forces that were sent to fight it. By the end of July, Ibrahim had captured the key cities of Acre, Damascus, and Adana and was poised to drive into the heart of Anatolia. Instead of urging his son to advance, though, Mehmet Ali ordered him to halt. Before marching on Constantinople, the viceroy hoped to negotiate an agreement with the European powers that would sanction his territorial gains, establish his independence, and prevent any outside interference with his imperial ambitions. These efforts failed, however, and Ibrahim resumed his offensive. In late 1832, he scored another huge victory near the city of Konya, capturing the grand vizier who led the sultan's army. When the war finally came to an end in May 1833, Ibrahim was only 150 miles from the Ottoman capital, where the situation appeared grim. "I doubt you can conceive the state of disorder and peril of this country," the recently arrived British ambassador reported to London. "The Sultan has no army, no money, no influence; he is detested and despised."[30] Although the Ottoman Empire had survived numerous losses at the hands of its European rivals, it was now at the mercy of one of its own provinces.

The events that were unfolding in the Levant had enormous consequences for British interests. Nevertheless, London did not intervene in any meaningful way. With an election looming at home and other crises to manage abroad, government officials paid relatively little attention to the conflict during its early stages. For his part, Palmerston hoped to avoid any involvement, at least until it became clear how the war would end and how Great Britain might be affected.[31] Therefore, he deliberately avoided choosing sides.

To the sultan, Mahmud II, the foreign secretary would only express Great Britain's "general wishes to maintain and uphold him as an ancient ally and old friend, and as an important element in the balance of power in Europe." Although Mehmet Ali might not have been an ancient ally and old friend, he had nonetheless tried to court the British; in Palmerston's words, he had communicated "his anxiety to be well with England, and his hopes that we should give him our protection." In response, the foreign secretary offered him "equally vague and general assurances of good will."[32] With his armies suffering loss after loss, however, the sultan appealed to Great Britain for assistance on multiple occasions. As one diplomat reported from Constantinople, "it was the co-operation of a British squadron that the Porte most earnestly desired" because the Royal Navy could easily cut the supply lines between Egypt and Syria that were sustaining Ibrahim's forces.[33] Yet London denied these requests in the fall of 1832 (before the disastrous battle between Egyptian and Ottoman armies at Konya) and again in January 1833 (after the magnitude of the Turkish defeat became apparent).[34]

The British government's refusal can be attributed to several factors. Even if it had wanted to assist the sultan, the Royal Navy was already busy conducting operations near Portugal and Belgium. As Palmerston later explained, "it would not have been possible to have found, at that time, a sufficient number of ships for that service." Thus, "the moral assistance of England" was all that London could offer. Policymakers also failed to appreciate the gravity of the situation until the war was almost over. At least initially, Palmerston recounted, the conflict "did not assume a character so different from that of the usual contests between the governors of provinces and the Sultan, as to lead to the supposition that the result would be very different from the usual results of those contests." The history of the Ottoman Empire, he argued, "was full of successive revolts of powerful vassals," which almost always resulted in "the reassertion of the authority of the Sultan."[35]

With his pleas for help falling on deaf ears, and increasingly desperate for material rather than moral support, the sultan eventually turned to Russia, which was more than willing to provide assistance. This development came as a surprise to many observers and for good reason; the two powers were longtime adversaries that had concluded their most recent war only three years earlier. As one of the sultan's advisors reportedly quipped to a French diplomat, however, "a drowning man will clutch at a serpent."[36]

In December 1832, shortly after the battle of Konya, a military envoy from St. Petersburg arrived at Constantinople to begin preparations for the deployment of Russian forces. Once Ibrahim reached the city of Kütahya and appeared determined to march on the capital, the sultan requested immediate assistance. A Russian naval squadron soon entered the Bosporus Strait, and not long afterward Russian soldiers were encamped just a few miles away. By late April, the presence of approximately fourteen thousand troops and three naval squadrons served as an unambiguous deterrent to further

Egyptian advances. Confronted with the prospect of taking on Russia if his army did not retreat and having squandered his opportunity to capture Constantinople before outside powers could intervene, Mehmet Ali was forced to make peace and withdraw his soldiers from Anatolia. To placate his opponent, though, the sultan named Ibrahim the governor of Damascus, Tripoli, and Aleppo, as well as tax collector of Adana, conditional on payment of an annual tribute to the Porte. This agreement was not expected to last; Mehmet Ali had not yet achieved his main goal of formal Egyptian independence, while the sultan had ceded territory that could be used to launch another invasion against him. It was widely assumed, therefore, that the start of a second conflict was just a matter of time.[37]

Not surprisingly, Russia's assistance came at a steep price. The czar and his advisors had already decided to pursue a new strategy toward the Ottoman Empire. Rather than attempting to undermine it, as they had in the past, they would try to preserve it, albeit as a relatively weak buffer state. In theory, this would allow St. Petersburg to achieve several objectives: avoiding a European war over the empire's remains, keeping the British navy out of the Black Sea, and avoiding the emergence of a much stronger Middle Eastern power that might be capable of checking Russian expansion.[38] The sultan's desperation provided an opportunity for the czar and his foreign minister, Count Nesselrode, to put this plan into action. On July 8, 1833, St. Petersburg and Constantinople signed the Treaty of Unkiar Skelessi, a defensive alliance that was intended to last for eight years. The treaty stipulated that each side would assist the other in the event of an attack by a third party. According to a secret protocol, however, which soon became widely known, the Porte did not actually have to fulfill this commitment. Instead, it needed only to close the Dardanelles Strait to foreign warships at St. Petersburg's request.[39] Several months later, Russia solidified its new relationship with Turkey by enlisting other European powers to sanction the treaty. On September 18, 1833, Russia and Austria signed the München-grätz Convention, while Prussia gave its assent one month later. Publicly, the three eastern powers agreed to uphold the integrity of the Ottoman Empire if possible. Privately, they singled out Egypt as the greatest threat to the empire and pledged to cooperate with one another if partition became necessary.[40]

These developments provoked considerable apprehension in London. Although the secret protocol in Unkiar Skelessi was not a major departure from the Porte's traditional policies or its prior agreements, including its 1809 treaty with Great Britain, closure of the Dardanelles at St. Petersburg's discretion would still benefit Russia in a major way, namely, by securing its Black Sea coast from British attacks during a war in which the Ottoman Empire remained neutral.[41] This was "a guaranteed immunity that she had never previously enjoyed," one that would handicap London in the event of a conflict.[42] Although Russia could not easily strike at Great Britain directly given the enormous distance that separated the two powers, it could always march its armies toward India if a war broke out between them. London, however, could not easily use its navy to attack Russia, given that St. Petersburg had no overseas colonies, limited naval forces, and little maritime trade. In fact, the Black Sea coast was "the only point at which England could touch Russia at all in case of conflict."[43] Unkiar Skelessi thus removed one of the few coercive options at its disposal.[44] Perhaps more important, the treaty created an impression that British influence at the Porte had been dramatically curtailed and that the Ottoman Empire had become a Russian satellite.[45]

This was particularly true for Palmerston. The treaty, he argued, would make Russia "the acknowledged umpire between the Sultan and his subjects" and allow it to "exercise a kind of protectorate over the Turkish empire."[46] These fears were not entirely unreasonable; Russia did aim to increase its influence over the Ottoman Empire at Great Britain's expense, even though it had abandoned its earlier strategy of "conquest or partition" for one of "penetration and control."[47] In Palmerston's words, the czar "perhaps thinks it better to take the place by sap than by storm."[48] Irrespective of Russian methods, the foreign secretary believed that St. Petersburg was "pursuing a system of universal aggression on all sides."[49] Unkiar Skelessi had demonstrated that Czar Nicholas I was "intently engaged in the prosecution of those schemes of aggrandizement towards the South, which ever since the reign of Catherine have formed a prominent feature of Russian policy." Palmerston therefore directed his ambassador at the Porte to warn the sultan "that by placing himself thus under the Protection of Russia, he will soon find himself under her absolute Control." Russia had already partitioned Poland. Turkey could be next.[50]

The Convention of Münchengrätz only fueled these concerns. Although Russia, Austria, and Prussia might have raised the issue of dividing the Ottoman Empire, this was not a course of action that any of them advocated or intended to set in motion. Yet it was unclear what had actually been discussed during the meeting, and this opacity bred suspicion. "An eventual partition of Turkey between Austria and Russia is thought to be one of the topics," Palmerston speculated at the time, "and this seems to me very probable."[51] If so, this would preclude the possibility of a general European settlement to the problem of Turkish decline since the eastern powers were already coordinating with one another on how to divvy up the spoils.[52] As a result, the British in general and Palmerston in particular came to view the agreement as further evidence of a Russian-led effort to weaken and perhaps eliminate the Ottoman Empire.[53]

Ultimately, the combination of Egypt's rise, the Ottoman Empire's defeat, and Russia's response placed Great Britain in a very difficult position. Policymakers in London had been reluctant to intervene in the Syrian War for a variety of reasons, but by standing on the sidelines they had allowed

St. Petersburg to exploit the situation to its advantage. As a result, Great Britain's entire approach to the Middle East was beginning to unravel. Given the need for a strong local partner, Palmerston had a choice: try to repair relations with the Porte or cut ties with an old ally and embrace a new one. Both options were dangerous. The Ottoman Empire had grown weak and was now under the czar's thumb. There was also no guarantee that it could regain its strength and restore its independence. Yet the only alternative to working with the Porte was siding with Mehmet Ali and using Egypt as a barrier to Russian expansion. The viceroy was ambitious, however, and well on his way to controlling the overland routes to India that ran through the Middle East. In other words, Great Britain faced a high risk of containment failure as well as a high risk of access denial, and one of the chief ways to mitigate the former would almost certainly exacerbate the latter.

How did Palmerston resolve this dilemma? He did so by reaching the conclusion that there was no dilemma at all. While the conflict in Syria was unfolding, the foreign secretary decided that Great Britain would be better off siding with Turkey, even though he was unwilling and unable to come to its defense. Once the war was over, his strategy for the region included three main elements: preventing Mehmet Ali from launching a war for independence; restraining the sultan from seeking revenge against his vassal; and helping the Porte to improve its economic, administrative, and military capacity.[54] Nevertheless, as he explained in 1834, the fate of the Ottoman Empire was largely in its own hands. "Our policy as to the Levant is to remain quiet, but remain prepared; time may enable the Turks to reorganize their resources."[55] Palmerston did have occasional doubts about the Porte's ability to check Russian expansion in the future. He even considered working with Egypt on a number of occasions. Yet the foreign secretary was optimistic about the Ottoman Empire's prospects. In his view, Turkey might be weak but was not condemned to decline. Because Palmerston believed that the Porte could remain the dominant local power and resume its place in Great Britain's containment strategy, London did not have to accept the increased risk of access denial that would come from supporting Egypt instead.

Palmerston, British Policy, and the Evolution of the Eastern Question

Palmerston's views on the Eastern Question were unsettled before, during, and to some extent even after Egypt's victory over the Ottoman Empire. For instance, although the Russo-Turkish War in 1828–1829 convinced many British policymakers that Constantinople was too weak to resist falling under St. Petersburg's control, Palmerston was not one of them. In fact, he reached a very different conclusion. "As to Russia and Turkey," he wrote to his brother in March 1829, "it seems pretty certain that the two parties are a tolerable match for each other." Russia undoubtedly had a military advantage over its longtime rival, "yet one's notion that she could eat up Turkey at a mouthful has been utterly dissipated."[56] At the start of his tenure at the foreign office, therefore, Palmerston supported the general principle of maintaining Turkish territorial integrity. Yet he began to doubt that the empire would stay intact and soon feared that it was "falling rapidly to pieces."[57]

These conflicting assessments likely contributed to Palmerston's bout of indecision when the war in Syria broke out.[58] Eventually, though, he decided that supporting the sultan and preserving the integrity of the Ottoman Empire was the best way to secure British interests. In September 1832, he explained to his ambassador in Paris that conquest by Egypt would have much more dangerous ramifications than a victory by the Porte. "It seems to me," he noted, "the inconveniences which might arise to Europe and to England from the dismemberment of the Turkish Empire would be greater than those which could follow from even the expulsion of Mehemet Ali from Egypt."[59] Several months later, he claimed that although the British could not provide military assistance to the sultan, "we are anxious to preserve his empire from dissolution or dismemberment, considering it to be an essential element in the general balance of power." It was, he argued, "very doubtful whether it could be for the advantage of England that the Sultan should be so weakened and that a new state should be created in Egypt, Syria, and Bagdad."[60]

Finally, after the Treaty of Unkiar Skelessi was signed but before he learned what the document contained, Palmerston publicly addressed the government's response to the war between Egypt and Turkey, Russia's role in the conflict, and the possibility of renewed violence in the region. According to the foreign secretary, "it was of the utmost importance for the interest of England, and for the maintenance of the peace of Europe, that the Ottoman empire should remain entire, and be an independent State." Thus, "his Majesty's Ministers would feel it to be their duty to resist any attempt on the part of Russia to partition the Turkish empire; and they would equally have felt themselves at liberty to interfere, and prevent the Pacha of Egypt from dismembering any portion of the dominions of the Sultan." Turkey, he declared, must not be allowed to collapse. "The integrity and independence of the Ottoman empire were necessary to the maintenance of the tranquility, the liberty, and the balance of power in the rest of Europe."[61]

Although Palmerston advocated siding with the sultan, others in the cabinet did not share his views. According to Paul Schroeder, "some British ministers, including the prime minister, Grey, were ready to write off the Ottoman Empire as doomed."[62] There was no longer any doubt that the distribution of power in the region had shifted markedly. Turkey's capacity to check Russian expansion was highly debatable, whereas Egypt's military strength was difficult to deny. For Grey, therefore, supporting Mehmet Ali was the sensible option, even if it increased the risk that the Ottoman Empire would disintegrate—a possibility that did not seem to concern him.

"The truth is that the fate of the Turkish Empire has long ago been sealed," he wrote to Palmerston just as Russia was coming to the sultan's aid. Several months later, Grey maintained that Great Britain should side with the viceroy if, as many predicted, the sultan were overthrown and his son became a figurehead emperor who answered to Egypt. "There can be no question," he wrote, "that our true interests would engage us to support the new Government," which "would afford a prospect of a really efficient Government, capable of resisting the designs of Russia."[63] For his part, the Egyptian ruler was more than willing to play this role.[64] As early as 1830, Mehmet Ali attempted to convince Great Britain's consul in Egypt that he could raise an army 125,000 strong and would use that force to check Russian expansion against the Ottoman or Persian Empires. "The Porte is gone," he cautioned, "and England must be prepared to raise a force in Asia to meet the Russians and where can she find it but with me and with my son after me?"[65]

Palmerston understood that Egypt was willing and able to provide Great Britain with military assistance. For example, one contingency that began to worry him was a civil war in Turkey, which could lead the sultan to request assistance from the czar. If St. Petersburg were about to intervene, however, London might have to seize the Straits so that they did not fall into enemy hands. Doing so would be difficult without the support of a local ally. British forces, Palmerston observed, "should not find it easy to force the Dardanelles unless we had troops to land." Mehmet Ali, however, "could lend us plenty and would be ready enough to do so."[66] This scenario also reflected a deeper fear, namely, that the Ottoman Empire might be too weak to survive as an independent actor. If that were the case and he had no other option, Palmerston repeatedly suggested that he would be willing to embrace Egypt as an ally, indicating the extent to which he was determined to contain Russia, even if this meant accepting a greater risk to other British interests in the region.

In December 1833, for example, Palmerston instructed John Posonby, Great Britain's representative to the Porte, to warn Mahmud II and his advisors that London would not permit St. Petersburg to gain de facto control over Constantinople. So long as the Sultan remained independent, Great Britain would be on its side. "But if the British Govt. should ever be reduced to the necessity of choosing between the Establishment at Constantinople of the Power of Mehmet Ali, or the subjection of that Capital to the Power of Russia, it would be impossible that we should not prefer the former of these alternatives."[67] Nearly a year later, he offered similar guidance to the British ambassador at Vienna. Palmerston's main concern, he wrote, was to ensure "that the Countries which constitute the Turkish Empire, by Whomsoever or howsoever they may be governed, should form an independent and substantive political State, capable of bearing its proper part in the adjustment of the general balance of power." Although the foreign secretary did not say so explicitly, he strongly implied that Egyptian rule over Constantinople was a more acceptable alternative than Turkish subservience to St. Petersburg.[68]

These warnings were intended to encourage Turkish resistance to Russian influence (by introducing the threat of abandonment) and drive a wedge between Austria and Russia (by raising the possibility that St. Petersburg's ambitions could trigger a wider European crisis).[69] It would be wrong to dismiss them as mere posturing, however. For example, there was a clear strategic rationale underpinning Palmerston's threats. If the sultan were to lose control over Constantinople, Great Britain was far more concerned about the prospect of a Russian occupation than an Egyptian takeover because St. Petersburg was far less vulnerable to British coercion than Alexandria. Preventing the czar from seizing the Straits and controlling access to the Black Sea—which remained one of the only places that London could apply military pressure against its great power rival—was critical.[70] Just as important, Palmerston had genuine doubts over which local actor would make the best ally in the region.

In May 1833, even before the Treaty of Unkiar Skelessi had been signed, Palmerston admitted that Great Britain should have intervened on behalf of the Porte when it had the chance. By missing the opportunity to do so, however, the situation had grown so dire that Egypt was looking more and more like London's only option. "Now that the Sultan has thrown himself so completely into the arms of Russia, and now that it seems so evident that it is Mehmet and the whole Turkish people on one side, and Mahmoud and the Russian garrison on the other, one's view of the matter begins to alter, and one begins to doubt whether England and France ought not rather to try to make something out of the Egyptian, as an element of future resistance to the undisguised, though most emphatically disclaimed, ambitious intentions of Russia."[71] Several months later, as he considered the likelihood that Austria and Russia might attempt to partition the Ottoman Empire, he argued that Great Britain could, "with the assistance of Mehmet Ali," create "a strong barrier against the accomplishment of this project."[72] As late as September 1834, more than a year after the crisis had passed, Palmerston was still intent on preserving the option of working with Egypt, even as he attempted to deter renewed conflict in the region, discourage Mehmet Ali from declaring his independence, and bolster the strength of the Ottoman Empire. "It is quite true," he wrote to the British representative at Alexandria, "that the relative situation of Mehemet Ali and the Sultan is unnatural and not likely long to last." Both sides were almost certainly biding their time until they could settle their dispute once and for all. Nevertheless, "it must be our business to postpone any change as long as possible, and to leave ourselves free to take what course may appear the best for our interests when that change comes on."[73]

Despite these recurring concerns, Palmerston did not depart from his decision to side with the Ottoman Empire. What explains this course of action?

Beginning in 1832, the foreign secretary would cite a host of reasons for his position, including skepticism that the viceroy could establish himself as caliph and replicate the ideological foundations of the sultan's rule;[74] concerns over Mehmet Ali's advanced age and questions about who would succeed him after he died;[75] suspicions that Egypt might align with France or Russia to further its imperial ambitions;[76] and fear that an Ottoman collapse could, in his words, "lead to a general war in Europe."[77] Given Palmerston's habit of "painting a supposed threat in its darkest colours," it is difficult to determine which of these factors mattered most or which ones mattered at all.[78] Yet the argument that he returned to again and again over the years was his belief that the Ottoman Empire could be reformed and therefore that Great Britain did not have to endanger its access to the Middle East to contain Russian expansion in the area.

Egypt was clearly an attractive ally in certain respects, particularly when it came to military power. It is hardly surprising, then, that Palmerston seemed willing to support Mehmet Ali if the Ottoman Empire were in irreversible decline and there was no other local actor capable of counterbalancing Russia—that is, if a hegemonic and complete power shift took place in the region. Yet Great Britain also had to worry about maintaining its access to the Middle East, and from this perspective Egypt represented a potential threat. During the 1830s, London was exploring alternative routes to India that could supplement or replace the lengthy trip around the Cape of Good Hope. One of these routes involved a journey across Suez to board steamships on the Red Sea. Another entailed traveling across Syria and taking a steamship down the Euphrates River to the Persian Gulf. Yet Mehmet Ali already controlled both coasts of the Red Sea due to his previous expansion in the Arabian Peninsula and the Sudan. There was also a widely held assumption that he would attempt to conquer Baghdad in the near future, which could give him control over the Euphrates route as well.[79]

In January 1833, Henry Ellis, a member of the Board of Control (the government organization charged with managing the East India Company and, with it, British affairs on the subcontinent), wrote to the foreign secretary and warned him about the potential consequences of Egypt's rise. Ellis, who was influential in shaping Palmerston's thinking on these matters, suggested that Great Britain should be leery of Mehmet Ali extending his rule beyond the Arabian Peninsula and the Levant. It was not in London's interests, he argued, "that a powerful Mahommedan state should be placed at the mouth of the Euphrates." His fear was that a strong local actor might cooperate with Russia to divide Persia, undermining another barrier to an assault on India. In addition, if Egypt moved into Mesopotamia, it might "spread its influence throughout Arabia" and soon "become a maritime power of importance." This was not an outcome that Great Britain could tolerate. "The absence of such a power is at present a complete security against any attack upon our Indian possessions from the Southern parts of the Indus."[80] Several months later, Palmerston explained to Great Britain's new representative in Alexandria that an independent Egypt would represent a serious threat to the Persian Gulf.[81] By comparison, an Ottoman presence in the area was much more tolerable. As the historian Harold Temperley explains, "Mehemet Ali had been threatening the Persian Gulf, which the Sultan could not do, and might impose a high tariff which the Sultan was bound by treaty not to do."[82] In other words, an ambitious rising power might pose a danger to Great Britain's regional interests that a declining power like the Ottoman Empire would not.

Of course, it might have been necessary to accept that danger if there were no other way to contain Russia. Indeed, this was precisely the trade-off that Palmerston appeared willing to make when he noted that Mehmet Ali's control over Constantinople was preferable to the czar's influence there. Yet the foreign secretary never really had to make this choice. Despite his occasional doubts, he continued to believe that the Ottoman Empire had not been permanently weakened and could once again contribute to a strategy of containment. In his assessment, therefore, a complete power shift had not yet taken place.

Palmerston's position on this matter was strongly influenced by Stratford Canning, who was a past and future British ambassador to Constantinople, as well as a persistent opponent of abandoning the Ottoman Empire.[83] Canning's own conclusion that the Porte was capable of meaningful reform dated to 1826, when the sultan massacred his Janissaries—a cadre of elite soldiers that had become little more than a barrier to any institutional changes that would put their privileges at risk. For Canning, who was the British minister in Constantinople at the time, this "auspicious incident" left a strong impression. "The head of the nation," he later recalled, "was once more a Sultan not only in title but in act and power."[84] His respect for the sultan would only continue to grow, as would his confidence in the prospects for Turkish reform.[85]

In March 1832, with the war in Syria under way, Canning wrote to Palmerston and made the case that Ottoman reform was possible, although it was not guaranteed. "The Sultan," he explained, "has long sought to render his authority independent of the restraints to which his more immediate predecessors . . . were obliged practically to submit." These efforts, moreover, had so far "been eminently successful." His "great end and aim," Canning claimed, "is the formation of a military force capable of maintaining his authority at home and enabling him to recover the station which he has lost for the present with respect to foreign countries."[86] Later that year, just before the Turkish defeat at Konya, Canning provided the British cabinet with a formal memorandum outlining his views. "The Turkish Empire," he argued, "has reached, in its decline, that critical point, at which it must either revive and commence a fresh era of prosperity, or fall into a state of complete dissolution." In his view, the former outcome should not be dismissed. The

Ottomans already had greater legitimacy and more territory than Egypt, both of which could be translated into economic and military power if the Porte took the right steps. Should Great Britain intervene on its behalf, moreover, "the spirit of improvement, thus encouraged and directed, could hardly fail to revive the overlaid resources of a country so rich in natural advantages."[87] This document did not convince a reticent cabinet to intervene on the side of Turkey. Yet Palmerston's guidance to his new ambassador at Constantinople the following year clearly reflected Canning's influence. "Our great aim," the foreign secretary declared, "should be to try to place the Porte in a state of internal organization compatible with independence, and to urge the Govt. to recruit their army and their finances, and to put their navy into some order."[88]

Because Palmerston believed the Ottomans could be strengthened over a relatively short period of time, the downsides of supporting the sultan were minimized and the dangers of siding with Egypt appeared unnecessary.[89] As Palmerston explained to his brother, Mehmet Ali's "real design is to establish an Arabian kingdom, including all the countries in which Arabic is the language." That, however, would mean "the dismemberment of Turkey," which was "as good an occupier of the road to India as an active Arab sovereign would be." Therefore, Great Britain "must try to help the Sultan in organizing his army, navy, and finances; and if he can get those three departments into good order he may still hold his ground." Ultimately, Palmerston argued, "if the Sultan really has any stuff in him, he might in a few years make himself independent."[90]

Palmerston versus the Pasha

Following his early bouts of uncertainty, Palmerston's attitude toward the Eastern Question hardened between 1834 and 1839.[91] "My own opinion is, and has long been made up; we ought to support the Sultan heartily and vigorously," he declared in 1839, the year the Porte initiated a second round of fighting against Egypt.[92] That does not mean that the British government devoted a tremendous amount of attention to the region during this period. In fact, it was generally preoccupied with other matters closer to home, at least until the outbreak of another conflict in Syria revived the specter of a Turkish collapse. Nevertheless, under Palmerston's guidance, the cabinet adopted and implemented a consistent strategy between the two wars, one that was intended to preserve the integrity of the Ottoman Empire, undermine Russian influence over the Porte, and strengthen the sultan so that he could eventually reclaim his lost territory.

One of the best ways that Great Britain could aid the Ottoman Empire was by preventing Egypt from inflicting any further losses, especially while the Porte was trying to get its own house in order. Palmerston's immediate goal, therefore, was to discourage both sides from beginning another war. This was no easy task. With Egypt determined to gain its independence and the Ottoman Empire resolved to seek revenge, the status quo in the region was extremely fragile. As Palmerston observed, "Mehemet Ali has too much, not to wish for more; and the Sultan has lost too much, to be able to sit down contented with his loss."[93] Although another war might have seemed inevitable, the foreign secretary hoped that it could be postponed. There was little doubt that the Ottoman Empire was still at a disadvantage and little chance that it could achieve a clear victory over Egypt. "It would no doubt be a capital thing for the Sultan to crush and exterminate Mehemet Ali," Palmerston lamented, "but the heel is not yet hard enough for the viper's tooth." Moreover, a defeat for the Porte could have disastrous consequences. "If the Sultan makes the attack he will have the worst of it," Palmerston predicted, "and if he is again beaten by his Pasha," it would mean "an end of him and his Empire."[94] Even more worrisome, though, was the possibility that the Porte might invoke Unkiar Skelessi and appeal to St. Petersburg for help. In that case, the czar's forces would likely seize control of Constantinople as well as the Dardanelles Strait, "and once in possession of those points, the Russians would never quit them."[95]

Just as important, continued peace would give the sultan time to shift the distribution of power back in his favor, if he were up to the task. Palmerston estimated that within only a year or two the Ottoman Empire might be in a position to defeat Egypt.[96] In the meantime, however, "the only thing for the Sultan to do . . . is to remain quiet."[97] Rather than provoking a conflict he was unlikely to win, the sultan had to realize "that the only certain way of restoring the Turkish Empire" was "to increase the public revenues of the state" and "apply those revenues in paying and organizing an efficient army and navy," along with building fortifications that would help protect Turkey from another attack.[98] During an audience with the Porte's representative the following year, Palmerston cautioned restraint and advocated reform. "I strongly urged upon him how expedient it is for the Sultan to abstain from attacking Mehemet Ali, because Mehemet's army is now probably better than, or at least as good as that of the Sultan," he recalled shortly after the meeting. The foreign secretary also advised the sultan "to employ himself in organizing his army and navy, and in improving his revenue," so that he could "make himself strong enough to be able to beat Mehemet Ali by his own means."[99]

In addition to preventing renewed conflict in the region, the British government undertook steps to help the Ottoman Empire revitalize its institutions, which were the key to enhancing its relative power. For example, whereas Egypt had deliberately set out to emulate European militaries, Ottoman armed forces clearly were not up to modern standards. Palmerston concluded, therefore, that foreign advisors could play an important role in closing this gap, and Great Britain, along with other nations, dispatched personnel to provide advice and training. The British and Ottoman navies also conducted a joint cruise in the eastern Mediterranean, in the hope that direct exposure to the Royal Navy would lead Turkish sailors to improve their performance. Yet these efforts were mostly ineffective and unsuccessful. This was due in large part to the extremely poor state of the Ottoman military, which simply could not be transformed in a short period of time. It could also be attributed to domestic political barriers, such as the Porte's reluctance to allow European military officers to command its own troops.[100]

One measure that was slightly more successful was economic rather than military in nature. In 1838, Palmerston and his ambassador to the Porte, John Posonby, convinced the sultan to sign the Balta Liman Treaty. This commercial agreement not only regulated import and export duties between the two nations, but it also committed the sultan to abolishing monopolies throughout his domains—including Egypt, which technically was still under Ottoman jurisdiction. From London's perspective, the treaty was expected to have several benefits: enhancing British influence over its ally; encouraging the sultan to continue the process of reform; and enabling the Porte to extract more resources from society that could be directed toward military modernization. From Constantinople's perspective, the treaty was a stepping-stone to what it truly wanted, namely, an offensive alliance with Great Britain that was directed against Egypt. At the very least, signing the agreement increased the odds that London would come to the Porte's aid when the next war began. For both sides, Balta Liman also represented an opportunity to erode Egypt's strength. After becoming governor, Mehmet Ali had created a system of monopolies over agricultural products and other commodities, "running Egypt as a single, vast, capitalistic enterprise, on the profits from which he was able to assure the stability of the new regime and also to finance his growing imperialist ambitions."[101] By outlawing these monopolies, the treaty would undermine the viceroy's main source of revenue and make it more difficult for him to maintain a large army and navy. It was, therefore, a way to strike indirectly at the heart of his power.[102]

In sum, Palmerston had embarked on a process of state building in the Ottoman Empire and state breaking in Egypt. Although the commercial convention provided some grounds for optimism that this approach would succeed, Great Britain's ability to encourage Ottoman reform was limited, and the end result of its efforts was modest at best. At the time, however, Palmerston was still convinced that the Porte's struggles were exaggerated. "People go on talking of the inevitable and progressive decay of the Turkish empire, which they say is crumbling to pieces," he wrote. While he was willing to concede that the Porte was weak, at least in comparison to the European powers, he denied that it was growing any weaker. "In the first place, no empire is likely to fall to pieces if left to itself, and if no kind neighbors forcibly tear it to pieces." Moreover, "I much question that there is any process of decay going on in the Turkish empire; and I am inclined to suspect that those who say that the Turkish empire is rapidly going from bad to worse ought rather to say that the other countries of Europe are year by year becoming better acquainted with the manifest and manifold defects of the organization of Turkey." Striking an optimistic note, he observed that despite these defects, "the foundations at least of improvement have been laid."[103] In short, there was still hope for the Porte. "A little addition of order, organization, and force to the scale of the Sultan, and a little less of sagacity, vigour of intellect, and administrative capacity on the part of the usurping Government of Egypt, would place Syria again at the command of the Sultan."[104] The notion that the Ottoman Empire was on the verge of collapse was, in Palmerston's words, "pure and unadulterated nonsense."[105]

The Second Syrian War and the Straits Convention

Although the Porte had not made much progress when it came to internal reform, the Balta Liman Treaty seemed to indicate that Great Britain was committed to siding with the Ottoman Empire against Egypt, as did Palmerston's repeated efforts to dissuade Mehmet Ali from declaring his independence. Encouraged by these signs of support, the sultan pressed his luck. In November 1838, an Ottoman official came to London in pursuit of an alliance. Specifically, the Porte wanted British assistance for a military campaign to recapture territories lost during the first Syrian war. Yet this request went far beyond what Palmerston was willing to consider. A defensive alliance directed against Egypt was acceptable to the foreign secretary because it would reduce the likelihood of conflict while undercutting Russia's influence over the Porte. An offensive alliance was another matter entirely and would only embolden the sultan to launch a war that he was unlikely to win.

Dissatisfied with London's conditional support and unwilling to wait any longer, the sultan went ahead and deployed Turkish forces into Syria the following year. His apparent calculation was that London would come to his aid despite the absence of any formal alliance between the two powers and regardless of whether he initiated hostilities. Palmerston's concerns about Ottoman military weakness proved to be well founded, however, as the Turkish forces suffered another rout at Egypt's hands. What's more, the situation quickly grew worse. Just days after Ibrahim scored a decisive victory at the battle of Nezib in June 1839, Sultan Mahmud II died. His son and successor, Abdul Medjid, was a feeble sixteen-year-old who was not prepared for his new position. Adding insult to injury, the Ottoman navy then sailed to Alexandria and defected to the Egyptian side. In a remarkably short period of time, therefore, "Constantinople learned that she had lost a battle, an army, a fleet and a Sultan."[106]

This string of calamities seemed to throw Great Britain's regional strategy into shambles. Yet it created an opportunity to undo the damage from the first Syrian war. Palmerston's initial concern was that the Porte might attempt to reach a settlement with Mehmet Ali on its own. Given its desperation to end the conflict, the foreign secretary feared that Turkey would offer "unnecessary and injurious concessions" that would jeopardize its security even further.[107] To head off this prospect, the British, French, Austrian, Prussian, and Russian ambassadors at Constantinople presented Abdul Medjid's ministers with a collective note, which essentially forbade the Porte from concluding any agreement with Egypt unless it had the consent of all five nations. The document proved to be the first step toward establishing a new status quo in the region, particularly with respect to the Ottoman Empire's role in Europe's great power rivalries. It also marked the start of nearly two years of intense diplomacy that would eventually bring this phase of the Eastern Question to a close. Before that happened, however, Great Britain would lead a military campaign against Egyptian forces; London and Paris would nearly come to blows; and Mehmet Ali would lose his empire.

As these events unfolded, Palmerston had two main objectives. In the near term, he needed to prevent Russia from coming to the Ottoman Empire's defense, which would jeopardize its independence. Over the long run, he wanted to undermine St. Petersburg's influence over the Porte, which meant getting rid of Unkiar Skelessi. Even before the sultan launched his unsuccessful bid for revenge, Palmerston concluded that the best way to achieve these goals was to replace this bilateral treaty with a collective agreement among all of the European powers.[108] Unkiar Skelessi, which would soon expire unless renewed, provided the legal justification for the czar to intervene in Turkey on his own. A multilateral treaty would remove this risk.

Like Unkiar Skelessi, the agreement that Palmerston envisioned would ban foreign warships from transiting the Dardanelles Strait. It would also extend this prohibition to the Bosporus Strait. Russia's Black Sea coast would therefore remain secure in peacetime, while the Russian fleet would no longer be able to enter the Sea of Marmara. In Palmerston's words, Constantinople would become "as secure as paper can make her against uninvited visitors from the Black Sea," while London's naval preponderance in the Mediterranean Sea would remain intact.[109] Moreover, if the Ottoman Empire found itself in a war with Russia, there would be nothing to stop the Porte from requesting British aid.[110] A precondition for this arrangement, however, was that Mehmet Ali would have to relinquish some, if not all, of his territory in Syria, removing the threat of an Egyptian army crossing the Taurus Mountains and marching on Constantinople. Despite his hostility toward the viceroy, Palmerston was willing to leave him with hereditary possession of Egypt if he cooperated. Although the foreign secretary maintained that it would be best if the Pasha "could be got rid of altogether," it seemed unnecessary to remove him from power "if he is content to spend the rest of his days there as a faithful servant."[111] The key question was whether all the European powers would consent to rolling back Mehmet Ali's empire.

Great Britain, France, and Austria had already explored the possibility of a European conference to settle the Eastern Question, and they appeared close to reaching an agreement amongst themselves. Russia, therefore, was an obvious candidate for obstructionism. Its decision to participate in the collective note thus reflected a significant shift in its policy toward the Ottoman Empire, one that stemmed from the realization that Great Britain would not rest until Unkiar Skelessi was no longer in effect.[112] Despite Russia's efforts to extend its influence over the Porte, as well as Palmerston's enduring fears that it might seize Constantinople, policymakers in St. Petersburg were reluctant to live up to their end of the bargain and come to the sultan's aid. As the British ambassador to St. Petersburg reported when the second Syrian war began, "I am convinced that this event has caused surprise and great annoyance to the Imperial Government; that the Emperor will not seek, but will avoid, as far as he can, recognizing any *casus foderis*, that the Sultan may allege to have arisen under the Treaty of Unkiar Skelessi." Russia simply was not eager to fight a war against Great Britain. Moreover, it had insufficient resources to finance a large military expedition. In the end, Nesselrode concluded that a bilateral agreement with Great Britain to neutralize the Straits was a better alternative than a de facto Russian protectorate over Turkey. Eventually, he agreed that a five-power arrangement would be acceptable as well.[113]

Although St. Petersburg was willing to support Palmerston's plan, Paris was not. During the early stages of the crisis, Great Britain and France coordinated closely with one another. For instance, both nations ordered their fleets in the Mediterranean Sea to cut off communications between Egypt and Syria. Both were also prepared to enter the Dardanelles, even without authorization from the Porte, to prevent Russia from sending its forces into Constantinople. In August 1839, however, the French government refused to compel Mehmet Ali to return the Turkish ships that had arrived in Alexandria, something that Palmerston was prepared to do. From that point onward, it became increasingly apparent that France would not support the threat or use of force against Egypt, which had not instigated the recent war, had not lost on the battlefield, and was extremely popular in Paris given the close ties between the two nations. Some in France even viewed Egypt as a potential maritime ally against Great Britain in the Mediterranean Sea and thought that it could be a useful proxy for extending French influence throughout North Africa.[114]

On September 30, 1839, the cabinet met to discuss Palmerston's plans, which now included using force to end Egypt's occupation of Syria, as well as replacing Unkiar Skelessi with a multilateral treaty. A majority of cabinet members consented in principle, although many were reluctant to offer their support given the possibility of causing a rupture in Anglo-French relations. No formal decision was reached, however. The details of the military operation had yet to be established, and a possible Austrian commitment to participate had yet to be secured. As a result, there was no resolution for another nine months. During this period, Palmerston presented France with a number of proposals to secure its cooperation. Each of these offers would have enabled Mehmet Ali to retain a portion of his empire. Paris remained intransigent, however, assuming that Palmerston's opponents in the British cabinet would eventually succeed in vetoing his plans or, if they did not, that any British efforts to coerce Egypt would ultimately fail.[115]

Although the latter assumption proved to be mistaken, the former was not far off the mark. According to Kenneth Bourne, the September 1839 cabinet meeting was just the start of a lengthy debate in London over what course of action the government should adopt, one that pitted "those who wanted to pursue coercion at the price of the Anglo-French Entente" against "those who wished to preserve the entente at the price of the Anglo-Russian rapprochement."[116] At the center of this debate were competing assessments regarding the distribution of power in the Middle East. It was not clear, however, that Palmerston's case for siding with the Ottoman Empire over Egypt would win the support of his colleagues. As the prime minister, Viscount Melbourne, wrote to his foreign secretary, "The more I think of the matter the more I am convinced that you will not be able to persuade a majority of the Cabinet to concur in measures which may lead to long and difficult operations." Some cabinet members, he reminded Palmerston, were "entirely for Mehemet Ali."[117]

One of those members was Lord Clarendon, who drafted a memo for Palmerston questioning the assumptions that underpinned his Middle East policy, including his sympathy for the Porte. Clarendon denied that he was partial to Mehmet Ali, claiming instead that his inclinations were actually "in favor of the Sovereign and against the Vassal." Nevertheless, Egypt's power "can neither be denied or despised." The same could not be said of the Ottoman Empire. Clarendon agreed with Palmerston that Great Britain's chief aim in the region was and should be containment. In his view, "fear of Russia and desire to keep her out of Constantinople is at the bottom of all, and most properly so." Yet he doubted that Turkey could help to counterbalance its stronger neighbor, even if it regained control of Syria. It was, he argued, "a fallacy to consider accession of territory synonymous with accession of strength." In fact, when it came to British interests, "I cannot but think they lie more in the direction of Egypt than of Turkey." Not only was Mehmet Ali stronger than the sultan, but he also stood ready to become Great Britain's ally. By opposing him, the British government would only force the viceroy to declare his independence and drive him into the arms of France. Finally, Clarendon was extremely skeptical that the Ottoman Empire could successfully implement its plans for reform, which would require overcoming "the vices that a brutalising government have almost made inherent in Turkish nature."[118]

Palmerston would hear nothing of it. In his view, Egypt was still far weaker than his opponents believed—whether those opponents were in his own cabinet or in the French government. The viceroy's power, he argued, was "built upon delusion and fancy, as much as upon injustice, a bubble which will burst as soon as it is strongly pressed."[119] At the same time, he continued to believe that reforming the Ottoman Empire remained a realistic possibility. Throughout the crisis, Palmerston sent additional military advisors to Constantinople as well as to the Ottoman forces operating in Syria, provided arms and munitions for Turkish troops, and encouraged the Porte to allow British or Prussian officers to command Ottoman army units.[120] Even the disastrous battle of Nezib and the death of Mahmud II did not undermine his confidence, although they did suggest that the Porte would not be able to restore its strength as quickly as he had hoped. "As to the Turkish empire," he wrote in September 1839, "if we can procure for it ten years of peace under the joint protection of the five Powers, and if those years are profitably employed in reorganizing the internal system of the empire, there is no reason whatever why it should not become again a respectable Power."[121]

Months later the Turkish government issued the Rose Chamber decree, which initiated a series of reforms that were collectively known as the Tanzimat, or "reorganization." The Tanzimat was not just a mechanism for strengthening Ottoman institutions; it was also meant to serve as a clear demonstration to the European powers and Egypt alike that the Porte "could produce a liberal and modern régime." Specifically, it abolished tax farming, announced the government's intention to implement rule-based systems for conscription and criminal justice, and declared that laws would be applied equally throughout the empire to people of all religions.[122] Afterward, Palmerston wrote to Posonby and credited his ambassador as the driving force behind the edict. He also reaffirmed his confidence in the prospect of a much more capable Ottoman Empire. "Your Hathi Sheriff was a grand stroke of policy," he exclaimed, "and it is producing great effect on public feeling both here and in France. I never have despaired of seeing Turkey rear her head again as a substantive element in the balance of power."[123]

After a long delay, rumors that the Porte and Mehmet Ali were on the verge of reaching a separate peace (and that France was behind the effort) finally convinced Austria to participate in a military campaign against Egypt. At the same time, reports of a local rebellion against Ibrahim's occupation created an opportunity to push his forces out of Syria.[124] On July 4, 1840, Palmerston pressed the cabinet to take action. Once again, however, no agreement was reached. The failure to achieve a consensus led the foreign secretary to write Melbourne the next day, reiterating his views and offering his resignation. "The immediate result of our declining to go on with the three Powers because France does not join us will be, that Russia will withdraw her offers to unite herself with the other Powers for a settlement of the affairs of Turkey, and she will again resume her separate and isolated position with respect to those affairs; and you will have the treaty of Unkiar Skelessi renewed under some still more objectionable form." That, in turn, would result in "the practical division of the Turkish empire into two separate and independent states, *whereof one will be the dependency of France, and the other a satellite of Russia; and in both of which our political influence will be annulled, and our commercial interests will be sacrificed;* and this dismemberment will inevitably give rise to local struggles and conflicts which will involve the Powers of Europe in most serious disputes."[125] Palmerston's threat worked. The cabinet agreed to support his proposals despite the risk of a conflict with France. As for his chief critics, they opted to submit an official dissent to the queen rather than resign in protest.

On July 15, 1840, Great Britain, Russia, Austria, and Prussia signed an agreement that would govern use of the Straits, as well as an ultimatum that would be delivered to Mehmet Ali. In exchange for military and diplomatic support from the European powers, Abdul Medjid consented to bar the passage of foreign warships through the Dardanelles and Bosporus during peacetime. As for the viceroy, he was offered hereditary tenure of Egypt along with the southern part of Syria for the remainder of his life, if he formally submitted to the sultan within ten days. After ten days he would lose all of Syria and after twenty days he risked losing Egypt as well.[126]

These developments were the precursor to a military assault that would eventually bring the entire episode to a close. On September 9, 1840, British naval forces launched a barrage against the city of Beirut, where Egyptian forces were based. Two days later thousands of Turkish troops, supported by British and Austrian marines, landed on the Syrian coast. By early November, Ibrahim had lost control over Beirut as well as the fortress of Acre. With his hard-won empire crumbling under the weight of European intervention, Mehmet Ali attempted to negotiate a way out of the crisis before he lost everything and managed to reach a settlement with the British officer in command of the Royal Navy squadron stationed off the coast of Alexandria. Although he agreed to return the Turkish fleet and withdraw his troops from Syria in exchange for hereditary tenure of Egypt and protection for Ibrahim's retreating army, the pact with Great Britain's "man on the spot" was not harsh enough for the sultan and his ministers, who wanted the right to choose which of Mehmet Ali's sons would govern Egypt after he died—a condition that the viceroy refused to accept. By this point, however, the end was in sight. After a period of back-and-forth, an acceptable agreement was finally reached between the two sides. As for France, which was now isolated, it abandoned Egypt and joined with the other European powers in an agreement that neutralized the Straits.

Between 1831 and 1841, the Middle East was wracked with massive internal changes due to the power shift that was taking place between a dominant nation in decline and a rising challenger that wanted to supplant it. As a result, Great Britain was forced to reevaluate its entire strategy toward the region, including its long-standing support for the Ottoman Empire—an important bulwark against Russian expansion and an unobtrusive guardian of the overland routes to India. Although it considered siding with Mehmet Ali and acquiescing to Egyptian hegemony, the British government eventually chose to preserve its alliance with the Porte, irrespective of the growing body of evidence that the Ottomans were no longer strong enough to resist pressure from local rivals or major powers. This was not an easy decision, at least at first. Great Britain's principal concern was to check Russian expansion, especially with India vulnerable to attack and St. Petersburg determined to extend its influence over Turkey. Moreover, because Egypt managed to defeat the Ottoman Empire, there was a good chance that it could be a useful military ally in the region. Yet supporting Egypt was a dangerous proposition. As an ambitious rising power, there was a realistic possibility that it might take actions that were averse to British interests, for example, by challenging London's access to the lines of communication that passed through the region. By contrast, the Porte had neither the incentive nor the ability to pose this type of threat. As he weighed the risks of containment failure and access denial, Palmerston focused sharply on the type of power shift that was taking place. In his view, Ottoman decline was not nearly as steep as other observers believed, while Egypt was not nearly as strong as its partisans maintained. Despite his occasional doubts about the Porte's resilience, especially between 1833 and 1834, Palmerston repeatedly argued that the Ottoman Empire could be reformed and that with only modest outside assistance and several years of relative calm it would be able to resume its place as an informal ally against Russia. In short, the foreign secretary did not believe that a hegemonic and complete power shift had occurred. Instead, the power shift was more limited in scope; Egypt's advantages were certainly real, but the new status quo was a fragile one. Given that the Ottoman Empire had the potential to remain a local hegemon and a British ally, there was seemingly no need to accept the perils of siding with an aggressive and expansionist rising power.

The Confederacy's Quest for Intervention and Independence, 1861–1862

Perhaps more than any other conflict, the American Civil War illustrates how the changing distribution of power in a peripheral region can capture the attention of the world's leading state, how a global leader can influence the outcome of a local power shift through its actions or its inaction, and how intervention decisions can shape the international system over the long run. Despite taking place in a relatively isolated area far from Europe, the war between the Union and the Confederacy drew intense scrutiny from several major powers, including Russia, France, and, most important of all, Great Britain, where everyone from factory workers to aristocrats followed the conflict with a close eye. While it raged on, debates over the merits of outside involvement as well as the potential effectiveness of any intervention played out in daily newspapers and on the floor of Parliament. Meanwhile, members of the governing cabinet wrestled with a handful of policy options, namely, recognizing the Confederate States of America as a sovereign nation, offering to mediate an armistice between the opposing sides, or simply allowing the war to continue without directly interfering.

Regardless of which option it chose, London's position on intervention was bound to have an enormous impact on the conflict in North America. For instance, official recognition would have enabled the South to sign formal treaties with foreign governments, increasing the likelihood that it would receive significant external support—especially if Great Britain acted in concert with other European powers or if those nations followed its example. External support, in turn, might have enabled the Confederacy to carry on the war against an opponent that enjoyed a considerable advantage in resources—and perhaps would have convinced the Union that forcibly reincorporating secessionist states was no longer possible. Not surprisingly, the South was desperate to gain foreign recognition, while the North was determined to prevent it. By contrast, an offer of mediation was ostensibly a much less intrusive measure. Because it would have constituted a de facto acknowledgment of Southern independence, however, all sides viewed it as a logical and perhaps necessary precursor to de jure recognition.

In short, either form of involvement would have benefited Richmond given its status as the weaker actor, increasing the prospect of Confederate success.[1] Moreover, a victory for the South would have had enormous geopolitical implications by permanently dividing North America between two bitter rivals. Although its continued rise was by no means a foregone conclusion, the United States had all the ingredients to be more than just the strongest nation on the continent. Given its nearly limitless resources and favorable geography, it was also well positioned to extend its dominance throughout the Western Hemisphere, to establish the sphere of influence that it already claimed but could not yet enforce, and perhaps to become a global power on par with Great Britain. In addition to undermining its primacy in North America, therefore, losing the war—and, along with it, nearly 40 percent of its total population and almost 50 percent of its territory—could have brought its great power prospects to an early end.[2]

Ultimately, Great Britain was willing to acknowledge the Confederacy as a belligerent, which was consistent with contemporary international law, enabled Richmond to purchase naval vessels from English shipyards so long as they were armed elsewhere, and immediately fueled anticipation of greater involvement in the near future. Yet it refused to officially recognize Southern independence, despite efforts by the Confederate diplomatic mission in London and its supporters in Parliament. Nor did the British government attempt to negotiate an end to hostilities, notwithstanding proposals by France for a joint mediation effort. Although these alternatives were seriously considered, British policymakers dismissed them and opted to stay on the sidelines. Nevertheless, as the war appeared to turn in the Confederacy's favor during the summer of 1862, London nearly decided to intervene before key cabinet members reconsidered their stance and chose to preserve their original strategy of strict neutrality. "Here, and only here," one study notes, "Great Britain voluntarily approached the danger of becoming involved in the American conflict."[3]

What accounts for these changing views? Throughout the war, and especially during the critical months in 1862 when some form of intervention was seriously considered, Foreign Secretary Earl Russell and Prime Minister Viscount Palmerston were guided by their shared interest in restoring regional stability as well as their evolving assessment of the war's likely outcome. Because the risks of containment failure and access denial in the region were both relatively low, ending the bloodshed trumped strategic and economic concerns, particularly as the casualties continued to mount. Of course, Russell and Palmerston had their own inclinations when it came to the future order in North America; for different reasons, both would have been satisfied to see the continent divided. Yet this concern was secondary, and restoration of the Union was still preferable to separation if it meant that peace would prevail. Because their main interest was regional stability, they were not prepared to accommodate the South until it could demonstrate that its position was sustainable and its independence was no longer in doubt—especially Palmerston, who was "the pivotal figure in any interventionist effort."[4]

Put differently, a necessary condition for intervention on behalf of the Confederacy was clear evidence that a complete power shift was taking place in the region, that parity between the North and the South was on the horizon, and that a durable balance of power could be firmly established. Only then would outside intervention stand a good chance of ending rather than extending the war. Although the Confederacy nearly reached this threshold when Robert E. Lee's Army of Northern Virginia launched an invasion of Maryland in September 1862, the costly Union victory at the Battle of Antietam was a major setback to the Confederate cause and effectively ruined any chance of British involvement in the war. Because of its impact on British policy, therefore, "Antietam, not Gettysburg, was the lynchpin of Southern success or failure."[5]

Great Britain's Interests in North America

British interests in North America during the Civil War era included a mixture of strategic, economic, and normative concerns. Many of these interests also divided the popular and political classes within Great Britain, although not always along clear lines. For instance, with a number of potentially vulnerable colonies across the border from the United States, the conflict became intertwined with imperial defense and was the catalyst for thorny questions such as whether to dispatch reinforcements to the region and how to finance the added cost of deploying more troops abroad. Given the nature of British industry and its dependence on American cotton exports, the economic consequences of the war were also felt deeply at home once trade across the Atlantic Ocean was interrupted. Moreover, the conflict cast a spotlight on other controversial issues that had implications for both domestic and international affairs, including whether American-style republican liberalism was inherently unstable and dangerous, when it was appropriate to embrace independence movements rebelling against foreign governments, and how Great Britain's opposition to slavery should influence its foreign policy. Sorting through these varied and sometimes competing interests leads to several conclusions regarding London's views on the Civil War and its overarching strategy toward North America: that it did not face a significant risk of containment failure or access denial; that its chief concern was the mounting humanitarian cost of the conflict; and, most important, that it was impartial when it came to the war's impact on regional order. In other words, policymakers did not particularly care whether the fighting resulted in a restoration of the United States or independence for the Confederacy. What mattered most was that it came to an end as quickly as possible.

For instance, one of the more pressing issues raised by the outbreak of the Civil War was the defense of British North America against a possible invasion.[6] Although the likelihood that the Union would start another major conflict before defeating the Confederacy might have been low, policymakers in London could not dismiss the possibility outright, particularly given the influence of William Seward, President Abraham Lincoln's secretary of state. Many British leaders viewed Seward as bombastic and aggressive; they were also aware of his long-standing and very public support for annexing Canada. This contributed to lingering concerns that the Union might instigate a war in the north despite its ongoing contest with the South.[7] In fact, it might even expand the conflict in the hope of rallying Confederate states to Washington's side in the face of a common enemy.[8]

Fears of a direct clash between the Union and Great Britain waxed and waned during the first year of the Civil War. By 1862, however, they had largely dissipated. Until this point, the precarious status of the Northern cause made a diversionary attack of some kind seem like a plausible threat. Palmerston, for one, was clearly worried about the possibility that the Union might provoke a fight and was therefore determined to maintain an effective military deterrent overseas. Relations between the two nations were "in a ticklish condition," he noted several months after the war began. "No reliance can be placed on Seward and Lincoln from week to week. The only security we can have against wrong insult and aggression on their part must consist in our being strong in our provinces, and in our squadron off their coast."[9] Yet other cabinet members were far less concerned about the situation and attempted to assuage Palmerston's anxiety. Secretary of State for War George Cornewall Lewis, for example, repeatedly argued that the North was too preoccupied with the conflict against the South to further divide its forces and risk a confrontation with Great Britain.[10]

In the end, Lewis's assessment proved to be the correct one. That was hardly certain at the time, however. Tensions between the two nations peaked during the final months of 1861 after a Union naval officer illegally detained a pair of Confederate envoys bound for London and Paris aboard the British mail packet *Trent*. Although the situation was eventually resolved peacefully, it was the closest that the United States and Great Britain had come to blows in decades. Aware that escalation might risk a war, London was still determined to address the matter head-on once it learned about the incident. The decision to board a neutral vessel and seize passengers without taking the ship to a prize court for adjudication was not only viewed as a significant insult to British honor (and perhaps a deliberate provocation intended to spark a conflict), but it was also considered a serious violation of international law. London therefore demanded that Washington release the captured diplomats and apologize for the actions of its naval officers. Convinced that it could handle only "one war at a time," in Lincoln's famous words, the Union ultimately freed the prisoners after an internal debate and avoided a conflict that it was not prepared to fight.[11]

Meanwhile, other considerations loomed even larger as the war unfolded, in particular, economic considerations. English textile mills that employed a large portion of the nation's work force and represented the backbone of its industry were heavily dependent on cotton produced in the American South. In total, nearly 80 percent of the cotton spun in English mills was imported from the United States.[12] By 1862, however, these exports had more or less ceased thanks to a pair of developments. First, the Union declared a maritime blockade of Confederate ports. Although Richmond attempted to discredit Washington's cordon as a "paper blockade," which did not need to be recognized by neutral powers according to international law, the British government chose not to openly challenge the quarantine. Not only was it eager to avoid becoming involved in the conflict once it began, but it was also fearful that denouncing the blockade would establish a precedent that could one day be used against it. Cutting off an enemy's seaborne commerce was a key element of British military strategy, and London did not want to provide third parties with a ready excuse to ignore its own blockades in the future.[13] Over time, however, the Union's encirclement became more effective and fewer blockade-runners were able to break through. Second, Richmond exacerbated the situation during the first year of the war by implementing an unofficial embargo of its cotton shipments in the futile hope of exploiting Great Britain's dependence on the Confederacy and forcing London to intervene out of economic necessity.

This interruption in trade had broad ramifications. The prospect that many laborers would soon be out of work not only threatened the British economy but also raised fears of internal unrest if significant and sustained unemployment led to protests or riots. Unlike strategic interests such as the defense of Canada, however, economic considerations were not a major source of concern for the British government at the start of the war. This was due in large part to the surplus of cotton that was still on hand from the previous year's "bumper crop," which mitigated the impact of supply disruptions from America, at least for a time. In 1862, however, a "cotton famine" contributed to a downturn in the textile sector, which was forced to put thousands of people out of work. As a result, the economic impact of the Civil War began to play a larger role in the calculations of British policymakers, who predicted greater hardship in the months and years to come if the conflict continued. By the summer of 1862, for example, Benjamin Disraeli, a leading conservative member of Parliament, complained to an acquaintance that the war in North America was "impoverishing Europe." Disraeli painted a grim picture of the issues confronting London (along with less urgent matters, such as the weather): "Lancashire & Lyons are both distressed; the trade returns fall off, the revenue declines, & the rain never ceases."[14] Before long, however, the situation began to improve. Other suppliers soon emerged, including India, Egypt, and Brazil, all of which began to reorient their agricultural sectors for the commercial production and export of cotton, replacing the lost American imports.[15]

Finally, there was a profound aversion among the general public as well as British policymakers to the human costs of the conflict, a topic that was the subject of detailed press reports in addition to diplomatic correspondence. Throughout Europe, one historian notes, most observers "regarded the American Civil War as useless, inhumane, and insulting to the civilized standards of the nineteenth century."[16] These views were strongly held throughout Great Britain due to the close cultural and economic ties between the two nations and only became more deeply felt as the war persisted, the casualty figures climbed, and the death toll continued to mount. According to Howard Jones, "as the conflict ground on, increasing numbers became repulsed by its human and material destruction and simply wanted the hostilities to end, regardless of who won."[17] That included key cabinet officials. "There can be but one wish on the part of every man in this country with respect to this war in America," Palmerston argued in 1862 as Parliament debated whether London should recognize the Confederacy as an independent nation, "and that is that it should end."[18] A durable peace, however, could be achieved in two very different ways: through a Union victory that guaranteed U.S. primacy in the region or a Union defeat that led to regional parity. Either one was acceptable in London. As Russell explained the following year, the only outcome that truly undermined British interests was perpetual conflict, because war between the Union and the Confederacy "disturbs commerce, it puts to hazard the peace of the world, and it afflicts America herself."[19]

This overview of British interests provides support for the theory's emphasis on the linkage between risk assessments and preferred regional orders. For instance, Great Britain did indeed have to worry about access denial as the Civil War unfolded, for two reasons. First, a Union assault on its colonies in Canada might have pushed it out of the region. Second, its dependence on Southern cotton was a source of economic vulnerability. Neither of these problems was especially serious, though. Not only was Washington too preoccupied with its fight against Richmond to start another war, which became apparent during the *Trent* affair, but shortfalls of cotton were mitigated by adjustments in the global economy, which created new suppliers in a relatively short period of time. The risk of access denial was also more of a near-term concern than a long-term challenge because a resolution to the conflict in North America would eliminate the threat of a diversionary attack and remove the main barriers to trade. At the same time, concerns about containment failure were even lower and therefore were not a major factor in Great Britain's foreign policy during this period. Because of North America's remote location, outside powers would need to commit enormous resources to mount a serious military intervention, even while the region was in upheaval and Washington was distracted. Intervention would also mean accepting significant opportunity costs, including a diminished ability to manage more pressing threats from rivals in Europe.[20] Although that might not have stopped other great powers a century earlier, by this point the era of serious competition for positional advantage in North America was basically over.

Given these relatively modest risks, it is not surprising that British policymakers were highly motivated to end the war on humanitarian grounds, especially since the costs of the conflict rose substantially as time went on. Nor is it surprising, therefore, that they were impartial between a Union conquest of the South that would reestablish its primacy and a Confederate victory over the North that would leave the region divided because either outcome would end the bloodshed. Of course, some policymakers did seem to favor the latter outcome, which was somewhat appealing from a strategic point of view. Simply put, as long as the North and the South remained focused on one another, neither could pose a serious challenge to London's interests in North America or the Western Hemisphere more broadly. Palmerston, for one, clearly recognized that the collapse of the Union could put Great Britain in a favorable position. "If the North and South are definitely disunited," he wrote in 1862, "and if at the Same Time Mexico could be turned into a prosperous Monarchy I do not know any arrangement that would be more advantageous for us."[21] William Gladstone, who served as chancellor of the exchequer while the Civil War was under way, also recalled that Palmerston would have been happy to see parity reign in North America because it would have resulted in the "diminution of a dangerous power." Despite this view, Palmerston "prudently held his tongue."[22] Thus, his preference for parity was not a very strong one. In fact, as detailed below, he was the key opponent of any intervention that might have divided the continent. For his part, Russell was also willing to see the Union separated and was even more willing than Palmerston to pursue some type of diplomatic intervention, although he was driven more by normative concerns than by strategic considerations. Yet the foreign secretary's preference for a balance of power was quite weak as well, and while animosity between the two sides made it difficult to imagine them actually setting aside past grievances and coming back together as one nation, he eventually concluded that it was not worth standing in their way if they did. "If it were possible that the Union could be reformed" and "if the old feelings of affection and attachment towards it could be revived in the South," Russell maintained, "I for one would be glad to see the Union restored." At the same time, if "the North were to feel that separation was finally decreed by the events of the war, I should be glad to see peace established upon those terms." Looking forward, he concluded, "I trust that we shall see at the close of this struggle *either one great republic or two great republics* in the full enjoyment of freedom and all the advantages of a great and independent Power."[23]

The Rationale for Neutrality and the Requirements for Intervention

With no clear preference for a victor and no desire to be drawn into the war, in May 1861 London formally announced its intention to remain neutral. At first glance, neutrality should have benefited the Union as the stronger party. By conferring belligerent rights on the Confederacy, however, London's decision spurred fears of imminent diplomatic recognition in the North as well as hopes for outside assistance in the South. Even though it was consistent with international practice and reflected the obvious fact that war in North America was far more than a minor rebellion, the announcement received a hostile reaction in Washington and guaranteed that the issue of intervention would not go away.[24] As Russell argued emphatically at the time, however, "We have not been involved in any way in that contest by any act or giving any advice in the matter, and, for God's sake, let us if possible keep out of it!" He hoped, therefore, that if a full-scale war could not be avoided, it would, at least, "be a short one, and not interfere with the ultimate prosperity of the country."[25]

Palmerston concurred with his foreign minister, even when the likelihood of a short war began to decline. Writing some months later, he offered his opinion that "our best and true policy seems to me to go on as we have begun, and to keep quite clear of the conflict between the North and South."[26] The prime minister still remained committed to nonintervention the following year, as the two sides fought in the west while the situation remained comparatively quiet in the east. Great Britain had maintained a policy of strict neutrality, he explained in the House of Commons, "and from that position of strict neutrality it is not our intention to depart." Palmerston did not deny that the economic and humanitarian consequences of the war were bad for America and bad for Great Britain. Yet they were not bad enough that he was ready to cast aside neutrality and opt for intervention. "We regret, no doubt, the calamities which that war is bringing upon the population of the United States; we lament the pressure which incidentally that war has produced upon the commercial and manufacturing interests of this country; but we do not think that that is a sufficient reason why we should depart from a course which a sense of prudence and a sense, I may say, of national honour, have imposed on us, or why we should interfere in a quarrel with which originally we had nothing to do."[27]

The reticence of British policymakers to become involved in the Civil War stemmed from a number of factors, aside from their initial hope that the conflict would be brief and from their consistent desire to avoid a military confrontation with the Union if possible. There was, for example, a widely held view that the South might not require outside assistance and therefore that intervention might not be necessary because the North would eventually realize that its objective was unachievable. Although policymakers in London did not have a strong preference when it came to regional order in North America, that does not mean they thought parity and primacy were equally likely outcomes. Rather, the former appeared to be a much better bet than the latter. Especially during the first year of the war, there was a general sense throughout Europe that the North could not win the conflict because reincorporating the South was an impossible task. The only questions that seemed to remain, then, were whether and when the Union would give up and how many losses both sides would suffer before it did.

This conclusion stemmed from two preconceptions. First, despite Washington's obvious advantage in resources such as transportation infrastructure and manufacturing capacity, not to mention Richmond's inability to close this gap by gaining international recognition and outside support, there were persistent doubts about the Union's ability to translate its enormous latent power into effective military power. These questions were fueled by the relatively poor performance of Union armies in a number of early engagements, as well as the inactivity of its armed forces in the east. The Confederacy, by contrast, seemed to have the edge on the battlefield, which was usually attributed to greater motivation (because Southern soldiers were fighting to defend their home territory from an invading force) and military skill (because Southerners were generally thought to have a greater aptitude for fighting than their Northern counterparts). Second, even if Union armies were able to defeat Confederate forces and compel them to surrender, few observers thought that they could actually hold Confederate territory and subdue a hostile population over an extended period of time. At some point, the costs of occupation would simply prove to be too great. Both of these sentiments were reflected in popular commentary. For example, according to the *Times*, which was the most influential daily in London, "The South is not absolutely so strong as the North, but it has hitherto been stronger in the field, and it will always be strong enough, in all human probability, to resist subjection, if not to enforce its will."[28] Likewise, the failure of General George McClellan to capture Richmond in the summer of 1862 caused another paper to conclude that "the North, with its boundless resources and immense territory, is utterly unable to reorganise its army for the conquest of the Southern Confederacy."[29]

Another consideration that made London reluctant to intervene—and arguably the more important one as the war dragged on, Washington dug in its heels, and hopes for a swift resolution faded away—was that any effort at mediation would almost certainly fail unless the situation on the ground started to change. So long as Union and Confederate war aims were completely incompatible and both sides could sustain their military efforts, there was little to be gained from becoming involved. Although the South would welcome any intervention, the North would simply ignore it and continue to pursue its goals by force. If the South secured a major victory, however, then the North might begin to reconsider its position, particularly if the general public turned against the conflict, antiwar Democrats increased their power in Congress, or Lincoln lost confidence in his strategy. Under any of these conditions, the Union might be receptive to an offer of mediation by an outside party; not only would it become apparent that reincorporation was a lost cause, but Washington would also be unlikely to provoke a conflict in response to a friendly gesture that could end a failing war. Alternatively, if the Union still held out the hope of a decisive victory despite mounting losses, recognition of the South could deal the Northern cause a fatal blow. Absent Confederate success on the battlefield, however, any intervention would be futile and perhaps even counterproductive.

"The danger," Palmerston warned early on, "is that, in the excited state of men's minds in America, the offer of anyone to interpose to arrest their action, and disappoint them of their expected triumph, might be resented by both sides; and that jealousy of European, especially of English, interference in their internal affairs might make them still more prone to reject our offer as impertinent."[30] The prime minister continued to express these concerns the following year when calls for intervention grew louder. As he explained in Parliament, the British government "would be delighted" to help the two sides reach some type of accord, but only if there were an opportunity to do so that had a reasonable chance of success. That still seemed unlikely. Rather, "in the present state of the contest, while the two parties seem animated with the most bitter feelings and angry resentment against each other, I am afraid that any proposal of that kind would not be well timed, and would be sure to meet with rejection on both sides." Yet he did leave the door ajar to intervention in the future if "a different state of things should arise."[31] In other words, if Northern military defeats caused the Lincoln administration to reconsider a negotiated solution, Great Britain might rethink its commitment to neutrality. Russell agreed with this sentiment, even while he suggested that permanent division seemed to be the logical and likely outcome of the war. Not only would the prospects of a negotiated agreement remain dim until the Union suffered enough losses to finally abandon its cause, but any agreement that was reached under pressure from external parties would be a fragile one. Although he hoped that both sides would eventually be willing "to form a treaty by which the independence of the Southern States should be acknowledged" rather than continue to fight, he also argued that it would be "far better that this conviction should come from the failure of their own efforts than from the intervention of any foreign Power."[32] It was the relative strength of the two sides, not the actions of third parties, that would determine when and how the conflict would end.

Ultimately, as the British cabinet watched the war unfold between 1861 and 1862, its calculus on intervention was "coldly pragmatic."[33] London's willingness to recognize the South or to propose mediation terms that included independence for the Confederacy was highly contingent on the level of success that Richmond could achieve on the battlefield. If it could compel Washington to abandon its chief wartime objective of reunification and if it were strong enough to deter future attempts by the North to reacquire lost territories, then international intervention could help the two sides reach a lasting accord. If not, then British involvement stood little chance of success because the Union would refuse to concede.

When the Confederate commissioner to Great Britain arrived in London and petitioned the British government for official recognition, Russell made this position clear. As the foreign secretary later recalled telling him, "if the military operations of the Southern States had been attended with great success; if their victories had been brilliant and decisive; and if the powers of Europe were generally disposed to acknowledge that they had fairly acquired the position of an independent power, the British government might fairly be asked for recognition." At the time, however, "none of these factors were proved, and there was no case to justify the British Government in acceding to the proposal he had made."[34] Or, as Palmerston told another Confederate representative, "Break through this blockade, get some decisive advantage, and no country will recognize you more cheerfully when you have earned your right to it, than England will."[35] Consistent with the theoretical arguments in chapter 1, because Great Britain was mainly concerned with restoring stability in North America, it would accommodate an RRP and intervene on its behalf only when it became clear that a complete power shift had taken place, the region had been transformed into a balance-of-power subsystem, and a durable peace rather than renewed conflict was the most likely outcome.

These conditions were almost met in September 1862. With the North experiencing serious reversals on the battlefield and the South launching a military campaign on Union territory, it appeared as though Washington was on the verge of suffering a large enough defeat that it would be unable to resist secession any longer. Moreover, British policymakers believed that the shifting tides of battle were creating an opportunity for intervention. As a result, they began to consider an offer of mediation that might secure Confederate independence and, they hoped, bring the war to an end. The Confederacy's failure to capitalize on the military success it had achieved during the preceding months brought this debate to its conclusion, however, and left policymakers to continue watching the conflict from a distance.

The Shifting Military Balance and the Buildup to Antietam

By the middle of 1862, barely one year after the start of the Civil War, the prospects for a Northern victory were looking more and more favorable. In the western theater, where most of the fighting took place during the first twelve months, the Union was finally making significant progress. Under the command of Flag Officer David Farragut, naval forces had seized New Orleans, the Confederacy's largest city and seaport. This not only dealt the South a symbolic blow, one that captured the attention of observers overseas, but it also enabled Washington to tighten its maritime blockade and make its strategy of economic strangulation more effective. Union armies were beginning to score their own victories as well. For instance, by capturing Forts Henry and Donelson earlier in the year, they had secured the border state of Kentucky and set the stage for an invasion deep into Tennessee. They also managed to repel the Confederate counterattack at Shiloh, albeit at great cost, and then take the critical rail junction of Corinth, which was a key step toward attacking Vicksburg and gaining control over the Mississippi River. Meanwhile, in the eastern theater, General George McClellan's Army of the Potomac began a major campaign in March, sailing down the Chesapeake Bay, disembarking at Fort Monroe, and then moving up the Virginia Peninsula toward Richmond. McClellan's objective was to capture the Confederate capital, a blow from which the South might not recover. By the end of May, Union forces were encamped just a short distance from the city and enjoyed a numerical advantage over the defenders, although McClellan insisted, as he often did, that his army was outnumbered.[36]

With its seaborne commerce increasingly threatened, enemy armies scattered across its territory, and the fate of its capital in jeopardy, the outlook for the Confederacy seemed grim. Not surprisingly, then, British policymakers saw no reason to become involved in the conflict, although they still declined to rule out the possibility of intervention in the future if circumstances changed. According to Russell, "the present time would be most inopportune" for outside intervention. "No good could come of it, and in the present state of the war, and in the present embittered state of feeling on both sides, such an offer would rather tend to prevent any good result from being attained, if it should be deemed desirable to attempt such mediation hereafter."[37] Yet the tide of battle soon turned back in the South's favor, especially in the east, which appeared to confirm earlier suspicions that the North could not win.

Although Union victories during the first half of 1862 seemed to provide grounds for optimism, in reality the situation was precarious. Lincoln believed that a limited aims strategy—one characterized by a maritime blockade, the seizure of key Confederate cities, and no immediate efforts to tackle the slavery problem—would eventually turn Southern moderates against secession. Yet this assumption was proving to be unfounded. Instead, resistance was much more robust, widespread, and enduring than the president had anticipated, and Washington was not much closer to winning the war.[38] This became apparent to all, especially to outside observers, when the Union's progress suddenly stalled in the east and Confederate forces went on the attack. McClellan's Peninsular Campaign had generated lofty expectations, especially as Union forces moved toward Richmond and Confederate forces pulled back to protect their capital. Following the Battle of Seven Pines at the end of May, however, his offensive ground to a halt, and Union troops settled in for a lengthy siege of the city. In addition to breaking McClellan's momentum, the battle had another notable consequence. One of the casualties on the Southern side was General Joseph Johnston, commander of the Army of Northern Virginia. Confederate President Jefferson Davis chose his military advisor, Robert E. Lee, to succeed him. Within a month, Lee's forces launched a series of attacks against the Army of the Potomac, known as the Seven Days Battles, which drove McClellan back and led him to establish a new camp at Harrison's Landing, roughly two dozen miles from Richmond. One month after that, with Lincoln's tolerance of McClellan's languid pace, aversion to risk, and overreaction to any setbacks nearing an end, the president recalled the Union forces to Washington.

McClellan's campaign was closely monitored in Great Britain, where his requests for additional troops and overly optimistic assessments made him the subject of biting criticism in the press. More generally, the Union's inability to capture Richmond when its forces were so close to the Confederate capital suggested that time was running out for the North. "Ever since the beginning of this unhappy conflict," the *Times* observed, "the crowning victory which was to restore the South to Federal supremacy has always been dancing like a Will-o'-the-Wisp before the eyes of the Northerners. It has led them through a boundless waste of blood and money, it has caused them to stir up hatreds which a century perhaps will hardly appease, and it now glimmers before them as deceptively as ever, while they are sinking slowly but surely into the slough of national disorganization and bankruptcy." Despite a string of battles across multiple theaters, up to the present the Union had proven largely ineffective. "Though the future maps of America may be marked abundantly with the crossed swords that distinguish the battlegrounds in the maps of the Old World, the chronicles cannot speak of many Federal victories." On the basis of Washington's record of futility, the paper argued, it was time for negotiation, because "the worst settlement of the dispute cannot be so fatal as the war."[39]

Likewise, the *Morning Post*, described by one historian as the "semi-official voice of the Palmerston government," was extremely skeptical about the North's chances of success given the outcome of the Peninsular Campaign.[40] Even before McClellan's withdrawal to Harrison's Landing, his decision not to attack Richmond until more troops arrived indicated that a successful offensive was probably impossible. "The clouds are beginning rapidly to collect over the Federal cause," the paper declared. In particular, it was difficult to understand why an army that was expected to "crush down all opposition" would instead "shrink from a contest on the grounds of intrinsic weakness." Soon afterward, as the Union forces retreated from the outskirts of Richmond, and as Lincoln's call for another 300,000 volunteers appeared to be going unanswered, the paper voiced even deeper pessimism: "The time seems now to be fast approaching when the Government at Washington must confess their utter helplessness to conduct the affairs of the country." Nevertheless, it was not yet prepared to call for outside intervention, which still seemed premature. Although "a conviction is beginning to dawn upon the Northern population that the effort will be a vain one to subjugate the South," taking advantage of the Union's faltering position might backfire by creating a rally effect among those who were growing weary of the conflict. European involvement, the paper cautioned, "might fan into a flame the flickering spark, which otherwise will soon expire."[41] Better, then, to postpone any involvement until the North was ready to accept that separation was inevitable.

The Union's declining fortunes resulted in even greater pressure on the cabinet to intervene in the conflict. In mid-July, Parliament engaged in a lengthy debate over a motion calling for the government to mediate between the North and the South. Palmerston, who opposed the motion and helped defeat it, highlighted the uncertain military situation in North America as the reason for British inaction. Despite the Confederacy's recent success, the outcome of the war remained unclear, and the South had yet to prove that it could survive against the North. He argued, therefore, "that up to the present moment, whatever may be the opinion which anybody may entertain of the determination of the South to fight to the last for the maintenance of its independence, practically the contest has not yet assumed that character which would justify this country in assuming that that independence was permanently and fully established." Nevertheless, the prime minister refused to speculate on the future course of the conflict or to rule out intervention if it turned more sharply in the Confederacy's favor. "The events of this war have been so contrary to all anticipation, from time to time, that he would be a bold man indeed who should attempt to prophesy from month to month what character the war would assume." The British government, he claimed, would gladly consider intervention "to establish peace between the two parties who are carrying on this desolating and afflicting contest," although it would do so only when the chances for success seemed reasonable.[42] In fact, even as Palmerston remained opposed to any involvement in public, he and Russell planned to have a cabinet meeting to discuss the possibility of intervention, once the foreign secretary returned from a planned trip to Europe alongside Queen Victoria.[43]

Before policymakers could formally consider the issue, though, events on the ground provided additional evidence that an opportunity for intervention might be at hand. Following his victory during the Seven Days Battles, Lee reorganized the Confederate forces under his command and began to lay the foundation for an offensive campaign. By late July, with McClellan's army still regrouping at Harrison's Landing, Lee had dispatched nearly half his forces to monitor and engage the Union's Army of Virginia, which had just been established and was tasked with defending the approaches to Washington from the area south of the Rappahannock River. Both Lee and Davis feared that once the new army was brought up to full strength it could cut off Richmond's supply lines through the Shenandoah Valley and perhaps even combine with McClellan's forces to envelope the capital. Despite the risks, therefore, they gradually weakened the defenses around Richmond, sent more troops north, and prepared to exploit a fleeting window of opportunity to attack. Calculating that the ever-cautious McClellan could be kept at bay, and therefore that Richmond was not in excessive danger, Davis allowed many of the remaining forces to head north in early August, while Lee remained behind to direct the defense of the capital. Lee did not stay in Richmond long, however, departing once he learned that the Army of the Potomac planned to evacuate the peninsula.[44]

These movements culminated in the Second Battle of Bull Run, which took place near Manassas, Virginia, at the end of August. Lee nearly achieved his objective during the clash, scoring a clear victory and compelling Union forces to retreat toward Washington. The turnabout was remarkable. Less than two months earlier, Richmond had been under siege. Now the Union's capital seemed to be at risk. Press reports cast the engagement in dramatic terms. "A careful perusal of the details of the battles fought in America on the 29th and 30th of August only confirms our first impressions of the immensity of the encounter, of the magnitude of the interests involved, and of the importance of the consequences to which the issue must inevitably lead," declared one paper.[45] Shortly afterward, Palmerston wrote to Russell and conveyed his impression that the military balance seemed to be shifting in the South's favor. The Union forces, it appeared, "got a very complete smashing." He also predicted that it was "not altogether unlikely that still greater disasters await them, and that even Washington or Baltimore may fall into the hands of the Confederates." If the South were able to capture a major Northern city and especially the capital, then circumstances might finally be ripe for intervention. Following such a major defeat, he wondered, "would it not be time for us to consider whether in such a state of things England and France might not address the contending parties and recommend an arrangement upon the basis of separation?" In sum, it appeared that the Confederate victory at Manassas and the growing likelihood of future victories might be sufficient to convince Washington that subduing the South was simply not possible. Russell concurred, arguing that "the time is come for offering mediation to the

United States Government, with a view to the recognition of the independence of the Confederates." Moreover, if Washington continued to oppose negotiations and pursue its military campaign instead, the foreign secretary felt that the British "ought ourselves to recognise the Southern States as an independent State," a plan that the prime minister deemed "excellent."[46]

The Battle of Antietam and the End of the Intervention Debate

While the Second Battle of Bull Run was an important battle in its own right, the biggest consequence of the engagement was that it served as the springboard for an even more ambitious Confederate offensive, which culminated in the Battle of Antietam near Sharpsburg, Maryland, in mid-September. Lee and Davis had several objectives in conducting an invasion into Union territory: prompting unrest in a border state where pro-Confederate sentiment was believed to be high, providing ammunition for antiwar Democrats in the hope that they would make major gains in the upcoming congressional elections, and perhaps even convincing the European powers that they should finally intervene on the Confederacy's side.[47] Indeed, word that Lee's troops had crossed the Potomac River and moved into Maryland lifted the spirits of Southern partisans and raised expectations that the war would soon be over. As one daily waited for reports on the outcome, it predicted that the confrontation would be a turning point in the war. "It is to be hoped," the editors wrote, "that at last some faint prospect of 'the beginning of the end' has commenced to manifest itself." It did not seem possible that the two sides could continue fighting much longer. While the Union was "utterly bankrupt," the Confederacy was "bleeding at every pore."[48]

Lee's Maryland Campaign also gave British policymakers, especially Palmerston, a reason to wait a bit longer before pursuing any intervention. "It is evident that a great conflict is taking place to the north-west of Washington, and its issue must have a great effect on the state of affairs," he told Russell.[49] A major clash in Maryland so soon after the South's victory at Manassas had the potential to be a decisive event. Should the Union lose, Palmerston argued, its cause "will be manifestly hopeless." Should the Confederacy lose instead, however, its forces might be stranded.[50] Either outcome could alter the course of the war and, as a result, tip the scales in favor of British intervention or against it. "If the Federals sustain a great defeat, they may be at once ready for mediation, and the iron should be struck while it is hot," the prime minister declared. "If, on the other hand, they should have the best of it, we may wait awhile and see what may follow."[51] Unfortunately for Richmond, Antietam proved to be a major setback. At the tactical level, the rematch between Lee and McClellan (who was placed in charge of Union forces despite his failure on the peninsula and his demotion from general-in-chief) was nearly a draw. Both sides suffered heavy casualties, and while his campaign was unsuccessful, Lee was able to salvage most of his army and retreat back across the Potomac, due in large part to McClellan's reluctance to pursue him. Strategically, however, the battle was a tremendous defeat for the Confederacy, not only because it had to withdraw from Union territory and go back on the defensive, but also because of its impact in foreign capitals.

Early reports on Lee's Maryland Campaign seemed to confirm the growing sense in Great Britain that conditions might be auspicious for outside intervention. As Palmerston noted at the end of September, the most recent information available suggested that "the Forces of the North & South are pretty equally balanced & that neither are likely to overpower the other." If so, this was "just the Case for the Stepping in of Friends."[52] It was not long, however, before news of the Confederate defeat reached London. Lee's failure left a significant impression on foreign observers, one that was magnified by their relatively low opinion of the North's military prowess and the lofty expectations created by the South's recent victories. "An Army demoralized by a succession of failures and a long retreat has suddenly proved at least equal, and we may probably say superior, to an army elated with triumph and bent upon a continuation of its conquests," the *Times* explained. "The forces of the Confederates have suffered their first important check exactly at the period when they might have been thought most assured of victory." Despite the Union's enormous advantage in men and materiel, until recently "every pitched battle had been more or less in favour of the Confederates, and their final advance from Richmond to the Potomac represented one continuous victory." Yet "the best army, in the best condition, which the Confederates have ever arrayed on a field of battle stood last month on the soil of Maryland," and "it was worsted by an army of which we can give no account, commanded by a General who had never won a victory before."[53]

The outcome of the battle quickly caused Palmerston to revise his views and, in the end, renounce his support for diplomatic intervention. With Confederate forces now in retreat, there was little chance that the Union would ever accept Great Britain's proposal. "There is no doubt that the offer of Mediation upon the basis of Separation would be accepted by the South," he observed. "Why should it not be accepted? It would give the South in principle the points for which they are fighting." Nevertheless, the North "would be unwilling to give up the principle for which they have been fighting so long as they had a reasonable expectation that by going on fighting they could carry their point." Thus, recognizing Richmond would only antagonize Washington without lessening its commitment to a military solution. Ultimately, Palmerston observed, "the condition of things . . . which would be favorable to an offer of mediation would be great success of the South against the North. That state of things seemed ten days ago to be approaching. Its advance has lately been checked, but we do not yet know the real course of recent events, and still less can we foresee what is about to follow. Ten days or a fortnight more may throw a clearer light upon future prospects." The issue of intervention was "full of difficulty," he lamented, "and can only be cleared up by some more decided events between the contending armies."[54]

Although the cabinet had generally been united to this point, internal divisions began to emerge following the Battle of Antietam. Gladstone, for one, seemed to contradict the government's position when he outlined his personal views on the Civil War in a public speech. There was "no doubt," he declared, that Confederate leaders had "made a nation," which strongly implied that Richmond had met London's benchmark for meriting recognition.[55] Nor was the chancellor of the exchequer alone. Russell privately advocated intervention even after the Confederate defeat. The foreign secretary had long been concerned about the growing costs of the conflict, which the staggering losses at Antietam only highlighted. In mid-October, he circulated a memorandum for cabinet members outlining the case for British involvement on humanitarian grounds. Because neither side could completely defeat the other, Russell argued, and because there was a strong prospect of even greater violence in the near future, "it has become a question . . . whether it is not a duty for Europe to ask both parties, in the most friendly and conciliatory terms, to agree to a suspension of arms for the purpose of weighing calmly the advantages of peace against the contingent gain of further bloodshed and the protraction of so calamitous a war."[56] Yet Palmerston remained convinced that conditions on the ground no longer favored British intervention. He was, he told Russell, "inclined to change the opinion on which I wrote to you when the Confederates seemed to be carrying all before them, and I am very much come back to our original view of the matter, that we must continue merely to be lookers-on till the war shall have taken a more decided turn."[57] The cabinet therefore rejected Russell's plea for intervention, as well as a subsequent French suggestion that the European powers jointly propose a temporary armistice.[58]

There is another possible explanation for Palmerston's change of heart, however, namely, that his decision to forgo intervention was not due to the military outcome at Antietam but was instead a reaction to the preliminary Emancipation Proclamation that was announced by Lincoln almost immediately after the Confederate defeat. On the advice of Seward, the president had chosen to wait for a convincing Union victory before issuing the proclamation, which he had first revealed to his cabinet two months earlier. Seward's main concern was that the edict might be interpreted as an act of desperation absent success on the battlefield. Although McClellan was unable to destroy Lee's army, repulsing the Confederate advance into Maryland gave Lincoln the victory that he needed. Just days after the battle, the president declared that any slaves in rebel states would be free at the start of the following year. This decree was bound to have an effect abroad. Great

Britain had outlawed the slave trade in 1807, used its Royal Navy to enforce the prohibition by interdicting suspected slave ships traveling across the Atlantic Ocean, and pressed other nations to follow its example. Slavery itself was banned throughout the British Empire in 1833, with the exception of several territories where it remained legal for another decade. These actions were a mark of pride for officials in London, including Palmerston, who was a staunch opponent of the institution. Policymakers also had to take into account public sentiment, which was mostly antislavery as well.[59] Yet there is little evidence that opposition to slavery had a significant impact on the cabinet's debate over intervention in the fall of 1862.

British policymakers were highly skeptical about Lincoln's intentions when it came to this issue. From the very start of the war, the president's chief rationale for opposing secession had been restoring the Union, not ending slavery. As he famously wrote in the *New York Tribune* following a public broadside by the paper's editor, Horace Greeley, his "paramount goal" was "to save the Union," not "to save or destroy slavery." "If I could save the Union without freeing any slave, I would do it, and if I could save it by freeing all the slaves, I would do it, and if I could save it by freeing some and leaving others alone, I would also do that."[60] Although Lincoln was personally opposed to slavery and believed that it should be eliminated eventually, his decision not to build the case for war on the goal of emancipation made sense for a number of reasons, not least of which included keeping opposition Democrats on his side and slaveholding border states in the Union camp. This came at a cost, however, because there was no guarantee that a Confederate defeat would lead to the end of slavery throughout the United States. This not only created tensions within the president's own Republican Party, but it also prevented Washington from seizing the moral high ground overseas. In fact, some British policymakers, including Russell, believed that an independent Confederacy would eventually be compelled to abandon slavery on its own, while a restored Union might leave it intact.[61]

Lincoln's preliminary Emancipation Proclamation did little to alleviate these doubts. By declaring that he planned to free all slaves in rebel states, where his order could not be enforced, the president left many observers in Great Britain with the impression that he was cynically grasping for ways to destroy the South and win the war. As the conflict dragged on, many British officials had grown fearful of emancipation, which they thought might be used to spark an insurrection. After receiving a report in the summer of 1862 that Seward counted on a slave revolt to weaken the Confederacy and believed that an uprising was close at hand, Russell recorded his opinion that "the prospect of a servile war will only make other nations more desirous to see an end of this desolating and destructive conflict."[62] Given these concerns, the preliminary Emancipation Proclamation actually heightened support for British involvement in some quarters, at least initially.[63] In fact, in his October memorandum to the cabinet, Russell cited this "act of punishment and retaliation" as one of the chief reasons why Great Britain should intervene.[64] The decision to free Southern slaves, he later argued, was "a measure of war, and a measure of war of a very questionable kind . . . I venture to say I do not think it can or ought to satisfy the friends of abolition, who look for total and impartial freedom for the slave, and not for vengeance on the slave-owner."[65]

As for Palmerston, the slavery issue appears to have reduced rather than increased his willingness to intervene in the conflict, but it was only a secondary factor in his deliberations. According to one historian, "in his letters to Russell, Palmerston made no mention of slavery as an obstacle to mediation, until the northern victory at Antietam made him more cautious. *Once he decided against mediation*, Palmerston concluded that slavery, and especially southern demands for the return of fugitives, would be difficult for the British government and people to accept."[66] After the debate over intervention was over and the official Emancipation Proclamation was announced in January 1863, public and political opposition to slavery did become a more important constraint on British decision making.[67] Nevertheless, this all suggests that antislavery views merely reinforced Palmerston's initial decision not to become involved. That decision, moreover, was influenced primarily by his assessment of the military balance between the North and South. The Battle of Antietam convinced the prime minister that a complete power shift had not yet occurred in North America. Because the South was not strong enough to impose its will on the North, the Union would continue to seek a total military victory and continue to oppose any negotiated solution premised on Confederate independence. Intervention, therefore, would only increase hostility between Washington and London without resolving the underlying conflict between Washington and Richmond.[68]

Even Russell held a similar point of view. Although the foreign secretary had been the most important and vocal advocate for British involvement in the war, he eventually returned to his earlier position that intervention was unwarranted because it stood little chance of success. "I must confess I remain in the same persuasion as before," he explained the following year, "that there is nothing this country could do usefully and wisely which would tend to the termination of the hostilities on the other side of the Atlantic." Any proposal for the two sides to accept a cease-fire and begin negotiations was likely to be rejected in Washington and "by causing irritation" would only exacerbate the conflict. Moreover, the South had still not proven its independence, while the North was still unwilling to accept anything less than the total restoration of the Union. Any solution imposed by outside parties, therefore, would not be sustainable. "Depend upon it, my Lords, that if that war is to cease, it is far better it should cease by a conviction, both on the part of the North and the South, that they can never live again happily as one community and one republic, than that the termination of hostilities should be brought about by the advice, the mediation, or the interference of any European Power."[69]

Although the Civil War was principally an internal affair, it also had significant international ramifications. By the 1860s, the United States had long since established itself as the strongest nation in North America as well as the dominant actor in the Western Hemisphere, although its primacy beyond the continent was underwritten in part by Great Britain. It even had the potential to become a major global power in the future. Yet the outbreak of the Civil War raised the possibility of a continent divided. If the Confederacy could attain its independence despite Union opposition, then the region would be split between two nations locked in a perpetual competition for security and influence. Although the war was monitored in many quarters abroad, the British paid particularly close attention. As the conflict unfolded, policymakers in London weighed a variety of factors—from strategic considerations to their positions on slavery—in an effort to determine whether and how they should intervene. In the end, the absence of British intervention can be explained by two factors. First, Great Britain's overriding interest in the region was not preventing containment failure or avoiding access denial but restoring stability. Therefore, its chief hope was that the war would come to an end, irrespective of who won. Second, in the view of British policymakers, the best opportunity for intervention would come if the Confederacy were able to dissuade the Union from opposing secession through force of arms. Only by defeating Northern armies on the battlefield could the South convince Washington to abandon its objectives and accept permanent division, even if permanent division also meant enduring rivalry. At that point, a British offer to mediate or a decision to officially recognize Confederate independence would help the two sides reach a final agreement or, if the Union still held out some hope of victory, put the final nail in the reunification coffin. Although circumstances appeared favorable for outside intervention between August and September of 1862, as the South stemmed Northern advances and took the fight into Union territory, the failure of Lee's Maryland Campaign at the Battle of Antietam cracked the image of Confederate strength and led British policymakers to forgo any involvement—a decision they never seriously revisited. The result was, in effect, an implicit vote to accept "the re-assertion of American supremacy."[70]

Japan and the Creation of a New Order in East Asia, 1894–1902

From the end of the nineteenth century until the early twentieth century, the British government confronted a geopolitical environment in East Asia that was complex, dynamic, and very similar to the one that it faced in the Middle East many decades earlier. In both cases, policymakers were extremely concerned about Russian expansion into areas where Great Britain had considerable economic and strategic interests. Due to a combination of global commitments, resource limitations, and logistical constraints, officials also relied on preponderant powers in these peripheral regions to help mitigate the risk of containment failure. Finally, London's informal alliances with local hegemons had to be reevaluated once rising powers attempted to alter the status quo.

Just like the Ottoman Empire, the Chinese Empire was "the traditional supreme power" in its neighborhood.[1] These once great powers shared a number of more notorious characteristics as well. Both had extremely weak central governments that struggled to control their extensive territories; they suffered from institutional decay and domestic unrest that sapped their strength; and they became inviting targets for stronger actors that sought territorial concessions, exclusive economic spheres of interest, or both. In fact, by the end of the century, "China had taken the place of Turkey as the pre-eminent Sick Man."[2] Meanwhile, Japan was in the midst of sweeping political, economic, and military reforms, not unlike Egypt under Mehmet Ali. The need to fend off encroaching outside powers triggered a process of defensive modernization and drove it to emulate many of the Western institutions and technologies that it had shunned during more than two centuries of self-imposed isolation. As a result, Japan soon emerged as a rising power that was on pace to supplant the Middle Kingdom, even if many observers did not recognize it right away.

Although Great Britain opposed a rising Egypt and supported the declining Ottoman Empire when the distribution of power was changing in the

Middle East, the power shift that was taking place in East Asia provoked a very different response. This time, Great Britain not only accommodated a rising Japan and abandoned the declining Chinese Empire, but London and Tokyo also formed an alliance that was widely regarded as a major departure from the British tradition of "splendid isolation," or the avoidance of formal commitments to defend other nations. What explains this variation? During the 1830s, Palmerston was convinced that although Egypt was on the verge of achieving regional primacy, the changes he was witnessing could be undone easily and were unlikely to last. Thus, there was no need for Great Britain to cast aside an old ally in favor of an ambitious and unreliable new partner. During the 1890s, however, British leaders eventually concluded that Japan's bid for local dominance was a clear success and could not be reversed. In their eyes, a hegemonic and complete power shift had transformed the Far East, and London had little choice but to work with Tokyo if it wanted to safeguard its interests there.

A key turning point for British policymakers was the Sino-Japanese War of 1894–1895.[3] As George Curzon would later recall, "The whole face of the East was changed by the results of that war. It exercised a most profound and disturbing effect upon the balance of power, and upon the position and destinies of all the Powers who either are situated or have interests around the China Seas."[4] When the fighting first broke out, influential voices throughout Great Britain offered similar predictions regarding the likely outcome. While they expected the qualitatively superior Japanese military to defeat the quantitatively superior Chinese forces, they also assumed that China's enormous population, natural resources, and strategic depth would wear down Japan over time and limit its progress. In short, there was little concern that the war would upend the existing local order. Before long, however, the actual implications of the conflict became clear. Not only had Japan achieved a decisive military victory over its ailing rival, but China's internal weaknesses were also revealed to be much more severe than most observers had assumed. Under pressure from several European powers to intervene against Japan and help roll back its wartime gains, Great Britain refused. Once it recognized that China could no longer serve as an effective barrier to Russian expansion, it was determined to avoid any measures that might alienate Japan.

This assessment did not prompt the immediate reorientation of Great Britain's Far Eastern policy, thanks to a change of administration that took place shortly after the war came to an end. Over the next several years, however, the scramble for concessions that carved China into foreign spheres of interest, the Boxer Rebellion that swept across the northern part of the country, and the Russian military occupation of Manchuria provided additional evidence of the Middle Kingdom's deep decline, increased the risk of containment failure, and created new incentives for Great Britain to find an effective local ally. Thus, the 1902 Anglo-Japanese Alliance can be traced directly back to the war between China and Japan—a conflict that highlighted China's inability to defend against external aggression, provided Russia with the opportunity to expand at the expense of its vulnerable neighbor, and laid the foundation for increased collaboration between London and Tokyo.

The Evolution of the Anglo-Russian Rivalry: From Near East to Far East

The Anglo-Russian rivalry was a persistent feature of international politics during the second half of the nineteenth century, particularly in the Middle East. For instance, the Crimean War of 1853–1856, the completion of the Suez Canal in 1869, the Russo-Turkish War of 1877–1878, and the British occupation of Egypt in 1882 all ensured that the region would remain a key arena of great power competition. Yet London and St. Petersburg began to clash in other areas as well, including East Asia and Central Asia, where China played a critical role due to its status as the dominant local power and its proximity to British India, respectively.

Beginning in 1847, Russia set its sights on the east and began to encourage increased settlement in Siberia, the large and sparsely populated territory bordering Manchuria. In 1858, with China suffering from a massive internal revolt and fighting a war against Great Britain, St. Petersburg took advantage of its neighbor's weakened state to reach an agreement with Peking, one that adjusted the poorly defined border between the two massive empires in Russia's favor. Two years later it gained direct control of adjacent territory and founded the outpost of Vladivostok.[5] For the next several decades, Russia's attention was focused elsewhere, but in the early 1890s, it embarked on a major program of economic industrialization, one that depended on finding new markets for Russian goods in the Far East. A key element of this program was the construction of a railway linking the European and Asiatic halves of Russia. The chief advocate of the Trans-Siberian Railway was Sergei Witte, who took over as finance minister the year after it began. Although the project was expected to increase Russia's economic ties to Japan, Korea, and China most of all, it had considerable strategic value as well; with the railway in place, St. Petersburg could accelerate the colonization of its eastern territories and rapidly transport additional troops there if necessary.[6] In either case, the main objective at the heart of the project was clear: "domination of the Chinese empire."[7]

Russia's eastward expansion was a cause for concern in London. Motivated by a strong demand for Chinese exports such as tea and silk, as well as the promise of an enormous market for its own manufactured goods, Great Britain gradually established itself as the most influential outside power in the Middle Kingdom. This position was achieved by fighting a pair of wars that opened the Chinese economy to foreign trade; it was exemplified by the British role in establishing and running a local customs service that provided China's central government with significant revenue; and it was underwritten by Great Britain's forward naval presence.[8] In fact, nineteenth-century Anglo-Chinese relations represented one of the most prominent and, according to historian Kenneth Bourne, most successful instances of "informal empire," or efforts to expand British economic and political influence abroad without incurring the costs associated with territorial control and colonial administration.[9] St. Petersburg's economic penetration of the region therefore represented a serious challenge for British policymakers. So too did its ongoing search for a warm-water port that, unlike Vladivostok, was not closed for several months each year due to icing. If Russia were successful in this quest, it would be able to expand its own naval presence in the area and erode Great Britain's military advantage. Consequently, London opposed St. Petersburg's efforts to establish a year-round naval base on multiple occasions, even before this concern became acute during the 1890s.[10]

Ultimately, Russian designs on China and its broader ambitions in the Far East had a significant impact on the relationship between London and Peking. As William Langer explains, "there was, in fact, a sort of unofficial Anglo-Chinese entente in the decade following 1885." Once little more than a market, the Middle Kingdom became an important barrier against outside expansion into its neighborhood.[11] Meanwhile, Great Britain had other regions to worry about as well. Between the 1860s and the 1880s, Russia was focused on extending its southern frontier and enhancing its influence throughout Central Asia. Its goals included creating a secure border along a traditional invasion route; preempting British expansion into the area so that Russia would be the one to dominate its trade; and creating a strategic advantage vis-à-vis Great Britain by establishing a military presence within striking distance of India, the vulnerable continental "underbelly" of its maritime rival.[12] As one study notes, "whereas in 1863 the Russian frontier was still some 500 miles from the Oxus," the river along Afghanistan's northern border marking the outermost boundary that British forces might attempt to counter a Russian invasion, by 1886 St. Petersburg had expanded as far as the city of Merv, "an excellent jumping-off point for the invasion of India."[13]

Russian expansion in Central Asia provided an added incentive for Great Britain to view China as a strategic partner. With St. Petersburg's reach extending toward the subcontinent, policymakers in London grew increasingly concerned that it might instigate an uprising or launch an attack. After it annexed the khanate of Khokand in 1875, British officials began to fear that Russia would soon capture Kashgar and Yarkand in western China—cities that were only sporadically under Peking's control and that were strategically located near mountain passes leading to Ladakh and Kashmir. If so, "the ring around India's northern frontiers would be complete, allowing the Russians to strike southwards from almost any point or points of their choosing."[14] Later, it was discovered that a previously unexplored portion of the Pamir Mountains—which marked the intersection of Russia, China, Afghanistan, and British India—was not the insurmountable barrier to invasion that most had believed. Rather, its passes could be used for a northern thrust into India, creating a new source of concern in addition to the traditional invasion routes through the Khyber and Bohlan Passes to the southwest.[15]

Rumors that Russia intended to annex this area, along with the discovery of Russian troops there, triggered a series of crises between London and St. Petersburg beginning in 1891 and continuing over the next several years. The Earl of Rosebery, who was Great Britain's foreign secretary and later prime minister during this period, sought to avoid a conflict with Russia while continuing to protect India. One way he planned to resolve this dilemma was by relying on China as a buffer state. Peking technically had jurisdiction over the mountain passes at the center of these disputes according to an 1884 agreement. Moreover, while it was strong enough to impose a heavy toll on any Russian forces transiting its territory, it was not capable of posing a threat to India on its own.[16] By the late nineteenth century, therefore, preserving London's influence in the Middle Kingdom and defending the Indian subcontinent could no longer be viewed in isolation from one another; Russia's expansion and China's location ensured that they were closely interconnected, while Peking emerged as an important barrier to St. Petersburg in both theaters. It is hardly surprising, then, that Rosebery considered China to be Great Britain's "natural ally."[17]

The Shifting Distribution of Power and the Sino-Japanese War

While the Far East was emerging as a new arena for the Anglo-Russian rivalry, it was also experiencing a dramatic change in the distribution of power. China had been the dominant nation for hundreds of years, thanks in part to its sheer size and considerable resources.[18] It had long been in decline, however, and this trend became more pronounced during the early nineteenth century due to a host of developments: massive population growth and internal migration, a rigid bureaucracy that failed to expand or respond effectively to new challenges, endemic corruption and uncontrolled patronage networks that drained money from the government's coffers, and a series of large-scale rebellions.[19] Although the Middle Kingdom's growing weakness stemmed primarily from internal rather than external factors, its two conflicts with Great Britain—the Opium War from 1839 to 1842 and the *Arrow* War from 1856 to 1860—highlighted the inferiority of its military forces relative to those of more advanced European nations.[20]

China's steep decline was only one-half of the transformation that was taking place in the region; the other was the rapid rise of Japan. Isolated from foreign influences and possessing only modest natural resources, until the mid-1800s, "Japan seemed destined to remain politically immature, economically backward, and militarily impotent in World Power terms." By the end of the century, however, "it had become a major player in the international politics of the Far East" and was fast approaching great power status.[21] Since the early seventeenth century, Japan had been a feudal society that was ruled by a series of military advisors to figurehead emperors. By the 1650s, these shoguns from the Tokugawa clan had almost completely prohibited foreign contacts. Thus, Japan had limited exposure to modern developments in science, technology, medicine, and warfare. Dissatisfaction with the shogunate became increasingly intense by the middle of the nineteenth century, however, due to a variety of factors, in particular the government's failure to deter Western nations from imposing treaties that opened Japanese ports to overseas trade, fixed low customs dues, condoned foreign settlements in treaty ports, and ensured that foreigners would not be subject to local laws. In 1868, pro-reform officials overthrew the shogunate and, consistent with their slogan "enrich the country, strengthen the military," embarked on a program of political centralization, economic industrialization, and military modernization.[22]

These converging trends set the stage for an international conflict that would reshape the entire region. The Sino-Japanese War of 1894–1895 was "an epoch-making event in the history of the Far East."[23] Although the underlying cause was the power shift between the two sides, the proximate cause was a competition for influence on the Korean Peninsula. For nearly three decades after the overthrow of the Tokugawa shogunate, the imperial government in Tokyo was preoccupied with restoring and maintaining internal order, as well as pursuing much-needed reforms at home. Given these weighty demands, it avoided the temptation to expand beyond its borders and "approached questions of foreign policy in a manner which was calculated to avoid serious conflicts with the powers."[24] To the extent that Japan did consider building an overseas empire, its main target was Korea, an isolated nation that "clung persistently to the old ways, including its tributary relationship with China."[25] In 1885, following an attempted coup d'état in Seoul by pro-Japanese elements that was quickly crushed by the local Chinese garrison, Peking and Tokyo agreed to a mutual withdrawal of their forces based on the peninsula. They also pledged to inform one another before sending troops there in the future. This seemingly innocuous agreement was a tacit admission on China's part that its influence over a traditional vassal was eroding. Meanwhile, Tokyo's interests in Korea were growing; not only had the peninsula become an important source of food, but it was also a prospective export market for Japanese goods. Moreover, policymakers in Japan were becoming increasingly willing to use force in pursuit of their interests, especially once their military modernization efforts began to pay off.[26]

The crisis that ultimately led to war started in 1893, when a Korean movement opposed to foreign influences—the Tong-Hak—staged a revolt. In response to a request for aid, China dispatched several thousand troops; consistent with the 1885 agreement, Japan deployed thousands of its own forces as well. After the immediate crisis had passed, Japan refused to withdraw its soldiers unless China agreed to help reform Korea's judicial and taxation systems, as well as its military and police forces. This was a proposal that China was almost certain to decline, which it did.[27] Casus belli in hand, Japan officially declared war on August 1, 1894. Although early skirmishes between the two nations yielded inconclusive results, within six weeks Japan's armies captured Pyongyang and its navy gained control over the Yellow Sea.[28] Tokyo then proceeded rapidly along two fronts. Its forces crossed the Yalu River and marched into southern Manchuria by the end of October, while its troops landed on the Liaotung Peninsula at nearly the same time. By late November, the fortress at Port Arthur had fallen after a relatively short siege. Although several months of fighting still remained, the war was all but over and Tokyo had scored a huge victory.

The consequences of the conflict were profound, not only for the belligerents, but also for the great powers that were watching these events unfold. Although its military strength did not come as a total surprise to outside observers, "few suspected that Japan's superiority would be so marked."[29] Its initial peace terms were even more shocking, however. Not only did Tokyo require Peking to recognize Korea as an independent nation, but it also demanded a generous indemnity to cover its wartime expenses, as well as new commercial provisions that would grant Japan most-favored-nation status and lift restrictions on foreign trade within China's borders. Most important of all, it wanted China to cede control of Taiwan, the Pescadores Islands, and the Liaotung Peninsula. With the prospect of a Japanese attack on Peking looming, the Chinese government was forced to sign the Treaty of Shimonoseki on April 17, 1895, agreeing to all of Japan's conditions with only minor revisions.

Shimonoseki quickly prompted intervention by several great powers, the so-called Dreibund of Russia, Germany, and France. In this unusual coalition, Ian Nish explains, "Russia appears to have been the ringleader, Germany the enthusiastic supporter and France the independent-minded and reluctant follower."[30] Together, all three insisted that Tokyo return the Liaotung Peninsula, partly because they viewed a permanent Japanese military presence on the Asian mainland as a threat to China's territorial integrity, partly because they hoped their efforts would give them leverage over Peking that could be used to secure future concessions, and partly because Tokyo's demands interfered with their own designs. As Great Britain's ambassador to Russia observed at the time, "The notorious desire of Russia for a sea-port in some part of the world which would remain open all the year round" made it easy to see why "she should object most strongly to the acquisition by an energetic and well-organized nation like the Japanese of territory which she might perhaps hope to acquire eventually herself."[31]

Japanese leaders were faced with a dilemma. On the one hand, they felt entitled to the spoils of their victory. On the other hand, the continental European powers were united in opposition; there were few resources available to fund additional military operations if Russia and its coalition partners tried to impose their demands by force; and Great Britain, which was notably absent from the Dreibund, would not openly take Japan's side. As a result, officials in Tokyo agreed to abandon their claim to the Liaotung in exchange for a larger indemnity. The consequences of this decision would shape Japanese foreign and defense policy for the next decade.

British Assessments of the Distribution of Power

The Sino-Japanese War took place during the brief tenure of Lord Rosebery as Great Britain's prime minister. Rosebery was a leading figure in the Liberal Party who had previously served as foreign secretary in William Gladstone's final two administrations, first in 1886 and again from 1892 to 1894. In March 1894, Gladstone resigned and Rosebery assumed the premiership, selecting Liberal Party stalwart John Wodehouse, the Earl of Kimberley, to replace him at the Foreign Office. While the new cabinet was hardly united, especially given the sharp differences between the prime minister and his chancellor of the exchequer, William Harcourt, Rosebery and Kimberley were closely aligned with one another and clearly directed foreign policy.[32]

Great Britain had two immediate objectives as the crisis unfolded on the Korean Peninsula during the summer of 1894. The first and most important, at least at the outset, was to avoid any disruption to its commerce in the Far East. The second was to prevent Russia from exploiting the dispute to expand its territory in the region. Because a conflict had the potential to jeopardize both of these goals, London initially took steps to dissuade the Chinese and especially the Japanese from going to war. As they encouraged both sides to pursue negotiations, British policymakers and diplomats emphasized the possibility of Russian involvement, which, they argued, would pose a threat to Japan's long-term ambitions as well as Great Britain's economic and strategic interests. In late June, Kimberley spoke to the Japanese minister in London, cautioning him "that it would be most disastrous if a collision took place between the Chinese and Japanese forces" because "no possible advantage could accrue to either country from an appeal to arms." The outcome of any war, he pointed out, "might be an intervention by Russia in Corea."[33] The British minister in Tokyo was similarly instructed to warn his hosts that in a conflict between China and Japan, "Russia alone will reap the advantage."[34]

Policymakers in London also considered the possibility of a diplomatic intervention before and during the conflict, although they were not willing to act alone. In early July, for example, as tensions were mounting between China and Japan, Rosebery and Kimberley proposed forming a coalition "for the purpose of effecting a peaceful settlement of the question at issue between these two Powers." The United States refused to participate, however, while France and Germany preferred that Great Britain and Russia take the lead.[35] For its part, even if Russia had wanted to intervene alongside other nations, which appeared doubtful, both the czar and his foreign minister were seriously ill at the time. Rebuffed in their efforts, Rosebery and Kimberley chose to wait and see how the conflict would unfold. After Japan scored its first major victories, expelled Chinese forces from the Korean Peninsula, and appeared poised to assault Peking, Great Britain inquired for a second time about the possibility of a collective effort to end the war. Once again the powers were divided, however, and neither Great Britain nor Russia was willing to act without first knowing how its rival would respond.[36] Despite these efforts, officials in London discouraged either side from reaching any agreement that might avoid a clash but could undermine Great Britain's position in the region. Given Russia's growing interest in Korea, and thus the possibility of Russian intervention to ensure that it did not fall under Japan's direct control, rumors began to circulate that Tokyo might give St. Petersburg access to a warm-water port on the peninsula in exchange for its support. British policymakers responded immediately, warning the Japanese "that any Agreement with regard to Corea made by Japan with Russia, China with Russia, or by Japan with China and Russia, to the exclusion of England, could not be viewed with indifference by Her Majesty's Government."[37]

Although concerns about disruptions in commerce and Russian designs on Korea were hardly insignificant, British officials generally took a relaxed view of the crisis in the Far East. This attitude reflected their underlying assumptions about the regional distribution of power. Policymakers were certainly aware that Japan's capabilities had increased over the past two-and-a-half decades; Great Britain had even supported its military modernization efforts by constructing Japanese warships and training Japanese sailors.[38] Although China had tried to implement a similar program of reform, its history of stagnation and decline was also apparent.[39] Nevertheless, few people believed that a hegemonic and complete power shift was taking place in the region. Put differently, Japan did not appear to be on the verge of surpassing China or supplanting it. In fact, it seemed unlikely that a conflict between the two nations would alter the distribution of power very much at all, mainly because China's enormous territory, population, and natural resources seemed to offset Japan's military edge.

In the summer of 1894, many observers actually believed that China would defeat Japan if a war broke out, although victory was not expected to be easy and the price was sure to be high.[40] Shortly before the conflict began, the *Times* of London summarized the reasons why a Chinese victory was the most plausible outcome, notwithstanding Japan's advantages in military capabilities and training. The Japanese, it acknowledged, "are not unjustifiably proud of their army and their navy," while the limited information available on the Chinese military indicated "that its organization and equipment are very defective." Even if Tokyo achieved some early successes, however, it probably would not win in the end. "China has enormous staying power. She can go on pouring men into Korea in numbers which will be found very hard to cope with, even by greatly superior Japanese troops." Peking's determination to prosecute the war to the fullest was impossible to predict. Nevertheless, if the Chinese did become "thoroughly roused," they would "make a long fight, and will grow stronger as they go on." The *Times* even predicted that a Sino-Japanese war could trigger a serious program of reform in China, one that might lead it to pursue a more active role throughout the region.[41] The *Naval and Military Record*, published in Plymouth, England, offered a similar perspective on the relative strength of the two combatants. Because Japan's military was well trained and well armed, while China's forces were poorly organized and poorly equipped, the outcome of the war seemed to be "a foregone conclusion." Yet China still had "an overwhelming population and, possibly, limitless resources of wealth." Therefore, as the conflict wore on, "matters would become more doubtful, for the mere vastness of China as a part of her figting [*sic*] strength cannot be lightly esteemed."[42]

The British public was treated to a comparable assessment by George Curzon, the famed politician, world traveler, and Asia expert, who would go on to hold a high-ranking position in the next government. In his opinion, "the Japanese forces, both naval and military," were "greatly superior to the Chinese." He predicted, therefore, that Japan would win any early battles on land as well as at sea. Despite its apparent weaknesses, however, he made a convincing case that China "is a country that is hard to beat, as even European antagonists, and notably France, have found." Specifically, it could draw on huge material and intangible reserves of strength. "She pours upon the enemy an inexhaustible volume of men; her resources are almost illimitable; her patience is both colossal and profound." Equally important, China had a unique and powerful incentive to triumph. "In a war in which her entire prestige and her continued domination of Eastern Asia were at stake she would fight on and on, through defeat to victory, and would sooner perish than capitulate."[43]

The views of key policymakers, including Rosebery, did not differ markedly from these public appraisals. Cabinet members understood that the military balance in the region favored Japan and that China would confront enormous challenges during any conflict. Staff in the Foreign Office, for example, doubted that Chinese forces would be able to compel the Japanese to leave Korea, while Great Britain's minister in Peking, Nicholas O'Conor, reported that senior Chinese officials were extremely pessimistic about their nation's prospects in a war.[44]

Analysis of the two sides' military forces painted an even bleaker picture. Although Peking had taken steps to improve the quality of its fleet over the preceding years, including purchasing ships abroad, a comparative estimate of the Chinese and Japanese navies produced by the Admiralty in July 1894 left no doubt as to which side had the advantage: "Notwithstanding the greater figures of the Chinese tonnage and guns, the Japanese organization, discipline, and training are so superior that Japan may reasonably be considered the stronger Power on the sea." A review of the military balance on land was even more revealing. China did not have a national army. Rather, it had a number of regional armies that were not well integrated. Many of these forces were also composed of "undisciplined rabble" and were "so entirely lacking in training, organization, and leaders, that a war under existing conditions . . . could have but one issue." Japan's army, by contrast, was "well equipped and organized, and ready for work." On the whole, the report concluded that "the Japanese army bears comparison with the Chinese much in the same way as the forces of nineteenth century civilization compare with those of mediæval times." China's only path to victory would require "protracting operations indefinitely, say over a period of two or three years, in the meanwhile straining every nerve to reorganize on European models."[45]

Despite these assessments, Rosebery, like many other observers during the summer of 1894, still felt that China was too large and too resilient to experience a serious loss. He assumed, therefore, that while Japan might defeat China, a conflict between the two nations was unlikely to be quick or decisive and would not result in any major changes to the local status quo. Neither he nor Kimberley anticipated that Japan would completely overturn the existing regional order in less than six months. "It is quite true," the prime minister argued, "that China and Japan may weaken themselves by war, but that will not, I suspect, be a very violent process. The methods, at any rate, of China are too languid to admit of their being rapidly or seriously weakened."[46] As his biographer, Gordon Martel, explains, when Asian powers fought one another, "their wars were supposed to be slow affairs that did little to alter the actual situation—a supposition that helps to explain why Rosebery was prepared to countenance the Japanese attack when they finally declared war on 1 August."[47]

As the conflict progressed into late summer and early autumn, British officials started to reassess the situation and reconsider their long-standing support for the Chinese Empire. Japan's victories at Pyongyang and the Yalu River in September 1894 were not unexpected. Yet the scale of those victories did come as a surprise and brought the qualitative differences between Chinese and Japanese forces into sharp relief. They also began to turn the tide of British public opinion against China and toward Japan.[48] This is hardly surprising given the news coming out of Korea. After the battle of Pyongyang, for instance, press reports painted a grim picture of devastating Chinese losses, while editorials highlighted China's ineptitude at military affairs and suggested that additional setbacks were sure to follow.[49] Because of this "severe defeat," Kimberley inquired whether the conflict might soon lead to unrest in China, which could threaten the country's European residents. The answer he received was hardly encouraging. Japan's next step, O'Conor surmised, could be an assault on Peking, the "strain of which might be too great for [the] Central Government."[50]

By the end of the year, Japanese forces had captured the naval base of Port Arthur, and there was little doubt which nation was now the dominant local actor. In the Far East, "the sleep of centuries has been broken in a manner that has amazed the world," declared the *Times*. Japan, fighting against "the vast and torpid bulk of China," had "conducted by sea and land a victorious campaign with a swiftness, a scientific certainty, and an unchecked success to which even European history scarcely offers a single parallel."[51] This view was shared on the other side of the Atlantic. The *New York Times*, for example, had published a number of analyses before the war, some of which suggested that China would prevail thanks to its superior resources, while others maintained that Japan would succeed due to its superior forces.[52] After China's defeat at the Yalu River in mid-September, however, the paper reached a more definitive conclusion: "Few people can now be found to dispute what only a few weeks ago very many people disputed, that the advantage of numbers and resources possessed by China is not decisive either in a short war or a long war. In fact, it is the advantage of Japan over China in knowledge, enterprise, and patriotism that has been very nearly decisive already." Although European nations had persistently assumed "that China was the leading Asiatic power, and the only Asiatic power to be reckoned with," this view had been "exploded" by Tokyo's military victories, which revealed that Japan was "a first-class power."[53]

Official correspondence from Peking also grew increasingly alarming as the war progressed. Not only did the conflict confirm the severe weakness of China's military and the poor quality of its leadership, but it also cast doubt on the government's ability to learn from its failures, implement reforms, and meet future threats. According to Great Britain's representative in Peking, "The general foreign opinion when war broke out had been that China, though ill-prepared at the outset, would so bestir herself as to be strong enough, at least for self-defence, in a few months' time." That assumption had proven to be far off the mark. Instead, Chinese officials were virtually paralyzed. "The deficiencies now coming to light had been as much of a surprise to them as to any foreign observer; they had been miserably deceived in their estimates of troops and supplies, and had found weakness where they had expected strength." Even before the Japanese captured Port Arthur, O'Conor raised the possibility "that real progress on Western lines will only follow a total overthrow of the existing system of Government."[54]

Then, in early January 1895, the minister transmitted a much longer and much harsher assessment. Although he continued to have faith in "the latent strength of the Empire" and therefore recommended that Great Britain redouble its efforts to encourage reforms, O'Conor painted a bleak picture for policymakers in London. "It is beyond doubt that the Chinese Government has been seriously frightened by the general disorganization of the whole military system, which has been brought gradually to light by the progress of the war during the last six months." Nevertheless, it might not be frightened enough to do what was really necessary, namely, "bring about a radical and complete change in the vicious administrative system to which these misfortunes are mainly due." In fact, the situation had grown so hopeless that London might need to reevaluate its entire relationship with China. "Whether any political advantage is to be gained by a close and cordial understanding with a Power whose military weakness is rather a temptation to aggression than a factor in the solution of political difficulties in the East is highly problematical," O'Conor observed. Thus, "the time seems to be close at hand when it becomes a matter of vital importance to us to know whether China is going to break in pieces, or whether it is still possible to vitalize and restore the inanimate body, and to instill into it sufficient force for its own protection."[55] By the end of January, Kimberley was also expressing doubts about China's prospects. The country, he argued, was "rotten to the core, as regards its governing class," although the Chinese people were "an industrious race, who may have a future."[56]

A series of events over the next several months fueled the shift in public opinion that began in September, as Japan completed its rout of China's forces, captured the port of Wei-Hai-Wei, and compelled Peking to accept the humiliating peace terms contained in the Treaty of Shimonoseki. The *Times*, for example, claimed that the result of the conflict was no less than a "revolution" in the region, with the Japanese achieving "that primacy for which they pined."[57] Moreover, these developments put the question of intervention back on the agenda. This time, however, the other great powers were in the lead. Russia, France, and Germany wanted Great Britain's support as they opposed Japan's most ambitious demand: territory on the Asian mainland. Yet London opted for continued neutrality instead. Given the magnitude of Japan's success, the extent of China's weakness, and the possibility that Russia would exploit the situation to enhance its position in the area, the British government was determined to avoid any measures that might alienate Tokyo, which was quickly becoming its new "natural ally" in the Far East.

Great Britain and the Tripartite Intervention

China's defeat "shattered the pre-war illusion of its military power."[58] It also forced British policymakers to reconsider their assumptions about the role that it could play in a regional containment strategy. The idea of using China as a barrier to Russian expansion was now questionable at best and discredited at worst; in William Langer's assessment, it had proven to be "as mistaken as the older policy of bolstering up Turkey."[59] The *Times* effectively captured the situation confronting the government in London shortly after the Treaty of Shimonoseki was signed: "A new world has been called into existence in the Far East. We must live with it and make the best of it."[60] For Rosebery and Kimberley, living with this new world meant striking a delicate balance between their desire to avoid tensions with St. Petersburg and their wish to preserve friendly ties with Tokyo. Judged by these measures, their efforts were largely a success and laid the foundation for a new approach to the region, one in which Japan replaced China "as the nucleus of Oriental resistance to the expansion of the Russian empire."[61]

Even before the Sino-Japanese War began, officials in London had considered the possibility that Tokyo might become a useful strategic partner. For instance, after his first attempt to organize a diplomatic intervention failed, Rosebery declined to consider more forceful measures to preserve the peace. His reasoning was straightforward: those measures would have to be directed against Japan, which was clearly the aggressor, and therefore would "weaken and alienate a Power of great magnitude" in the Far East, one that was also "a bulwark against Russia."[62] In October 1894, however, Rosebery was still referring to China as Great Britain's "only natural ally" in the region.[63] That changed after Japan succeeded in capturing Port Arthur the following month. According to historian T. G. Otte, "Japan's military strength, combined with ineffectual Chinese countermeasures, convinced Kimberley and Rosebery that it was not in Britain's interests to obstruct the rising regional power," a conclusion that "implied a shift of policy away from Britain's traditional support for China."[64]

These changing assessments of the local distribution of power and Japan's potential value as a strategic partner were reflected in a number of decisions, including London's refusal to intervene on China's behalf when Tokyo's initial peace terms became known; its repeated suggestions that China should settle at nearly any price rather than risk a Japanese attack on Peking; and its decision not to intervene alongside Russia, France, and Germany once the Treaty of Shimonoseki was signed, despite repeated requests to participate by the continental powers. Per Rosebery's guidance, Kimberley told Japan's minister in London, Count Kato, that while the British government wished a conflict could have been avoided, it was still "animated by most friendly feelings towards Japan" and "admired the high qualities which Japan had displayed in the war." Yet it would not shield Tokyo from the Dreibund. Kimberley even warned Kato that Russia appeared willing to use force if Japan were to resist.[65] Nevertheless, Rosebery was determined to maintain a policy of "benevolent neutrality."[66]

Why did Great Britain stand aside as the Dreibund forced Tokyo to abandon many of its hard-won gains? There are a number of plausible reasons. First, it had "no special interest in that part of China," Kimberley explained to Queen Victoria, because its economic interests in the Middle Kingdom were concentrated far away from Liaotung in the Yangtze Valley.[67] This does not quite ring true, however, since any territorial changes on the Chinese mainland had broader implications, especially for which outside powers had the most influence over Peking. Second, Japan included a number of commercial articles in the treaty that further opened China to foreign trade and manufacturing, and these provisions would benefit all of the powers, including Great Britain, by virtue of the most-favored-nation clauses in their existing agreements with the Chinese government. Yet the treaty was not entirely a good-news economic story for policymakers in London. Peking could pay the indemnity that Tokyo required only through large foreign loans, and securing those loans would require raising customs dues, which would negatively affect British trade.[68] Third, there was always the possibility that Japan would refuse to abandon its claim to the Liaotung Peninsula and therefore that European intervention might lead to war. Rosebery and Kimberley were not anxious to take this chance given the stakes involved. Interestingly, though, London declined to join the Tripartite Intervention even after Russia suggested that it could be released in secret from any commitment to join military operations if Japan refused to comply with the Dreibund's demands.[69] Perhaps most important, remaining on the sidelines appeared to be the only viable way to meet the government's main objectives, which were suddenly in tension with one another: avoiding measures that would antagonize St. Petersburg and building closer ties with Tokyo.

Until the spring of 1895, Rosebery regularly sought to coordinate with the other great powers as the war unfolded and was determined to work with Russia most of all.[70] Although he feared that St. Petersburg might adopt unilateral measures that would harm London's interests in the region, Anglo-Russian rapprochement was a core objective of his foreign policy. Caught between the Franco-Russian Dual Alliance on the one side and the Triple Alliance of Germany, Austria-Hungary, and Italy on the other, Great Britain faced a dilemma. While the Dual Alliance threatened its overseas empire, the Triple Alliance helped to limit that threat by compelling France and Russia to concentrate their attention on their continental adversaries. Yet relying on the Triple Alliance, even informally, came at a cost. Convinced that Great Britain could not compete with the Dual Alliance on its own,

Germany sought British membership in the Triple Alliance. London had a long-standing aversion to formal security commitments that could reduce its freedom of action, however, and was not interested in the offer. Nevertheless, in response to the pressure coming from Berlin, British policymakers tried to cooperate more closely with Russia in the hopes of driving a wedge within the Dual Alliance and demonstrating to the Triple Alliance that Great Britain could contain Russian expansion on its own, albeit mainly through diplomacy rather than deterrence.[71]

Ultimately, Rosebery's decision not to participate in the Tripartite Intervention represented a potential setback for Anglo-Russian relations and thus for his general approach to managing this dilemma, although the consequences of openly siding with Japan could have been far more serious. Kimberley even cited the possibility of heightened tensions with Russia as one of the most significant drawbacks of continued neutrality, while Russia's representative in London issued a similar warning.[72] Joining the Dreibund could have poisoned relations between Great Britain and Japan, however, and might have led Tokyo to align with St. Petersburg at London's expense.[73] Rosebery was not willing to take that chance. Neutrality, therefore, appeared to be the best option available if Great Britain wanted to avoid a complete break with Russia but maintain the option of aligning with Japan.[74]

In the aftermath of the war, Kimberley's assessment of British policy in the Far East reflected just how much the situation had changed. Moreover, this assessment is consistent with the argument that a hegemonic and complete power shift was taking place in the region, which required London to find a new partner that could help manage the risk of containment failure. Just weeks after the conflict came to an end, the foreign secretary was explicit that Great Britain had to accommodate Japan. It was, he argued, "our natural ally" against Russia. He also emphasized "the desirability of a close understanding" between London and Tokyo in a private conversation with Japan's representative. Then, shortly before leaving office once the Liberal government fell from power in June 1895, he shared his views on the Far East with Ernest Satow, who would soon become the British minister in Tokyo. London's policy, Kimberley argued, "ought to be a close alliance with Japan, the combined fleets being quite able to cope with the Russians, while the Japanese army would be most useful." By contrast, China now had little to offer. "The Chinese alliance would never be of any use," at least not unless China's military was "thoroughly drilled and taught on European systems," which seemed doubtful. "China was unreliable and useless," Kimberly concluded. Great Britain "should keep on friendly terms with her, but not count on her as a factor against Russia." For his part, Satow also felt that China was "hopeless in the matter of reform" and that its system of government was "thoroughly rotten."[75]

Several years later, as the situation in the Far East was becoming even more perilous, Kimberley revisited the Liberal government's role in the Sino-

Japanese War. Looking back, he asked rhetorically, "did we foresee the position in which China would be placed by its collapse after the war with Japan, and did we take any measures to prevent the consequences which might follow from the collapse?" Indeed, he argued, the Rosebery government was "perfectly alive to the enormous change which must necessarily follow from the collapse of China, in consequence of her defeat by Japan." Aware that intervention would have significant ramifications for the region and for London's relationship with Tokyo, the government reached two conclusions: "first, that we were not justified in interfering, as regards a war in which we had taken no part, with the victorious power; and, secondly, we were of [the] opinion, looking to the great change impending in the Far East, that there was nothing more important to this country than to establish a friendly relation with the growing naval Power of Japan." He maintained, therefore, that "a more seriously mistaken policy could not have been committed than to have joined the other Powers in that action against Japan, thereby alienating her from this country."[76] After retiring from politics, Rosebery similarly claimed that one of the government's principal objectives during the Sino-Japanese War was to make sure that Japan would be "on our side."[77]

Despite the Liberal government's decision not to intervene in the conflict and its recognition of Japan as a potential ally against Russia, relations between London and Tokyo remained cordial but distant over the next several years. In fact, British policy in the Far East was even more erratic and reactive once the Liberal government left office. By 1901, however, the two nations were seriously discussing the possibility of a formal alliance, and an agreement was reached the following year. Notably, the sequence of events leading to this alliance was a direct legacy of the power shift in the region that was revealed by the Sino-Japanese War.[78]

Chinese Weakness and Russian Expansion

Following its defeat by Japan, China was viewed "as an impotent, decadent empire" by the great powers, which were quick to exploit this situation for their own benefit.[79] Over the next several years, France, Germany, and Russia each coerced Peking into granting exclusive economic concessions and territorial leases that were little more than "thinly-disguised annexations of Chinese territory."[80] This process began shortly after the Sino-Japanese War came to an end. For instance, Russia and France jointly loaned more than £15 million to the Chinese government, which allowed Peking to begin paying its wartime indemnity. The real purpose of the loan was twofold. First, both European powers wanted to erode Great Britain's preponderant role in Peking, which depended in part on its domination of the China trade as well as its financial strength. Second, the loan was "the golden bait that was eventually to catch the monstrous fish." That is, the largesse provided by the Dual Alliance would be a potent source of leverage, enabling Paris and St. Petersburg to extract lucrative concessions from the Chinese government in the near future.[81]

Then, less than a year later, Russia and China signed a defensive military alliance, which was intended to last for the next decade and a half. St. Petersburg's goal with the agreement was to deter a renewed assault by Japan, prevent Tokyo from seizing territory on the Asian mainland that it secretly coveted for itself, and undercut Great Britain's influence over the court at Peking. According to the treaty, if Japan were to attack China, Russia, or Korea, the two parties would assist one another. In return for Russia's protection, Peking would allow St. Petersburg to build the China Eastern Railway, an extension of the Trans-Siberian Railway that would connect the area near Lake Baikal to Vladivostok via Manchuria—a more direct path than the circuitous northern route that ran through Russian territory alone. Proponents of the agreement argued that this would enable St. Petersburg to help its new ally in a crisis because it could deploy its forces into China more rapidly. As A. J. P. Taylor notes, however, the treaty and the railway concessions were nothing more than a replay of Unkiar Skelessi, namely, an effort by Russia to subordinate a weaker neighbor by posing as its chief defender.[82]

These developments provided clear evidence that Great Britain faced a growing challenge to its position in the Far East. Yet their consequences for the stability of China, along with London's economic and strategic interests in the region, paled in comparison to the scramble for concessions that began soon afterward. In November 1897, German naval forces entered the bay of Kiaochow following the murder of two Catholic missionaries. Under the guise of seeking justice and protecting its citizens, but in reality searching for a coaling station to support its naval presence in the Far East and bolster its global aspirations, Berlin coerced Peking into leasing it the port for the next ninety-nine years. Germany also established a fifty-kilometer neutral zone in the surrounding territory and gained exclusive railway and mining concessions throughout the area. Thus, it acquired a naval base as well as an economic foothold in China's Shangtung Province, which had become "in all but name a German protectorate."[83]

For its part, the Russian government objected to Germany's demands, although not out of any sense of altruism. Instead, it feared they would trigger a rush for Chinese territory that St. Petersburg hoped to avoid, at least for the time being. Great Britain's ambassador to Russia relayed the frustrations of Sergei Witte, who considered Germany's seizure of Kiaochow "an act of brigandage" that would merely disrupt his own plans. From the finance minister's perspective, "Russia's geographical position must sooner or later secure her political predominance in the North of China," therefore Witte's preference was "to keep China intact."[84] Despite his objections, Russia ultimately chose to respond in kind. Shortly after German forces arrived at Kiaochow, it deployed a naval squadron of its own to Port Arthur—the same port that it had prevented Japan from acquiring several years earlier. In principle, St. Petersburg was fulfilling its alliance obligations to Peking. In practice, Russia convinced China to lease it Port Arthur as well as the nearby port of Talienwan for the next twenty-five years. At the same time, Peking also allowed St. Petersburg to construct a spur line connecting the China Eastern Railway to one of these ports. In concert with other exclusive economic concessions offered by the Chinese government, Russia acquired "something approaching monopoly rights in the southern half of Manchuria."[85]

Finally, the Boxer Rebellion and its aftermath offered additional evidence of China's weakness and Russia's ambitions. Motivated by the loss of territory to European powers, in 1898 Chinese leaders initiated a process of reform that was intended to modernize nearly every aspect of government administration, including the military. The program was brought to an abrupt end, however, following a palace coup by conservative officials led by the empress dowager, who had long been a key source of power and influence in Peking. Shortly afterward, violence escalated against Europeans and Christian converts throughout the country at the hands of the so-called Boxer movement. This was a loose organization that was eventually co-opted and encouraged by the reactionary Chinese leadership in an attempt to undermine European influence in China and oust foreign powers that now controlled so much of the country. With the government's support and encouragement, the Boxers laid siege to foreign diplomatic legations in Peking, which compelled several European powers, the United States, and Japan to dispatch troops and save their representatives.

Although Russia participated in the multilateral intervention, it quickly withdrew its soldiers from Peking and redeployed its forces to Manchuria, ostensibly in response to attacks against Russian railway interests by Boxers and Chinese army forces. This was also a calculated attempt to curry favor with the government in Peking by drawing a clear distinction between Russia and other nations, which continued to engage in punitive expeditions and demand compensation after their citizens had been rescued. Before long, Russia had nearly 200,000 troops deployed throughout Manchuria and was essentially engaged in a large-scale military occupation.[86] Moreover, press reports in early 1901 indicated that Russia and China had reached an agreement that would cede control over this territory to St. Petersburg. The rumored treaty never materialized and formal discussions between Russia and China came to an end several months later, thanks in no small part to British and Japanese pressure on the Chinese government to resist St. Petersburg's demands. Yet the Russian occupation continued, and negotiations to return control of Manchuria to Peking made little progress. As Japan's foreign minister reportedly noted at the time, "It had been constantly charged against Japan that her victories in 1894–95, having exposed China's weakness, were largely responsible for the subsequent exactions and aggressions suffered by the Middle Kingdom. But it now appeared to Japan that while she was blamed for leading European Powers into temptation by showing the frailness of China's armour, those same Powers were bent upon taking away China's armour altogether."[87]

All of these events in northern China were a culmination of two interrelated trends, both of which could be traced back to the Sino-Japanese War: the fragility of the Chinese government and the extent of Russian ambitions in the Far East. Moreover, St. Petersburg's military occupation of Manchuria, on top of its earlier decision to occupy Port Arthur, put to rest any hope that it would be satisfied with increasing its commercial influence in China and forgoing territorial control. Instead, "it now had all the appearance of seeking to hasten China's collapse, and to absorb Manchuria."[88]

Toward an Anglo-Japanese Alliance

Despite French, German, and especially Russian expansion in the Far East during the final years of the nineteenth century, the British government was slow to take these challenges seriously. The Liberal cabinet that was so intent on preserving good relations with Japan and perhaps even fostering some type of alignment between London and Tokyo fell from power shortly after the Sino-Japanese War ended. It was succeeded by a coalition of Conservatives and Liberal Unionists, with Tory elder statesman the Marquess of Salisbury serving as both prime minister and foreign secretary. Salisbury had a number of reasons for deviating from the Far Eastern policy envisioned by his immediate predecessors, not least of which was the distraction of events in other regions, especially the Near East, which rendered the fate of China a secondary priority when he returned to office.

Despite the many challenges that Great Britain confronted in Europe and throughout Asia, Salisbury also remained determined to avoid formal security commitments overseas unless it was absolutely clear that London stood to gain far more than it put at risk.[89] Equally important, in the aftermath of the Sino-Japanese War, Salisbury was not especially concerned by St. Petersburg's efforts to expand its influence over its neighbor to the south. Given Russia's proximity to China and the relatively feeble government in Peking, this process seemed nearly inevitable.[90] The only questions that remained were the degree to which Russia would extend its influence and the form that these efforts would take. Salisbury did not view the "peaceful penetration" of Manchuria as a significant threat to British interests. Rather, he had two main concerns. First, he wanted to ensure that St. Petersburg avoided outright territorial aggrandizement, which could precipitate efforts by other European powers to acquire Chinese territory and hasten the collapse of the Qing dynasty. Second, he also wanted Russia to respect Great

Britain's treaty rights, which meant forgoing exclusive agreements with the Chinese government and avoiding high tariff barriers that would discriminate against British goods.

If China's territorial integrity and the Open Door both remained undisturbed, Salisbury considered Russia's growing interest in that country to be a manageable problem, one that did not require departing from British foreign policy precedents. In his view, "as long as the Russians only looked for commercial advantages out there, we should not interfere, but if they contemplated any military movements we should have to take corresponding measures."[91] Along with Arthur Balfour, his nephew and chief deputy in government, Salisbury actually encouraged Russian economic activity in China, including its possible acquisition of a warm-water commercial port, at least until Anglo-Russian relations began to deteriorate badly in 1898. By treating Manchuria as a Russian sphere of interest, they hoped that St. Petersburg would return the favor when it came to London's own sphere of interest in the Yangtze Valley.[92]

While Salisbury's preference for isolation and his relatively sanguine view of Russian expansion help to explain why Great Britain did not seek out new allies or take firmer measures to preserve its position in the Far East between 1895 and 1897, his personal views on Japan and China also account for this relative quiescence. Publicly, the prime minister limited his criticism of British policy during the Sino-Japanese War and agreed that Rosebery and Kimberly were correct to avoid measures that could have driven a wedge between London and Tokyo. It would have been "greatly contrary to our policy to do anything that would alienate the rising power of Japan," he argued years after the conflict, "with whom we had so many grounds for sympathy and co-operation."[93] Privately, however, he regretted the decision not to aid China, which caused Peking to grow suspicious of Great Britain's motives and skeptical of its value as a patron and ally. From Salisbury's perspective, because it was St. Petersburg that came to Peking's defense, not London, the British were now viewed by the Chinese "as a people that cannot be trusted," even though they "had been their allies for many years."[94]

At the same time, Salisbury downplayed Tokyo's capabilities and voiced suspicions about its intentions. "My impression is that our strategic or military interests in Japan can easily be over-estimated," he wrote in the fall of 1895, not long after returning to office. "She may no doubt be of use in hindering Russia from getting an ice-free port. But how long would her obstruction be effective?" Although Japan could certainly challenge Russia's access to such a port from the sea, doing so from the land would be far more difficult. In addition, it was hardly obvious that British and Japanese interests were compatible. Japan's chief objective was control over the Korean Peninsula, and that could best be achieved through a condominium with Russia. Such an arrangement would almost certainly require Tokyo to condone

St. Petersburg's increasing control over northern China, however, as well as its growing influence in Peking. Ultimately, Japan seemed more likely "to join with Russia and perhaps with France in cutting up China, than to exchange platonic assurances of affection with us."[95] Nor was the prime minister alone in his misgivings. For example, although George Curzon recognized Japan as a rising power and suggested that London might need to work more closely with Tokyo in opposition to Russian expansion, he also thought that the Japanese were "untrustworthy" and that it was "difficult to have an alliance with them."[96]

Events soon demonstrated that Russia posed a more serious threat to British interests than Salisbury believed and that London needed a new ally more than the prime minister wanted to admit. Specifically, the occupation of Port Arthur was a turning point. St. Petersburg's decision to join the scramble for concessions was viewed as a major challenge to an already fragile and increasingly unfavorable status quo. Consistent with his earlier views on Russian commercial expansion versus military expansion, Salisbury acknowledged that the British government "would not regard with any dissatisfaction the lease by Russia of an ice free commercial harbour and its connection by rail with the Siberian Railway now under construction." Therefore it would not object to St. Petersburg's acquisition of Talienwan or its development of the South Manchuria Railway. Control over a military facility like Port Arthur, however, "opens questions of an entirely different order." Unless St. Petersburg abandoned the facility, the occupation would encourage other great powers to follow Russia's example while bringing Manchuria under its direct control. Moreover, a Russian fleet at Port Arthur would enable St. Petersburg to dominate the maritime approaches to Peking. As a result, it would gain "the same strategic advantage by sea which she already possesses in so ample a measure by land."[97] Similarly, Balfour suggested that Russia's acquisition of Port Arthur could "alter the balance of power at Pekin." Not only would this leave St. Petersburg with an "overwhelming" influence over the Chinese government; it would "discredit England throughout the Far East."[98]

China's capitulation to Russia also highlighted just how weak it had become. Interestingly, Salisbury was more optimistic about China's prospects than either his predecessors or some of his peers. During the Port Arthur crisis, for example, he acknowledged that Peking was not strong enough to resist St. Petersburg's demands; it was "prostrate" and had "no power at her command to range against the forces which Russia could have brought to bear against her." Yet he continued to place significant weight on the Middle Kingdom's enormous resources and could not discount it as an important factor in the regional distribution of power. "If you take a wider view," he argued, "you never could pronounce that 400,000,000 of men who, whatever else they are, are the bravest of the brave . . . could ever be absolutely prostrate. I do not in the least believe in the prostration of China in that wider sense."[99]

Other British policymakers disagreed, however, even if they were not willing to contradict Salisbury in public by advocating the total abandonment of China. Balfour, for example, described the Middle Kingdom's weakness in vivid terms: "I do not believe that in the history of the world such a spectacle has ever been presented as that which the Empire of China presents at this moment." The Chinese government was so feeble, he declared, that there was no precedent for its failure to resist the demands of foreign powers. "You may ransack and study the pathology of empires, and you will study it, I believe, in vain, before you find any example of so complete a paralysis."[100] Despite this harsh diagnosis, Balfour still hewed to the government's line that this fragile nation could somehow be reformed. In other words, he was "not ready to admit that China, either by inoculation from outside or by some spontaneous reform from within, is wholly incapable of changing her present unhappy condition for a better one."[101] Yet this was an increasingly difficult case to make.

Irrespective of these differences, Russia's seizure of Port Arthur compelled London to abandon its "unusually passive" approach to the region, although the government did not settle on a clear response right away.[102] Initially, Salisbury opted for rapprochement with St. Petersburg, which he hoped would stabilize the status quo in the Far East as well as the Near East, where the two powers were also in competition with one another. Thus, he proposed an agreement that would have effectively divided the Chinese Empire and the Ottoman Empire into British and Russian spheres of interest. In the case of China, Great Britain would maintain its dominant economic position in the Yangtze Valley, while Russia would exercise a controlling influence over Manchuria. "We aim at no partition of territory," he explained to the British ambassador at St. Petersburg, "but only a partition of preponderance."[103] These talks failed, however, leaving London in a difficult position.[104] Demanding that Russia withdraw from Port Arthur could lead to war. Yet doing nothing could harm Great Britain's position in China and the broader Far East. After lengthy deliberations, London eventually decided to participate in the scramble for concessions and acquire a lease over the port of Wei-Hai-Wei. Peking had actually suggested this move earlier in a preemptive effort to counter Germany and Russia. Salisbury refused, however, fearing that it would further erode China's territorial integrity and increase the likelihood of its collapse.[105] Yet his inability to reach an agreement with Russia left him with few options. Although the port had negligible strategic value, the move allowed Great Britain "to balance and compensate that which had been done by another Power," at least according to Salisbury's account.[106]

The crisis over Port Arthur also spurred an ongoing effort to establish an alliance with Germany. This strategy was strongly advocated by Joseph Chamberlain, the colonial secretary, who believed that Great Britain would have to abandon its isolation in a world dominated by militarized alliance blocs. Although the attempt to reach some sort of arrangement between the two powers was a recurring theme in British foreign policy from 1898 until 1901, the likelihood of success was always quite small given the inherent asymmetry of interests between them. In particular, Germany had little incentive to antagonize Russia and jeopardize its security in Europe by supporting Great Britain in the Far East. "As to making use of Germany to come between the Russians and ourselves in China," observed Francis Bertie, an influential staff member at the Foreign Office, "we are not likely to have much success."[107]

For his part, Salisbury remained a skeptic of any alliance, deriding the risk of isolation as *a danger in whose existence we have no historical reason for believing.*" Nor did he think that public opinion would allow Great Britain to make commitments in advance of actual threats.[108] The prime minister was particularly opposed to reaching an agreement with Germany, something he claimed would be "full of risks" yet have "no compensating advantage."[109] By late 1900, however, Salisbury was forced to relinquish his post at the Foreign Office in favor of Lord Lansdowne, due in part to disagreements with his colleagues over the merits of isolation. Although he was far more open to the idea of formal alliances and pursued the German option for a time, even Lansdowne was dubious about the likelihood of success, admitting that there were "great difficulties in the way of a full-blown defensive alliance with Germany . . . difficulties which are, I should say at the present moment, virtually insuperable."[110]

While the prospect of securing Germany's support against Russia in the Far East was becoming more remote, the dangers to Great Britain's interests in the region were becoming more pronounced. The Boxer Rebellion demonstrated that China was far closer to collapse than Salisbury had believed.[111] Moreover, Russia's subsequent occupation of Manchuria made it clear that St. Petersburg was not content with simply extending its economic influence over the Middle Kingdom. As the *Times* correspondent in Peking caustically observed, despite Russia's claim that it was only protecting its interests and helping the Chinese government to defend its territory against insurrectionists, "protection in such cases spells empire."[112] Lansdowne agreed. After Russia's efforts to negotiate a treaty sanctioning its occupation of northern China became public, the foreign secretary argued that the putative agreement would result in "the virtual establishment of a Russian protectorate over all Manchuria as well as Mongolia and Chinese Turkestan."[113]

In the face of worsening threats and dwindling options, Great Britain began to explore another approach, namely, an alliance with Japan. Discussions between Lansdowne and the Japanese minister in London, Count Hayashi, began during the spring of 1901. Initially, these conversations were conducted with an eye toward a trilateral Anglo-German-Japanese agreement, although the new foreign secretary soon abandoned that possibility in favor of a bilateral alliance. The key characteristics of a potential treaty remained the same, however; it would require the parties to observe "a strict neutrality in the event of either of them becoming involved in war" and to assist each other if any signatory was "confronted by the opposition of more than one hostile Power."[114] By late 1901, formal negotiations were under way, and on January 30, 1902, the treaty was signed.

Tokyo's interest in an alliance with London was obvious from the start. The Russian occupation of Manchuria seemed to presage a move against Korea, and, as the British government was well aware, ensuring that no other power controlled the peninsula was "a matter of life and death" for Japan.[115] The Japanese were confident in their ability to fight Russia alone, at least before the Trans-Siberian Railway was completed, but the possibility that France might support its Dual Alliance partner and use its naval forces to sever the lines of communication between their home islands and any troops on the Asian mainland gave them pause. A commitment on Great Britain's part to "hold the ring" and deter French intervention was critical, therefore, if Japan were to protect its interests. Without that commitment, Tokyo would remain paralyzed by the prospect of outside interference in a regional war.

For its part, London's willingness to consider an alliance with Tokyo was heightened in 1901 by a number of factors, not least of which were the difficulty of reaching an accord with Germany and the failure to arrange a modus vivendi with Russia.[116] For example, there were persistent fears in London that Tokyo and St. Petersburg might reach their own agreement at Great Britain's expense. As one Foreign Office official warned, "If we do nothing to encourage Japan to look to us as a friend and possible ally against Russia and France, we may drive her to a policy of despair, in which she may come to some sort of terms with Russia." If so, "our interests would greatly suffer."[117] During the first half of the year, however, Lansdowne was still not ready to accept the risks of an alliance.[118] As an emerging regional power, Japan was also a revisionist power, whereas Great Britain hoped to preserve the status quo, or at least prevent it from deteriorating any further. Admittedly, Tokyo shared many of London's objectives in China, specifically, restricting Russian influence to Manchuria and preserving what remained of the Open Door. Nevertheless, British policymakers feared the possibility that Japan might instigate a conflict with Russia to secure its dominant position in Korea, where London had few interests beyond preventing St. Petersburg from acquiring a naval base.[119]

In the end, military and fiscal considerations "tipped the scales in favour of an alliance" during cabinet deliberations that took place in the fall of 1901.[120] London was highly—although only temporarily—constrained by the ongoing Boer War. Not only did this conflict take a heavy toll on the British Army, but it also placed significant demands on the Royal Navy to transport troops, guard the sea lanes to South Africa, and deter adversaries from threatening the British Isles while London was busy fighting in the Transvaal and Orange Free State. Maintaining Great Britain's relative military advantage in the Far East was becoming more problematic as well, especially with Japan, Germany, France, and Russia expanding their shipbuilding programs and enhancing their naval presence in the region.[121] Lord Selborne, the First Lord of the Admiralty, produced a memorandum for Lansdowne (which was later circulated to the entire cabinet) highlighting these challenges and outlining three alternatives in response: (1) increasing naval expenditures, constructing additional ships, and continuing to disperse the Royal Navy's forces, which would enable Great Britain to preserve its advantages in Europe and peripheral theaters; (2) deploying additional ships to the Far East without increasing the overall size of the fleet, which would require accepting significant risk in home waters; or (3) forming an alliance with Japan, which would help Great Britain to offset the growth of French and Russian naval forces in the area without incurring additional expenditures or accepting greater risk at home. While Selborne made a compelling case for the third option, his arguments received added support from Michael Hicks-Beach, the chancellor of the exchequer, who wrote two memoranda of his own arguing against increases in defense spending unrelated to the war in South Africa.[122]

In addition to supplementing its naval strength in the Far East, an alliance with Tokyo had the potential to help London in other ways. Japan had already demonstrated the value of its ground forces, not only during the war with China but also during the Boxer Rebellion. Moreover, the threat of Russian expansion could be checked mainly on land rather than at sea. Perhaps not surprisingly, then, one of the chief points of disagreement in the alliance negotiations was the British hope that the Japanese would help to counter any Russian moves against India. As Ian Nish explains, "It is often said that on the British side the alliance was an Admiralty initiative." That is only part of the story, however. "To be sure, there was interest in some naval arrangement with Japan for budgetary and political reasons. But there were also strategic reasons connected with anxieties over Russian expansion in Asia, particularly Afghanistan, and the threat it posed to the defence of India. British politicians as a whole and the army in particular were conscious of the supreme difficulty of dealing with an expansive Russia on India's northern borders. For them, Manchuria and Korea were lesser concerns, though they were, of course, the prime source of Japan's anxieties."[123]

All of these considerations suggest that relative decline was an important factor in pushing London to form an alliance with Tokyo. Indeed, the challenge of managing multiple competitors with limited resources was an important one, although it is debatable whether policymakers actually viewed decline as a permanent condition rather than a short-term constraint that would wane after the Boer War came to an end.[124] Nevertheless, this should not overshadow the fact that a high risk of containment failure led Great Britain to rely on China as a local partner long before it sided with Japan. Nor should it obscure the underlying cause of London's decision to accommodate Tokyo, namely, the severe weakness of China, which removed a critical barrier to Russian expansion in the region years before the conflict in South Africa began. The landmark agreement between the two nations therefore had its roots in the shifting distribution of power, the Sino-Japanese War, and the decision by British leaders to avoid any measures that might preclude a closer Anglo-Japanese relationship in the future.

By the end of the nineteenth century, the Anglo-Russian competition that began in the Middle East more than eighty years earlier encompassed virtually all of Asia. In the aftermath of the Crimean War, St. Petersburg increased its territory and influence abroad in fits and starts, extending its southern frontier toward India and challenging Great Britain's dominant position in the Chinese Empire. These unfavorable developments were complicated by the regional power shift that was taking place in the Far East. China, which by the 1880s had become an informal British security partner against Russian expansion in both Central Asia and East Asia, was experiencing deep decline. Japan, however, which had been an isolated and strategically inconsequential nation for many years, emerged from the Meiji Restoration determined to modernize its political and economic systems, enhance its military capabilities, and establish itself as the preponderant local power. The Sino-Japanese War of 1894–1895 fully revealed and even magnified these trends, as Tokyo exploited a crisis in Korea to drive Chinese forces off the peninsula and impose harsh peace terms on Peking. The war demonstrated to most observers just how weak China had become. It also indicated that the prospects for reform along the lines of what Japan had accomplished were slim. In short, a hegemonic and complete power shift had taken place. Because China could no longer resist the pressure of foreign nations or local rivals, the British government opted not to intervene against Japan when Tokyo's demands became known in the spring of 1895. Instead, Rosebery and Kimberley sought to maintain British neutrality and, they hoped, preserve good relations with Japan, well aware that it might soon replace China as a bulwark against Russia's ambitions in the Far East. Serious cooperation between Great Britain and Japan did not occur right away, however; the Liberal government that was in power during the war fell soon after its conclusion, and Rosebery and Kimberley were succeeded by Lord Salisbury, who was a proponent of splendid isolation, a skeptic of Japan's value as a security partner, and an optimist that Russian expansion in China could be managed without resorting to military alliances or the use of force. Yet the seizure of Port Arthur, the Boxer Rebellion, and the occupation of Manchuria soon confirmed that Russia's plans for China extended beyond peaceful economic penetration and that China's weakness was indeed as crippling as Salisbury's predecessors had believed. Although Great Britain remained cautious regarding any formal arrangement with Japan, due in large part to the inherent risks of allying with a rising power intent on altering the status quo, the failure of other options to check Russian expansion made an alliance increasingly attractive and increasingly necessary.

India's Rise and the Struggle for South Asia, 1962–1971

South Asia has been a persistent flash point for more than sixty years. Ever since the partition of the subcontinent in 1947, India and Pakistan have been locked in an enduring rivalry, which has resulted in a series of major conflicts as well as countless minor skirmishes. Not surprisingly, this competition has had a significant impact on outside actors, including the United States. South Asia was rarely a high priority for U.S. policymakers during the Cold War, at least in comparison to regions such as Europe, East Asia, and the Middle East. While Pakistan was an episodic American ally in the global struggle against communism and India could hardly be overlooked given its size, neither of these nations commanded the level of attention that was reserved for more strategically or economically important actors. Nevertheless, Washington was rarely able to ignore the area and was drawn into several crises on the subcontinent, especially when local wars threatened to upend the distribution of power and transform the entire region.

In general, the political order that prevailed in South Asia was not always clear. India's large territory and population made it a natural candidate for local primacy, not to mention a broader role on the world stage. Yet its rigid bureaucracy and nonaligned foreign policy were formidable constraints that hindered New Delhi from realizing its potential, while conflicts with neighbors consumed its attention and resources. As for Pakistan, its smaller territory and population made it appear much weaker than India, at least on paper. Thanks in large part to external patrons, though, it enjoyed healthy economic growth throughout much of the Cold War, as well as a reputation for fielding well-trained and well-equipped armed forces. In short, both sides had notable advantages and disadvantages, which contributed to regional parity.

At two points, however, parity nearly gave way to primacy. In 1965, when India seemed to be on pace to overtake Pakistan by a wide margin and establish its dominance on the subcontinent, the two rivals went to war over the disputed territory of Kashmir. Then, in 1971, India launched a military intervention against its neighbor just as Pakistan was mired in a domestic crisis. These events were followed closely in Washington and provoked very different reactions. Although the United States condemned both parties and remained neutral in 1965, which represented a sharp break from its recent efforts to improve relations with New Delhi, it sided against India in 1971, even dispatching a naval task force to discourage an Indian assault on West Pakistan. What explains these polices? Answering this question requires looking at each case to identify the risks that the United States confronted, the type of regional order that it preferred, and the type of power shift that it believed was taking place.

Following the 1962 Sino-Indian border war, senior U.S. officials were deeply concerned about the possibility of Chinese intervention in South Asia. At that time, the United States enjoyed a close relationship with Pakistan, which was a military ally, but had weak ties with India, which was the only local actor with the potential to balance China on its own. Because the risk of containment failure was so high, Washington became increasingly inclined to accept India as the dominant power in the region, even at the cost of downgrading its alliance with Pakistan. New Delhi's failure to achieve a major victory during the Second Kashmir War in 1965 caused U.S. officials to rethink this approach, however. Although the result of the conflict was a defeat for Pakistan, the war took a heavy toll on both sides, left the region more vulnerable to Chinese expansion, and demonstrated that India was not actually capable of achieving uncontested primacy. In other words, the hegemonic power shift that was taking place was incomplete. Sobered by this outcome and disillusioned with India's prospects, U.S. officials largely abandoned their efforts to forge closer security ties with New Delhi.

Six years later the geopolitical landscape had changed substantially. The Soviet Union and China were now open rivals, while Beijing had emerged as a potential American partner against Moscow. For the United States, therefore, the risk of containment failure in South Asia had receded. Moreover, Washington no longer maintained important military facilities in the region and had few economic interests there either. Thus, the risk of access denial was low as well. Given this assessment, U.S. policymakers did not have a strong preference between local parity and local primacy. Rather, they simply wanted to avoid any crises that would be a distraction from higher priorities, in particular rapprochement with China. These hopes were dashed in 1971, when another conflict broke out on the subcontinent and India appeared ready to inflict a decisive blow against its rival. Consistent with my arguments, senior officials in Washington focused on the scope of the power shift. Specifically, they concluded that a complete change in the distribution of power was taking place, one that would undoubtedly leave India as the dominant actor in its neighborhood. Rather than supporting India, though, as my theory would suggest, they sided with West Pakistan to save it from defeat. Interestingly, U.S. officials seem to have been motivated by the same factors that I have identified, albeit in different ways than I would predict. Instead of worrying about stability in South Asia alone, which should have led them to accommodate New Delhi under these conditions, they were more concerned about maintaining stability in areas such as the Middle East and feared that a complete power shift in one region would embolden revisionist nations to instigate conflicts elsewhere.

The Kennedy Administration's Containment Dilemma

During the early stages of the Cold War, the United States forged close military ties with Pakistan as part of its global strategy to prevent Soviet expansion throughout the developing world. On the surface, this relationship yielded significant benefits and made Pakistan one of the United States' most important allies outside Europe. Not only was it a key member of two anti-communist alliance blocs, namely, the Southeast Asia Treaty Organization (SEATO) and the Central Treaty Organization (CENTO), but it also hosted facilities that were used for highly sensitive U.S. intelligence collection operations, including U-2 aerial reconnaissance missions over Soviet territory. In exchange for Pakistan's support, the United States became its principal supplier of military hardware, such as armored vehicles and fighter aircraft, which were ostensibly needed to counter threats from outside the region. By contrast, relations between the United States and India were much more distant, although New Delhi did receive economic aid from Washington. As Pakistan's patron, the United States was responsible for arming India's main rival and therefore posed an indirect threat to its security. At the same time, New Delhi was committed to a foreign policy of nonalignment, which many officials in Washington viewed as a de facto way of siding with the Soviet Union. Nevertheless, between 1962 and 1965, American strategy in South Asia underwent a major reevaluation. Due to the growing risk of containment failure, the United States distanced itself from Pakistan, with whom it had less and less in common, and courted India as a new partner, one that had the potential to dominate the region.[1]

This change was precipitated by several factors. First, while Soviet–American relations experienced a thaw following the 1962 Cuban missile crisis, Sino-American relations remained hostile. In fact, China arguably had supplanted the Soviet Union as the most immediate threat to U.S. interests in many parts of the world. Given its proximity to South Asia and its border disputes with India, Chinese aggression in this region became a major concern for U.S. policymakers, who feared that hundreds of millions of people would fall into the communist camp if local nations proved unable to defend themselves.[2] Second, it was becoming increasingly apparent that Washington's interests and Rawalpindi's were not nearly as compatible as U.S. policymakers had assumed.[3] For years, the United States had been arming Pakistan to create a bulwark against communist aggression, one that could prevent an invasion if possible and serve as the first line of defense if necessary. Despite these efforts, Pakistan's value as an ally was questionable, mainly due to its overriding emphasis on countering India at the expense of containing communism. Put simply, while the United States viewed its relationship with Pakistan through the prism of a global strategic competition, Pakistan viewed its ties to the United States through the lens of local threats. Third, as external dangers to South Asia grew and frustrations with Pakistan boiled over, U.S. officials began to grapple with a seemingly obvious but somewhat inconvenient fact: thanks to its geographic position, large size, and potential power, India appeared to be the only local nation that could become a counterweight to China. In other words, Washington was slowly reaching the conclusion that it had made the wrong bet in the region.

Spurred on by these developments, a number of civilian advisors began to lay the foundation for a reorientation of U.S. foreign and defense policy toward South Asia. At the center of these efforts was Robert Komer, an influential staff member for the National Security Council (NSC) who helped to guide U.S. relations with India and Pakistan during the John F. Kennedy and Lyndon B. Johnson administrations, before going on to play a key role in developing the United States' rural pacification strategy during the Vietnam War.[4] Komer laid out his main arguments in a January 1962 memo to National Security Advisor McGeorge Bundy—arguments that he would return to again and again over the next several years and that became key themes for senior policymakers who were wrestling with how to handle South Asian affairs and contain China at the same time.

Pakistan, Komer argued, was not a reliable ally in the struggle against communism. Its president, Ayub Khan, despite his claims to the contrary, "isn't really much interested in the larger conflict in which we are involved." Rather, he viewed his relationship with the United States as "insurance" against Indian hostility and "a means of leverage" in future negotiations with New Delhi. Thus, the two sides were not on the same page when it came to the fundamental purpose of their partnership. Moreover, even if Pakistan were more committed to the anticommunist cause, its utility as an ally was dubious. Although it was using American-supplied weapons to maintain a rough military balance with India, the United States received few tangible benefits from the alliance, "except a paper commitment to SEATO and CENTO on which it is hard to see how Ayub could effectively pay off in more than peanuts." It was, therefore, time for Washington to seriously consider whether it was "giving too much and not getting enough in return."[5]

Importantly, Komer did not advocate abandoning the U.S.–Pakistan alliance, nor did other policymakers who shared his views. Despite growing tensions between the two sides, Washington still needed to use intelligence facilities located on Pakistani territory, which could not easily be replaced.

Moreover, if Rawalpindi withdrew from SEATO and CENTO, it might cripple both organizations and increase the risk of future communist challenges in Asia. To make the best of a bad situation, Komer hoped that the United States could convince India and Pakistan to resolve their differences and work together against external threats, which far outweighed any danger that the two nations posed to one another, at least from an American perspective. Washington's main goal, Komer explained, was "a strong and stable subcontinent" that could be "a counterweight and counter-influence to the Communists in Asia." This would require efforts "to ameliorate and eventually dissipate the tensions between the countries within the subcontinent, not only in our long-range interest but in the interest of their own survival against a much larger threat." Conflicts over the disputed territory of Kashmir, for example, "distract and divert these countries from the goal we have in mind." Despite his hope that the two rivals might set aside their differences and collaborate in defense of the region, Komer made the case that India and Pakistan should not be viewed on equal terms. If the United States had to choose between Rawalpindi and New Delhi, "there is little question that India (because of its sheer size and resources) is where we must put our chief reliance."[6] Ultimately, the United States should be willing to accommodate New Delhi as the preponderant local power in spite of the ongoing India–Pakistan rivalry, a change he believed Pakistan would grudgingly accept given its continuing dependence on American military aid. As he later recalled telling then vice president Johnson, "Pakistan has a hundred million people. India has over five hundred million people and if we're going to try and do something with South Asia as a counterweight to China, we better look at India as a first priority and not at Pakistan which is one-fifth the size."[7]

Although Komer was the most vocal and thoughtful advocate of India's strategic importance in the region, he was not alone. President Kennedy, for example, already believed that India, along with Japan, was one of the two most influential noncommunist nations in Asia.[8] Over the following year, as policymakers in Washington grew increasingly disillusioned with Pakistan, and as tensions mounted along the poorly demarcated Sino-Indian border, the geopolitical significance of India was difficult to deny. For instance, assessments on the future of U.S. policy in the region noted that "India's weight in international affairs can do more to help us or harm us than can Pakistan's," while New Delhi's importance was so great "that little or no consideration can be given to a major retrogressive change in U.S. policy toward it." Still, U.S. officials hoped to repair or improve relations with both sides if possible, not only because of the United States' long-standing ties to Pakistan, but also because some type of reconciliation between the two rivals was considered "a sina qua non for full freedom in dealing with India."[9]

Arguments for a change in strategy gained added momentum in late 1962. While the world's attention was consumed by the missile crisis that was unfolding in Cuba, conflict broke out between China and India in the Himalayas. The two Asian powers had enjoyed more-or-less cordial relations over the preceding decade, notwithstanding their dispute over territory located along the flanks of Tibet. Yet the situation along their shared border had been deteriorating and dispelled any illusions of Sino-Indian unity. Beijing, for example, believed that New Delhi was secretly aiding rebel groups inside Tibet, which it had annexed in 1950 and was struggling to maintain control over. For its part, India attempted to stake its claim to contested territory by initiating a "forward policy" in 1961, which involved establishing under-strength military outposts in areas claimed by China. Following a series of small clashes, Beijing launched a two-pronged offensive in October 1962 and quickly overran opposing forces before eventually pulling back its troops. The result of the war was an embarrassing defeat for India, which managed to appear strategically provocative and militarily feeble at the same time. Nevertheless, the conflict helped to bring New Delhi and Washington closer together. Not only did it highlight the danger of Chinese aggression in both capitals, but it also transformed South Asia into the new frontline of the Sino-American rivalry.

Komer, for instance, immediately viewed the war "as potentially one of the most crucial events of the decade," a view that U.S. officials openly shared with their Pakistani counterparts.[10] Not long after the fighting began, the American ambassador to Pakistan, Walter McConaughy, was instructed to tell President Ayub that the "Sino-Indian border conflict is second in importance only to Cuba in [the] present global confrontation between the Free World and the Sino-Soviet bloc."[11] The following month, Assistant Secretary of State for Far Eastern Affairs Averell Harriman visited the region. For Kennedy, the trip represented "a major opportunity to show Ayub how radically the Sino-Indian confrontation has altered the situation on the subcontinent from our point of view." His guidance to Harriman was blunt. The United States previously had been willing to tolerate the "basic difference in viewpoint" that plagued its relations with Pakistan, namely, that Washington regarded the alliance as a barrier to communist expansion while Rawalpindi viewed it as a way to maintain parity with India. As a result of the border war, however, the subcontinent had emerged as "a new area of major confrontation between the Free World and the Communists," which required a shift in U.S. policy. Kennedy hoped that this demonstration of Chinese hostility would not only convince Pakistan that the communist threat to the region was indeed very real, a possibility Rawalpindi had discounted in the past, but would also be the catalyst for a settlement with India, which would enable the two rivals to establish a united front against outside aggression.[12]

While Kennedy pressured Ayub to accept the reality of closer U.S.–India ties and focus on the much more serious threat from China, he also pleaded with Indian prime minister Jawaharlal Nehru to pursue negotiations over the status of Kashmir. "We appreciate how difficult it is for you at this moment, when the memory of the recent Chinese attack combines with the prospect of a further one, to turn your attention to the old and troublesome problem of Kashmir," the president wrote in a letter to his counterpart. "Yet an effective defense against the Chinese threat to India depends on your ability to concentrate your full resources on meeting their aggression. Further, since the threat extends to the whole subcontinent, ultimately the efforts of the whole subcontinent will be necessary to meet it. A full commitment of your own resources and unity of effort against the Chinese can be reached if the issues which divide India and Pakistan, the most important of which is Kashmir, are settled."[13]

Despite attempts at evenhandedness and a desire to see local rivals unite against a common threat, the Kennedy administration used the opening created by the war to recalibrate its relations with India and Pakistan. Komer, for instance, noted that the conflict had created "a golden opportunity" for Washington to improve its image in New Delhi, one that policymakers seized on when Nehru desperately appealed to the United States for military support. In response, the United States (along with Great Britain) provided India with small arms and other supplies, enough to equip several army divisions.[14] At the same time, frustrations with Pakistan continued to grow, especially when it became clear that Rawalpindi was not willing to sit back and accept closer U.S.–India ties. As one State Department report explained, Pakistan was responding to this development with "a more independent foreign policy," which included pursuing better relations with the Soviet Union, undertaking negotiations with China over disputed border areas, and distancing itself from its alliance commitments. Although this shift in policy was motivated by recent events rather than deep pro-communist sympathies and although Pakistan was unlikely to end its relationship with the United States given its dependence on U.S. arms and the inability of other patrons to supply modern weapons of equal quality, the change that was taking place appeared to be an enduring one. No matter how U.S.–India relations evolved, the report concluded, Pakistan "will probably not return to a policy of whole-hearted collaboration with the West."[15]

Komer praised the report and passed it on to Kennedy, who voiced some of the same conclusions himself. By the end of the year, for example, the president was openly questioning the utility of Washington's alliance with Pakistan and seriously considering whether its departure from CENTO would really be that bad: "In return for the protection of our alliance and our assistance what do they do for us?"[16] By contrast, Kennedy argued that the United States "must recognize the importance of India." If it were to side with China, "we would have no free South Asia."[17] The president even admitted that "he couldn't see how we could stop communist China without India" and was willing to send American combat forces to help defend it if Beijing renewed hostilities and bombarded Indian cities from the air. U.S.

officials also began to reconsider their views on pushing India and Pakistan closer together. Up to this point, resolving the Kashmir dispute was considered a precondition for improving U.S.–India ties without destroying the U.S.–Pakistan alliance. Yet Washington had a fleeting opportunity to exploit New Delhi's growing fear of China as well as its recent request for assistance. Kennedy, therefore, was unwilling to hold military support hostage to progress on the Kashmir negotiations, which were ongoing but appeared unlikely to succeed.[18]

Secretary of State Dean Rusk agreed that military assistance should not depend on the status of Kashmir or reconciliation between India and Pakistan, no matter how beneficial these outcomes would be for U.S. strategy in South Asia. The United States, he argued, "must not lose sight of the long-term geopolitical significance of India as the only non-communist country in Asia capable of becoming a counterpoise to Communist China."[19] As for Pakistan, U.S. officials were still searching for a way to become less dependent on Rawalpindi without driving it into the arms of Beijing. In short, they wanted a modified U.S.–Pakistan alliance, one that was "compatible with continued Western military assistance to India designed to increase India's capacity to resist Chinese Communist pressure."[20] Whether they could actually strike that balance remained to be seen.

The Johnson Administration and the 1965 India–Pakistan War

With the death of President Kennedy in November 1963, there was no guarantee that U.S. officials would persist with their nascent efforts to embrace India as an ally. Nor was it clear that they would continue to reduce their dependence on Pakistan. In fact, President Johnson not only distrusted the Indian political leadership, but he also had a strong affinity for Ayub Kahn, which suggested that the United States might return to its pre-1962 approach to South Asia. Despite these personal preferences, the policies that were embraced over the preceding year largely remained intact. Most of Kennedy's senior advisors stayed in government, and their views had not changed. Komer, for example, continued to argue that "India, as the largest and potentially most powerful non-Communist Asian nation, is in fact the major prize in Asia." He therefore maintained that while the United States "can and should protect Pakistan against India," it could not allow a preference for dealing with Ayub "to stand in the way of a strong Indian policy."[21] President Johnson, Komer later recalled, generally agreed with this assessment. Although he was not quite as enthusiastic about India's prospects as his predecessor, he maintained "the basically pro-Indian policy of Kennedy—indeed went further along the same lines."[22]

As Johnson explained to Chester Bowles, who was serving as the U.S. ambassador in New Delhi at the time, he was "fully aware of the importance of consolidating the gains we have made vis-à-vis India." Likewise, Bundy counseled patience with Bowles, a strong advocate of closer U.S.–India ties, telling him that Washington was in the midst of "the painful transition of disengaging from the out and out pro-Pak policy of the 1950's, and shifting to one more consonant with our real strategic interests."[23] Notably, this growing support for India was rooted in geopolitical considerations. According to Secretary of Defense Robert McNamara, the United States needed Japan and India to contain China across the whole of Asia. As one assessment by the Joint Chiefs of Staff noted, these were the only two nations that had the potential to one day protect their territory from communist aggression without substantial American military aid.[24] The United States did not throw its entire weight behind India during this period, however, nor did it cut ties with Pakistan. Instead, officials in Washington still believed that they could somehow improve relations with New Delhi and preserve their alliance with Rawalpindi. While they provided India with modest military aid and more generous economic support, therefore, they also attempted to reassure Pakistan that these steps did not jeopardize its security; rather, they enhanced its security by creating a more effective regional defense against a possible Chinese invasion. This argument fell on deaf ears, however, and U.S. policymakers returned to the notion that reconciliation between India and Pakistan was the solution to their strategic dilemma. Thus, they encouraged both sides to negotiate a resolution to the Kashmir dispute and focus their attention on extraregional threats from communist powers, not one another.

Although the prospects for a Kashmir settlement were remote, U.S. policymakers remained convinced that a significant improvement in relations between India and Pakistan would prevent Rawalpindi from retaliating against Washington for pursing closer ties with New Delhi, either by restricting U.S. access to key intelligence facilities, withdrawing from SEATO and CENTO, improving relations with China, or all three. In theory, with Kashmir off the table, Pakistan would no longer oppose U.S. military aid to New Delhi and would no longer view its relationship with the United States as a bargaining chip rather than a genuine security partnership. Likewise, India would no longer see U.S. support to Pakistan as a threat and would no longer be tempted to adopt a pro-Soviet stance in response.[25] As Komer explained to Johnson, settling the Kashmir issue would "be a big step forward toward an Indian subcontinent strong enough to stand on its own feet against the Chicoms, if not the USSR." Encouraging some type of compromise, especially by putting pressure on Pakistan, seemed to be "worth the effort."[26]

Barring a major change in the status quo, then, the United States appeared determined to steer a middle course. This meant avoiding a showdown with Pakistan, gradually improving ties with India, and encouraging both nations to work with one another. Nevertheless, while policymakers made it clear to their Pakistani counterparts that U.S. assistance to India was not up for debate, Pakistan still tried to drive a wedge between the United States and

India by flirting with China.[27] This only fed doubts about its reliability, however, and fueled resentment in Washington. As one State Department report summarized the situation, the Pakistanis "signed an alliance with us for one expressed purpose (anti-Communism) while intending quite another (anti-India)." Under "the guise of an anti-Communist ally," Rawalpindi had cashed in on Washington's largesse, accepting billions of dollars in economic and military aid. "In market-place English," the report noted, "the Paks have taken us for a ride."[28] Just like his predecessor, therefore, Johnson began to question the value of U.S. military support to Pakistan, which exceeded the amount of support that Washington provided to India by a substantial margin. Not only was the Pakistani government's intransigence becoming a problem in South Asia, but Rawalpindi was also refusing to assist the United States in its fight against communist insurgents in Southeast Asia. Washington, it seemed, was not getting very much in return for its investment.[29] Johnson expressed his frustrations to Ayub. The United States, he cautioned, could not remain a good friend to Pakistan if the relationship between the two nations became "more and more of a one-way street."[30]

Despite this relatively evenhanded approach, before long the opportunity arose to make a clear choice in favor of one side or the other. The year 1965 was a pivotal one on the subcontinent. In April, Indian and Pakistani armed forces clashed in the Rann of Kutch, a disputed area that straddled India's western seaboard and Pakistan's southern border. Rawalpindi, which initiated the engagement, was attempting to probe India's capabilities and test its resolve, both of which were still tarnished from its defeat by China several years earlier. New Delhi refused to commit significant troops to counter the incursion, however, and both sides eventually settled for international arbitration under pressure from Great Britain. Yet India's irresolute performance did little to bolster its strength in Pakistan's eyes and set the stage for another round of fighting.

Moreover, although Rawalpindi was skeptical about New Delhi's ability to fend off a major assault, it understood that key long-term trends were clearly in its rival's favor. Not only was India enhancing its armed forces thanks to recent increases in defense spending and a new military modernization program, both of which were prompted by its loss in 1962, but it was also attempting to reduce Kashmir's autonomy and integrate the disputed territory into the Indian political system. In August, therefore, Pakistan launched Operation Gibraltar, infiltrating regular and irregular forces into Kashmir with the goal of instigating a rebellion. This was, in effect, a preventive attack undertaken in the hope of gaining control over additional territory and bringing New Delhi to the negotiating table before the relative power gap between the two sides grew so large that India could crush Pakistan and therefore ignore its demands. Over the following month, however, the conflict escalated substantially. Rather than just fighting an irregular conflict in Kashmir, the two rivals also found themselves in a conventional

111

war that included large armored battles in the Punjab region along their international border.[31]

The power shift that was taking place and the outbreak of war raised the prospect that India would soon achieve regional primacy. Yet Washington did not accommodate New Delhi, even though its potential to dominate the region was precisely why U.S. policymakers wanted to improve relations with India in the first place. Instead, the United States supported efforts to reach a cease-fire through the United Nations, suspended military aid to both sides, and even allowed the Soviet Union to serve as a mediator between India and Pakistan once a cease-fire took effect. Collectively, these steps marked the start of a diplomatic withdrawal from the region and the end of any serious efforts to establish India as a friendly barrier to Chinese expansion.

Why did the United States oppose India, especially given the widespread view in Washington that it was the strongest nation in South Asia and the only viable ally in the region against China? Two reasons stand out. First, U.S. officials grew increasingly frustrated that India and Pakistan were focusing all their attention on one another, not on the communist powers, and were jeopardizing the security of South Asia as a result. During the first half of 1965, as the two rivals engaged in border skirmishes in the Rann of Kutch, U.S. policymakers began to reconsider whether either one merited assistance. President Johnson, for example, was "terribly disillusioned" with both sides in the aftermath of these clashes and by August was suggesting that the United States should "get out of military aid to both Pakistan and India."[32] Renewed combat over Kashmir one month later hardly alleviated American disappointment. As Rusk later explained, Washington "took the view during the Indian-Pakistan fighting that since we had strongly urged the two sides to take steps that would avoid the conflict, that if they wanted to ignore our advice and go to war with each other that we wouldn't pay for it." The ongoing rivalry between these nations, he added, "has been a big burden to the United States."[33]

Second, despite the considerable relative power advantage that India seemed to enjoy on paper, it soon became apparent that New Delhi was not going to emerge as a local hegemon that could dominate South Asia, if it managed to achieve a victory at all. Rather, the Second Kashmir War demonstrated to U.S. officials that India would remain preoccupied with Pakistan because it was not yet strong enough to break free of the balance of power on the subcontinent. In short, the hegemonic power shift that was taking place was incomplete. This, in turn, forced Washington to revise its earlier assessments and reconsider its regional strategy.

For example, in September 1963—less than one year after the Sino-Indian war had concluded and less than two years before the India-Pakistan war began—McNamara predicted that the "Indians could reach a level when they could lick the Paks soon" thanks to their growing defense budget. Pakistan, however, could never hope to match India, even with increased assistance from the United States.[34] Then, in late 1964, a National Intelligence Estimate (NIE) observed that New Delhi was not only bolstering its defense spending but was now receiving military aid from the United States, Great Britain, and the Soviet Union. It concluded, therefore, that while the Indian army "still suffers from deficiencies of leadership and training, its combat effectiveness is improving and it could probably overwhelm its smaller Pakistani foe."[35] Yet the course of the war seemed to contradict these appraisals. By mid-September, the conflict had devolved into a stalemate.[36] In Washington, Komer reported to President Johnson that the military situation on the ground was "confused," that successful Pakistani counterattacks had New Delhi "quite worried," and that he and others believed that Pakistan "will do quite well militarily in the next week or so in the key Punjab sector," at least until its armed forces started to run short of supplies.[37] With neither side able to achieve a decisive victory, senior U.S. officials began to take a much darker view of the region as a whole and India's prospects as a rising power.

According to Secretary Rusk, "Pakistani-Indian warfare bites deeply into American interests." Although he did not abandon his earlier position that India was the more important nation because of its potential to balance against China, he still painted a dire portrait of the war's long-term consequences. "Fighting could exhaust one country or both," Rusk argued, "and subject the 50 million Moslems in India and upwards of 10 million Hindus in Pakistan to unbelievable blood baths. Collapse and communal chaos would call into question the future of the subcontinent itself and would certainly negate our effort to build there a viable counterweight to Communist China." If India were "to go down the drain," he warned, the United States "would face a new situation in many ways as serious as the loss of China." This was, of course, a worst-case assessment. Yet less dramatic alternatives seemed almost as bleak. In Rusk's opinion, even if the war did not lead either side to experience significant internal instability, a prolonged conflict would "bankrupt both."[38]

The view from the Pentagon was equally pessimistic. As fighting raged on in September, McNamara delivered an update to President Johnson. Although the situation on the ground was fluid and reliable information was scarce, Pakistan appeared to be winning. He also estimated that it would remain on the offensive for approximately four weeks. After that, India's quantitative military advantages would come into play and probably turn the tide in New Delhi's favor. Yet McNamara predicted that it would be twelve weeks into the war before India could gain a clear edge on the battlefield. Meanwhile, its forces would be suffering from attrition, while the domestic consequences of the conflict could be far worse. In other words, even though McNamara believed that India would secure a victory if given enough time, he worried that the price of victory would be enormous. As he explained to Johnson, the conflict might result in the "weakening if not destruction of the Indian political institutions." Specifically, the secretary of defense feared the "fractioning or fragmenting" of the nation, especially if individual Indian states exploited the chaos to declare their independence. Like Rusk, therefore, McNamara considered internal collapse to be a very real possibility. Should India suffer such a massive trauma, eventually there would be "no effective barrier to the Chinese" in South Asia, an assessment the president did not dispute.[39] These warnings illustrate just how fragile India now appeared in the eyes of American policymakers, many of whom were certainly aware of its serious weaknesses but had spent the past several years focused on its potential strengths.

In the end, New Delhi did fight more effectively in 1965 than it had three years earlier, and from the perspective of most observers it emerged from the conflict as the winner. Yet its victory came at a significant cost and was a minor one at best. As Dennis Kux explains, "Although both sides lost heavily in men and materiel and neither gained a decisive military advantage, India had the better of the war."[40] This provided little comfort to U.S. policymakers. India might have been a rising power with aspirations for local dominance, but its inability to overwhelm Pakistan indicated that the hegemonic power shift in South Asia was incomplete. The region was still characterized by rough parity between the two rivals, at least in the military sphere. Consequently, the war tarnished India's image in Washington's eyes and undermined its appeal as a potential ally. Even still, both Komer and Bundy continued to advocate a pro-India policy. Shortly after the conflict came to an end, they suggested to the president that the United States "make it quietly clear that we accept and indeed support [India's] primary role in the subcontinent." As Komer put it, the United States simply could not avoid the reality "that India is (with Japan) one of the two really key countries in Free Asia" and therefore "merits a comparable investment *almost despite the Indians*."[41] The opportunity to transform U.S.–India relations had passed, however. Many proponents of closer ties would soon leave government or move on to different portfolios, while the legacy of the Second Kashmir War provided little evidence that India warranted the time, energy, and resources that Komer and others had advocated.

How do these events stack up with the arguments in chapter 1? While the theory predicts that the United States would have accommodated India if it had achieved greater success on the battlefield and scored a major victory over Pakistan, it is impossible to know for certain how Washington would have responded under these conditions. Nevertheless, the concerns espoused by senior U.S. officials during the Second Kashmir War are consistent with the theory's emphasis on the direction and scope of regional power shifts when the risk of containment failure is high. So, too, is the decision by U.S. policymakers to abandon their goal of making India the centerpiece of a new containment strategy in South Asia. The conflict between India and Pakistan took place in a balance-of-power subsystem and New Delhi failed to achieve the type of victory that would have cemented its status as the preponderant local power. Observing this, U.S. officials feared that an exhausting and in-conclusive war would weaken both sides, reinforce their single-minded fo-cus on countering one another rather than outside powers, and erode the barriers to external intervention.

Nevertheless, there is another plausible explanation for Washington's de-cision to oppose New Delhi in 1965. Specifically, even though U.S. officials believed that India might become an effective counterweight to China over time, they could have feared that a local conflict would provoke a Chinese intervention, which it was not yet prepared to handle. From this point of view, a complete power shift would have made accommodation less likely rather than more likely because the pressure on China to intervene would only grow if Pakistan suffered a devastating loss and Indian primacy seemed assured. This argument is unconvincing, however. During the war, Johnson probed McNamara on how Beijing was likely to respond, which the presi-dent believed was "the 64 dollar" question. According to the secretary of de-fense, the United States had no indication that China was massing forces along its southern border and was confident that any movements would be detected by aerial reconnaissance. Although McNamara calculated that Chinese military units would be able to "clean up that area" and "push the Indians out" with only a few days of preparation, he was doubtful that they would actually interfere. An attack on India would almost certainly trigger increased Western support for New Delhi and could even provoke a coun-terintervention, precisely the outcomes that China wanted to avoid. Mc-Namara was not alone in this assessment. The U.S. intelligence community also concluded that Chinese intervention against India was unlikely, although it was more focused on the difficulties of conducting military operations in the Himalayas as well as Beijing's other priorities in Southeast Asia. "We believe that China will avoid direct, large-scale, military involvement in the Indo-Pakistan war," one assessment concluded. "An impending Pakistani defeat would, however, substantially increase the pressures for Chinese entry. Even in this circumstance we believe the chances are better than even that the logistic problems involved and the primacy of Vietnam in China's interests would keep China from undertaking a major military venture against India."[42]

Ultimately, the conflict diminished India's value as a security partner and seemed to heighten the long-term risk of containment failure in the region. Perhaps not surprisingly, then, it also marked the end of Washington's efforts to make India an informal ally against China, although the United States con-tinued to provide New Delhi with economic assistance and nonlethal mili-tary aid. In fact, when a third India–Pakistan war broke out six years later, the United States would openly side against India, a decision that damaged relations between the two nations for decades afterward.

The Nixon Administration and the 1971 South Asia Crisis

Following the conflict between India and Pakistan in 1965, American involvement in South Asia declined considerably, as did its influence over New Delhi and Islamabad.[43] Before long, however, the United States was drawn into another crisis on the subcontinent, one that attracted the attention and involvement of all the major powers. Unlike previous India–Pakistan wars, however, the conflict that erupted in late 1971 was not fought over the disputed territory of Kashmir. Instead, its origins can be traced back to the geographic and ethnic divisions that had shaped Pakistan since its inception and that ultimately caused the nation to unravel in front of the entire international community.[44]

The partition of British India resulted in a majority-Muslim nation split between two noncontiguous wings, with northern India lying between them. The challenges of preserving national cohesion given this highly unusual political geography were compounded by deep ethnic divisions, as the Bengalis of East Pakistan suffered from discrimination at the hands of West Pakistan's Punjabi population, which dominated the nation's economic, military, and political institutions. As one author notes, "Since the creation of Pakistan in 1947, West Pakistanis had treated the eastern wing of the country as a virtual internal colony."[45] Friction between the two sides increased during the late 1960s, as did tensions within West Pakistan between President Ayub and his political opponents. These developments led to a coup in 1969, which replaced Ayub with the army chief of staff, General Agha Muhammad Yahya Khan. After committing to hold free elections in late 1970 and removing the key institutional barriers that had ensured West Pakistan's commanding position within the National Assembly, Yahya and his advisors were taken by surprise when East Pakistan's main political party, the Awami League, swept the elections in the East and won enough seats to hold a majority when the National Assembly reconvened.

Faced with a growing threat to the West's privileged position, Yahya engaged in several rounds of negotiations with Sheikh Mujibur Rehman, the head of the Awami League, as well as Zulfikar Ali Bhutto, the head of the leading political party in West Pakistan. His objective was to devise a new constitutional structure that would grant East Pakistan significant autonomy but preserve national unity. The talks failed, however, and in March 1971 Islamabad launched Operation Searchlight, a bloody crackdown on Awami League members and supporters, along with East Pakistan's Hindu population. Although the Pakistani military gained control over the capital of Dacca and other major cities, the crisis persisted for months. It also triggered a massive refugee flow into northeastern India and created an insurgent movement inside East Pakistan. With a military solution untenable, a political solution unreachable, and the Indian government under growing strains from a refugee population that soon exceeded ten million Bengalis, tensions between Islamabad and New Delhi increased dramatically. Finally, on December 3, 1971, Pakistan's air force executed a preemptive attack on Indian air bases. In response, India conducted airstrikes of its own, imposed a maritime blockade, and began a ground assault in the East to liberate what would soon become the new nation of Bangladesh.[46]

Although members of the Nixon administration closely monitored the crisis as it unfolded, from the outset they opted not to interfere directly. According to an NSC staff memo written in early March, "we have so far attempted to remain neutral and uninvolved" while maintaining the position "that we favor the unity of Pakistan and that it is up to the Pakistanis to determine the future of their country." Despite hopes that the crisis would not lead to secession or civil war, both of which had the potential to result in "a blood-bath" if thousands of West Pakistani troops attempted to suppress millions of East Pakistani civilians, policymakers recognized that they could be "witnessing the possible birth of a new nation of over 70 million people in an unstable area of Asia." Should East Pakistan declare its independence, however, they preferred "to see the split take place with the least possible bloodshed or disorder."[47]

The argument for inaction came straight from the top. As National Security Advisor Henry Kissinger explained, the president's position was "the same as everybody else's. He doesn't want to do anything."[48] Even after negotiations between Yahya and the Awami League broke down and Pakistani forces initiated an operation in Dacca that inflicted heavy casualties, the president did not alter his opinion of the situation. The United States, Nixon declared, "should just stay out." "If we get in the middle of that thing," he predicted, "it would be a hell of a mistake."[49] As the months passed, however, and a political resolution remained elusive, U.S. officials began to side with Islamabad, at least behind the scenes.

The ultimate outcome of the crisis was never seriously in doubt. Given the limited number of troops that Islamabad had stationed in the East as well as the difficulty of pacifying a large population in revolt, NSC staffers concluded "that the breakup of Pakistan is inevitable." Similarly, Kissinger maintained that the United States had "no illusions that West Pakistan can hold East Pakistan and . . . no interest in their doing so."[50] Nevertheless, two interrelated trends led Washington to take a more active role. First, the influx of refugees from East Pakistan to India increased dramatically as the crisis progressed. With no end in sight, the scale of the problem outstripped New Delhi's capacity to provide relief. Meanwhile, the growing refugee population in border areas contributed to fears of unrest in states that were already unstable. Second, the Indian government began to go on the offensive. Although it denied accusations that it was actively assisting opposition groups, New Delhi was providing arms, training, and logistical support to Bengali guerrillas that were harassing occupation forces. By mid-November, the internal war in East Pakistan seemed highly likely to escalate into a full-scale international conflict. As the Central Intelligence Agency (CIA) reported, "Cross-border clashes continue, regular Indian Army forces have made at least one foray into East Pakistan, the Mukti Bahini guerrillas are making deeper inroads, and the morale of the Pakistani Army and police is showing signs of wear."[51]

These developments led U.S. policymakers to reconsider their initial assumptions. Originally, Kissinger and others believed that New Delhi (much like Washington) preferred to see Pakistan remain intact. An independent Bangladesh might fall under the influence of India's old adversary, China, which could use it as a base to support secessionist movements in states such as West Bengal. Yet it became increasingly apparent that India preferred a divided Pakistan, which would alleviate its multi-front war problem, allow Bengali refugees to return home, and leave a friendlier nation along its northeastern border. Toward that end, it attempted to stoke an insurgency that would make controlling East Pakistan far more difficult.

The growing humanitarian catastrophe, New Delhi's efforts to impose costs on Islamabad, and the protracted nature of the crisis all increased the probability of a direct clash between India and Pakistan, while the possibility of a third major war on the subcontinent raised the specter of outside intervention by China and the Soviet Union in support of their respective clients—scenarios that were all considered possible but unlikely when the crisis began. Under these conditions, the United States opted to forgo "genuine neutrality," which would have entailed halting the very limited military assistance it provided to India as well as the economic aid it supplied to both sides.[52] Instead, Washington adopted a dual-track approach. First, it encouraged Yahya to take measures that would stem the flow of refugees into India, which would ameliorate the proximate causes of a potential war. U.S. officials also wanted Islamabad to reach some type of political accommodation with Dacca, which would grant East Pakistan greater autonomy and resolve the underlying source of hostilities. Even if these efforts were not a complete success, they still could buy time for the crisis to be resolved in some other way. As Kissinger explained, President Nixon "felt that we should give President Yahya a few months to see what he can work out."[53] Second, it strongly discouraged New Delhi from escalating the situation by launching a war to liberate East Pakistan. In a meeting with India's ambassador to the United States, the national security advisor warned that Washington "would deplore this matter getting totally out of hand." As he later told his colleagues, "I want to be sure everyone understands that there is to be no India–Pakistan war if we can prevent it; we are to do absolutely nothing that might egg anyone on. There should be no doubt in anyone's mind that there will be a drastic U.S. reaction if anyone resorts to military measures." If India opted for war, Kissinger declared, "there will be un-shirted hell to pay."[54]

Although this two-pronged strategy might have appeared evenhanded (and the administration attempted to describe it in precisely those terms to the general public as well as the international community), Nixon made it clear that he wanted to support West Pakistan in the hope of preserving good relations with Islamabad, even at the expense of alienating New Delhi. This preference was driven by personal views as well as geopolitical consider-ations. For instance, the president had little fondness for Indian leaders such as Prime Minister Indira Gandhi, whom he often disparaged in private con-versations, but enjoyed a much better relationship with Pakistani officials such as Yahya. More important, Islamabad had been a key intermediary be-tween Washington and Beijing, which culminated in Kissinger's secret visit to China in July 1971 following stops in both India and Pakistan. "The Pres-ident," Kissinger observed, "is eager to avoid any break with Yahya."[55]

If New Delhi's growing involvement in the crisis led the United States to "tilt" toward Islamabad, the outbreak of war in early December put Wash-ington firmly into its camp. The Nixon administration had no illusions that it could prevent the emergence of an independent Bangladesh, which was quickly recognized by the government in New Delhi only days after Indian forces swept into East Pakistan; India's prospects for liberating its neighbor were quite strong given the relatively small number of Pakistani troops de-ployed there, along with the difficulty of reinforcing and resupplying those troops from the West. Kissinger, for example, told Secretary of State William Rogers that there was "no way [the conflict] can blow over without East Pakistan being separated from Pakistan."[56] Nevertheless, U.S. policymak-ers were readying themselves for the possibility that India would begin to shift its forces to the West following a victory in the East—transforming a holding action into a full-scale offensive and potentially triggering outside intervention by other major powers. According to Kissinger, "At this stage we have to prevent an Indian attack on West Pakistan."[57]

To deter New Delhi from pressing its advantage and launching a wider war, Washington pursued a number of different measures. Publicly, it sought to "put the burden on India," in Nixon's words, so that the international com-munity would side against it.[58] This entailed branding New Delhi as the ag-gressor while working through the United Nations to achieve a cease-fire that would prevent India from keeping any territorial gains it might achieve. Privately, the administration encouraged American allies such as Jordan to transfer combat aircraft and spare parts to West Pakistan in the hope of bolstering its badly weakened air defenses; it urged the Soviet Union to use its influence over New Delhi and counsel restraint; and it even prodded China to mobilize military forces along its southern border, which might distract India by creating fears of a war on several fronts. Finally, Nixon and Kissinger ordered a U.S. Navy carrier strike group, led by the USS

Enterprise, to deploy from Southeast Asia to the Bay of Bengal. Ostensibly, its mission was to evacuate American personnel from East Pakistan. In reality, though, it was an unmistakable symbol to India, as well as its supporters in Moscow, that the United States was determined to bring the war to an end.[59]

Explaining "the Tilt"

Why did Washington remain neutral at the outset of the crisis, tilt toward Islamabad during the summer and fall, and side firmly against India following its military intervention in East Pakistan? Certainly the role of key individuals mattered; Nixon and Kissinger were often volatile and could let personal animosities influence policy decisions. The demands of triangular diplomacy also played a part. U.S. officials were committed to improving ties with China as a means of containing the Soviet Union, and Pakistan was a crucial player in this larger drama. Yet U.S. interests in South Asia and the type of power shift that was taking place in the region mattered a great deal as well.

In general, Washington faced little risk of containment failure or access denial in the area. Rather, its principal concern during this period was to preserve stability in an unstable part of the world. As Kissinger recalled in his memoirs, "When the Nixon administration took office, our policy objective on the subcontinent was, quite simply, to avoid adding another complication to our agenda."[60] Although American officials viewed South Asia as one of the main Cold War battlegrounds following the Sino-Indian War in 1962 and although the Kennedy and Johnson administrations attempted to court India as a counterweight to Chinese expansion, the strategic importance of the area diminished substantially as the Sino-Soviet split became irrevocable and the Nixon administration opted for rapprochement with Beijing. Moreover, the United States was not dependent on the region in economic terms and no longer operated surveillance aircraft from Pakistani territory. As Kissinger told his hosts in New Delhi shortly before his secret trip to China, "Unlike the other major powers from outside the region, the US has an essentially disinterested concern in developments in South Asia" and "sincerely believes that it is not involving itself in the internal affairs of the subcontinent."[61]

U.S. interests and objectives were outlined explicitly in an NSC document produced during the crisis. The United States, according to the report, "has no vital security interest in South Asia but as a global power we are inevitably concerned about the stability of an area where such a large percentage of mankind resides and which is geopolitically significant in terms of the Soviets and Communist Chinese." Peace, therefore, "is essential for the maintenance of U.S. interests." Given this assessment, "our basic objective is to prevent hostilities between India and Pakistan. If hostilities do break out, it would be our objective to ensure that neither we nor any other major external power become directly involved."[62] Kissinger conveyed these views directly to India's ambassador in Washington. The United States, he explained, "had no interest in keeping East Bengal a part of Pakistan," but it "did have an interest in preventing the outbreak of a war and preventing that issue from turning into an international conflict." Put more bluntly, the United States did not "give a damn" if Pakistan broke up, so long as the separation occurred peacefully.[63]

In sum, U.S. officials did not express a strong preference over the type of order that existed in South Asia, which is consistent with the theory given that they no longer feared Chinese intervention, did not need to worry about local actors withholding valuable resources, and simply wanted to preserve regional stability. Under these conditions, policymakers should have been attentive to the scope of the power shift that was taking place, presuming they believed that the local distribution of power was actually changing. Indeed, it was widely understood that India was once again a candidate for primacy on the subcontinent, that it was likely to win any war against Pakistan, and that a victory over its rival could allow it to accomplish what it had failed to achieve six years earlier. According to one CIA report, if India were to liberate East Pakistan, seize Pakistani-controlled Kashmir, and seriously degrade Pakistan's air and ground forces, it would become "the dominant power in South Asia."[64] The president and his national security advisor also concluded early on that a complete power shift would be the likely outcome if India elected for war, a view that had a significant impact on U.S. policy as events unfolded. Both Nixon and Kissinger believed that India planned to use the ongoing refugee crisis as a pretext to launch major military offensives against both East and West Pakistan, effectively eliminating its longtime adversary and becoming the preponderant power in the region. In July, for example, Nixon voiced his suspicion that the Indians "would like nothing better than to use this tragedy to destroy Pakistan." Kissinger agreed. In his estimation, "the Indians seemed bent on war" and "appear to be thinking of using the war as a way of destroying Pakistan."[65] For its part, although India might not have set out to destroy Pakistan, it did see the civil war as an opportunity to weaken its rival by dividing it in two and was prepared to take advantage of that opportunity before the window slammed shut.[66]

Senior U.S. officials understood that Pakistan still suffered from a quantitative military disadvantage vis-à-vis India, which meant that any conflict would be an uphill struggle. Just as important, they recognized that Pakistan was an extremely fragile nation that suffered from deep internal fissures. This meant that the consequences of a military defeat might extend far beyond the battlefield. If India were to intervene in East Pakistan, policymakers anticipated that "in West Pakistan so many forces . . . will be turned loose that the whole Pakistan issue will disappear."[67] Moreover, Nixon and Kissinger concluded that the destruction of Pakistan was not simply a possible but unintentional outcome of any Indian military operation in the East; rather, it appeared to be one of India's explicit objectives. After New Delhi deployed brigade-size military units in support of Bengali insurgents in late November, an action that marked the start of the war from Kissinger's perspective, he warned the president that New Delhi hoped to impose "so traumatic a settlement on the East Pakistan situation that the West Pakistan situation starts unraveling also." Its goal, he argued, was "to reduce West Pakistan to something like Afghanistan status" and "to turn East Pakistan into a sort of Bhutan [an Indian client state]." India seemingly wanted to overturn the status quo in South Asia, break the balance of power in the region, and establish a new order in which it was "the only significant country."[68]

While there was little doubt that India would be able to successfully liberate East Pakistan barring outside military intervention by China or the United States, which seemed unlikely unless its war aims expanded beyond Bangladesh, New Delhi's ability to defeat West Pakistan also appeared relatively certain. For example, the deputy director of the CIA explained that "the Indians have superiority in everything" and predicted that they would win a war if they mounted an attack in the West. "The Paks have the bulk of their armor and most of their divisions there," he observed, "but they won't prevail."[69] Despite this assessment of the military balance, few officials other than the president and his national security advisor believed that India was actually bent on destroying Pakistan. Because Nixon and Kissinger directed U.S. policy, their perceptions obviously mattered most. How and why did they reach this conclusion, though? From their perspective, several developments raised serious questions about India's motives.

First, in early August, India and the Soviet Union signed a twenty-year "Treaty of Peace, Friendship and Cooperation." In his memoirs, Kissinger described the agreement as a "bombshell." "Its bland provisions," he wrote, "could not obscure its strategic significance."[70] In truth, when the treaty was announced, most policymakers, including Kissinger, acknowledged that it was little more than a symbolic effort by Moscow to counter Beijing's influence over Islamabad and exploit Washington's diminished sway over New Delhi. As the crisis on the subcontinent escalated, however, it seemed as though India might have had a hidden motive in signing the accord: neutralizing the prospect of Chinese intervention on behalf of Pakistan in a future South Asia war.[71] In short, Nixon and Kissinger believed that the agreement was intended to give India a free hand against its archrival. Second, during her trip to Washington in early November, Indira Gandhi made few references to the situation in East Pakistan, instead calling attention to longstanding tensions inside West Pakistan, such as separatist movements in Baluchistan and the Northwest Frontier.[72] For Kissinger, this deliberate omission was a cause for concern and suggested that the Indians might have aims beyond creating an independent Bangladesh. It appeared, he told the president, that "to them East Pakistan is no longer the issue."[73] Third, after the war began, U.S. officials were provided with intelligence that seemed to support this assessment. According to the CIA, Gandhi had informed her cabinet that India would not accept a cease-fire until East Pakistan became an independent nation, the southern portion of Pakistan-controlled Kashmir had been liberated, and Pakistan's air and armored forces were so badly weakened that Islamabad would "never again be in a position to plan another invasion of India."[74] This report heightened fears that New Delhi was preparing to conduct a major offensive in the West. As the president explained to Congress the following year, "during the week of December 6, we received convincing evidence that India was seriously contemplating the seizure of Pakistan-held portions of Kashmir and the destruction of Pakistan's military forces in the West. We could not ignore this evidence. Nor could we ignore the fact that when we repeatedly asked India and its supporters for clear assurances to the contrary, we did not receive them. We had to take action to prevent a wider war."[75]

Given these factors, Kissinger believed that the conflict had the potential to reorder the region. The United States, he declared, was witnessing "a country, supported and equipped by the Soviet Union, turning one-half of another country into a satellite state and the other half into an impotent vassal."[76] In his mind, therefore, there was little doubt that a complete power shift was taking place, one that would eliminate the only local counterweight to Indian supremacy on the subcontinent. Notably, the strong emphasis that Nixon and Kissinger placed on the scope of the power shift between India and Pakistan is consistent with the arguments in chapter 1. Yet their reaction to the changing distribution of power is not. According to the theory, policymakers in a leading state should adopt a strategy of accommodation when their main interest is stability and an RRP appears capable of establishing a new local order. In this case, however, the United States chose to support Pakistan and preserve regional parity, even though India was clearly on the verge of achieving regional primacy. What accounts for this discrepancy between the theory's prediction and the historical record?

Although South Asia was no longer critical for containment, Nixon and Kissinger still viewed events in nearly every corner of the world through the lens of the U.S.–Soviet rivalry and continued to believe that Washington's reputation was always on the line, even if its material interests in a crisis were marginal. This outlook shaped their response to India's military campaign. As Robert Dallek notes, "If a South Asian war were confined to the principals, Nixon and Kissinger saw it as of limited consequence."[77] In their view, however, a third India–Pakistan conflict had implications beyond the subcontinent. Should India prevail, the national security advisor asked his colleagues rhetorically, "what would be the impact in the larger theatre of world affairs?"[78] Part of the answer, according to Kissinger, was that China would use the contest to assess the reliability of the United States as a security partner, leaving the fate of Sino-American rapprochement and the strategy of triangular diplomacy up in the air. The Nixon administration saw China as a key counterweight to the Soviet Union and was reluctant to adopt a posture toward the India–Pakistan war that might cause Beijing to reconsider its own tilt toward Washington. After all, if the United States stood idly by as Pakistan was irreversibly weakened by India, it might do so again if China suffered a similar fate at the hands of the Soviet Union. Meanwhile, India had grown closer to the Soviet Union over the past several years, particularly as relations between Washington and New Delhi deteriorated. In short, the United States had few strategic incentives to abet India's rise but an important strategic rationale for keeping what was left of Pakistan intact.

At the same time, Nixon and Kissinger were also convinced that a major Indian victory over West Pakistan would destabilize other regions, regardless of the long-term impact it would have on the subcontinent. China was not the only nation that would be assessing American resolve: the Soviet Union and its proxies would be as well. If the United States stood aside and allowed India to crush Pakistan, the Kremlin could become more willing to challenge it elsewhere. It might, for instance, encourage its clients to instigate conflicts in other areas where Washington also hoped to preserve stability, especially the Middle East. Interestingly, at the height of the South Asia crisis, Nixon temporarily vacillated over U.S. policy and wondered why the United States was adopting such a hard-line against New Delhi and Moscow. In response, Kissinger outlined the logic behind Washington's position. "We're going through this agony," he argued, "to prevent the West Pakistan army from being destroyed. Secondly, to maintain our Chinese arm. Thirdly, to prevent a complete collapse of the world's psychological balance of power, which will be produced if a combination of the Soviet Union and the Soviet armed client state can tackle a not so insignificant country without anybody doing anything." The crisis, Kissinger maintained, was "our Rhineland."[79] If the United States did not react decisively to what could be "the dress rehearsal for a Middle Eastern war," conflicts in other regions were inevitable.[80] Nixon was convinced. As he cautioned several days later, should "India and the Soviet Union succeed in destroying Pakistan as a military and political entity, this can only have a devastating effect in encouraging the USSR to use the same tactics elsewhere."[81]

Ultimately, the 1971 India–Pakistan War provides mixed support for my theory and suggests other conditions that might be applied to the argument. Specifically, the combination of two attributes appears to distinguish this case: (1) the existence of multiple regions in which the leading state was determined to preserve stability and (2) the perception that these regions were closely linked. The degree to which regions are viewed as being interconnected can, in turn, be explained by a number of factors, from the expected salience of demonstration effects to the existence of a third party with the ability to provoke conflicts throughout the globe. In fact, both of these factors influenced Nixon and Kissinger in 1971. Whether correctly or not, the president and his national security advisor strongly believed that Soviet client states in other regions would draw a dangerous lesson from India's victory and the U.S. failure to stop it. With a diminished fear of retaliation, these proxies would be more inclined to launch their own wars of aggression, while Moscow would be emboldened to encourage them. In the end, these conclusions led the United States to oppose India, intervene on the side of West Pakistan, and stop a complete power shift from taking place in South Asia.

Although South Asia was hardly isolated from the geopolitical rivalries unfolding all around it, the region did not regularly capture the attention of U.S. officials during the Cold War. Nevertheless, events on the subcontinent did make their way to the top of the policy agenda on a number of occasions, particularly when local conflicts broke out and the distribution of power was in flux. During these critical junctures, Washington's reaction was shaped in large part by the risks that it faced in the area and its assessment of the power shift that was taking place there. In 1965, for example, the United States perceived a high risk of containment failure in South Asia. Following the Sino-Indian border war several years earlier, it became convinced that the region was the new frontline in its competition with Communist China. Despite having close ties to Pakistan, therefore, the United States attempted to improve its relationship with India, which was the only nation with the potential to dominate the area and therefore the best candidate to counter Chinese expansion. When India and Pakistan went to war over Kashmir, however, New Delhi's failure to achieve a decisive victory undercut its value as an ally. Not only did the conflict increase the subcontinent's vulnerability to external intervention, but it also reinforced concerns in Washington that India was an extremely fragile nation that could easily slide into chaos. In short, the power shift that was taking place in South Asia was hegemonic but incomplete. As a result, the United States was reticent to side too closely with India at the expense of its relationship with Pakistan and was unwilling to be a source of aid to both sides that they would use against one another. In 1971, by contrast, the United States only wanted to preserve stability in South Asia and avoid potential complications to more important priorities because the risks of both containment failure and access denial were low. When India liberated Bangladesh and then posed a threat to West Pakistan, however, the possibility of a complete power shift that would make it the dominant nation in the region was impossible to ignore. Contrary to the theory's predictions, U.S. policymakers did not accommodate New Delhi in this case. Rather, Nixon and Kissinger used the threat of military intervention against India to bring the war to an end—a decision that can be explained by their fear that a sweeping victory by a Soviet client would spark instability in other regions.

The Emergence of Iraq and the Competition to Control the Gulf, 1979–1991

During the second half of the Cold War, Southwest Asia emerged as an increasingly important area for U.S. national security policy, one that was not quite on par with Western Europe or Northeast Asia but was no longer a distant third. Of course, the United States had significant interests in the region dating back to World War II, when the Allies feared that the Persian Gulf's petroleum might be targeted by Axis powers in need of oil. Not long after that conflict came to an end, Washington assumed greater responsibility for ensuring peacetime access to these resources, which underpinned the economic health of friendly nations. Specifically, it helped guard vital sealanes, prevent local conflicts, and deter intervention by outside powers such as the Soviet Union. Nevertheless, Southwest Asia remained a relatively low priority for U.S. officials, who were focused on more pressing threats elsewhere. That began to change between the late 1960s and late 1970s, however, thanks to several developments.

First, in 1968, Great Britain undermined a key pillar of regional security by announcing that it would soon withdraw its armed forces from their outposts "east of Suez." This decision not only highlighted the limits of London's military power in the Cold War era, but it was also a sharp blow for the United States, which could no longer count on its closest ally to help manage potential threats against local nations. Later, in response to Washington's support for Israel during the 1973 Yom Kippur War, the Organization of Petroleum Exporting Countries (OPEC) reduced oil production levels and embargoed oil shipments to the United States. Although the cutoff did not come as a complete surprise, it did demonstrate the vulnerability of advanced industrialized nations to spikes in prices and disruptions in supplies. Finally, between 1977 and 1978, Soviet military assistance to Ethiopia and the communist coup in Afghanistan seemed to bolster Moscow's influence in the Horn of Africa and Central Asia, respectively. To some observers, the Soviet Union was not only enhancing its position along the flanks of the Persian Gulf, but it also seemed to be preparing for a military move against oil-rich territory.

Just as Southwest Asia was starting to command more of Washington's attention, a series of events thrust it even further into the spotlight and kept it there over the following decade: the collapse of the Pahlavi dynasty in Iran, the emergence of an ideological and aggressive regime in its place, the Soviet invasion and occupation of Afghanistan, the long and bloody conflict between Iran and Iraq, and, finally, the Iraqi annexation of Kuwait. This combination of revolution and war altered the entire landscape of the region by raising the specter of additional Soviet expansion, interrupting oil exports, and threatening the security of the Gulf Arab monarchies. It also upended the distribution of power. Until 1979, Iran was clearly the strongest local actor. For the next ten years, however, a balance of power existed between Iran and Iraq thanks to the former's self-inflicted wounds, the latter's military buildup, and the shifting fortunes of the war they were fighting against one another. Then, after it gained control over Kuwait in 1990, Iraq was suddenly poised to dominate the entire area.

Not surprisingly, U.S. policy toward Southwest Asia during the Jimmy Carter, Ronald Reagan, and George H. W. Bush administrations underwent a number of changes as these events unfolded. For instance, Tehran quickly went from being a highly valued American ally to an enduring American adversary. In addition, relations between Washington and Baghdad experienced a pair of reversals. Despite more than a decade of antagonism, the United States embarked on modest efforts to improve ties with Iraq after the Iranian revolution, adopted a policy of neutrality when the Iran–Iraq War began, and supported Iraq once the conflict turned in Iran's favor. Following the seizure of Kuwait, however, Washington imposed economic sanctions against Baghdad and launched a major military campaign to remove Iraqi forces and restore Kuwaiti sovereignty. I argue that this variation can be explained by the United States' preferred regional order and the direction of the power shifts that took place. Although U.S. policymakers were concerned mainly about the risk of containment failure until the early 1980s, those concerns receded as the Soviet intervention in Afghanistan proved to be a costly failure and the Cold War started to wind down. Meanwhile, the risk of access denial only increased as Iran and Iraq struggled to dominate their neighborhood. Under these conditions, Washington's preference for regional primacy gave way to a preference for regional parity. Determined to prevent any local actor from withholding the area's resources, it accommodated Iraq when it was a counterweight to Iran and opposed Baghdad when it made a bid for hegemony.

The Risk of Containment Failure and Iranian Regional Primacy

Traditionally, the United States has had two main objectives in Southwest Asia: "first, to ensure access by the industrialized world to the vast oil resources of the region; and second, to prevent any hostile power from acquiring political or military control over those resources."[1] For many years, these goals went hand in hand. Moreover, the biggest threat to both came from outside the area. Local nations could withhold energy shipments in response to U.S. policies and regional conflicts could result in export interruptions. Nevertheless, the most significant danger from a U.S. perspective was the prospect of the Soviet Union capturing Iranian oil fields or seizing Pakistani territory astride critical sea-lanes. Not only would these developments provide Moscow with valuable resources, but they would also enhance its ability to deny those resources to nations that relied on them. Simply put, the United States was focused on preventing external intervention, although containment failure would have very likely resulted in a loss of access as well.

Burdened with more urgent and important responsibilities in other areas, however, Washington could not easily achieve these objectives on its own. At first, London was expected to provide assistance. For more than a century, Great Britain had been the most important outside power in this part of the world. To protect the land and sea lines of communication linking Europe to the Indian subcontinent, it had established a permanent military presence in the region, provided security commitments to the smaller Gulf sheikdoms, and carved out a sphere of interest in Persia.[2] Although its influence waned over time, particularly after the Suez crisis in 1956, Great Britain's continuing involvement in local affairs enabled the United States to concentrate its attention and resources elsewhere. From Washington's perspective, London's peacetime military presence helped "to exclude unfriendly major powers from the Gulf and to dampen intra-regional antagonisms and internal instabilities."[3] When they learned that the British planned to retrench, U.S. policymakers were left scrambling to find new ways of either shouldering or sharing the burdens of containment. With an escalating nuclear arms race, a deteriorating conventional military balance in Europe, and an ongoing conflict in Vietnam, the former option did not seem viable. Instead, the United States opted to rely on local actors that could serve as bulwarks against Soviet expansion into Southwest Asia, especially the "Twin Pillars" of Saudi Arabia and Iran—a decision that epitomized the Nixon Doctrine's emphasis on enabling allies rather than fighting directly on their behalf.[4]

At the time, however, Iran was widely recognized as the more important of the two pillars. In one author's words, it was "an obvious candidate for regional police officer."[5] Not only did it appear to have a stable government, but it was also a capable military power, at least in comparison to other

U.S. partners in the region. In addition, its location along the Soviet Union's southern perimeter meant that it was well positioned to block an overland incursion and to support intelligence collection operations. According to a State Department report produced in early 1970, Iran was "the strongest and most effectively ruled state in the area" and was "determined to assume responsibility for the maintenance of security in the Gulf after the British leave." By contrast, Saudi Arabia's ability to counter Soviet influence was much more limited because of "its military weakness relative to Iran" as well as "questions about the country's long-term stability."[6] Unlike his counterparts in Riyadh, the shah was also willing to cooperate openly with the United States on sensitive national security issues. This was due to a number of factors, including the history of U.S.–Iran relations. In 1946, during one of the first crises of the Cold War, the United States pressed the Soviet Union to withdraw its military forces from the northern portion of Iran, which Moscow had occupied in 1941 as part of a joint Anglo-Russian effort to keep the Axis powers out of the region. Then, in 1953, Washington and London helped overthrow Iran's prime minister, Mohammed Mosaddegh, who was attempting to nationalize the British-controlled oil industry and was suspected of having pro-Soviet sympathies. As a result of this coup, the shah was able to consolidate his rule and gain near-total control over the nation. He was, therefore, doubly in Washington's debt.

Ultimately, the United States was determined to enhance Iran's military capabilities and ensure its continued loyalty through massive arms sales.[7] In other words, to mitigate the risk of containment failure, U.S. officials were willing to strengthen a local power that was aiming for regional primacy. "Our main worry in the Gulf, as elsewhere in the Middle East, is the danger of Soviet penetration," explained National Security Advisor Henry Kissinger. He therefore believed the United States should "recognize that Iran is in fact the preponderant power in the Gulf" and support Tehran as the "keeper of stability" there.[8] This assessment became the foundation for U.S. policy in the region. According to the National Security Decision Memorandum outlining Washington's strategy for Southwest Asia in the wake of Great Britain's withdrawal, the United States should encourage greater cooperation between Iran and Saudi Arabia but accept that the former was the strongest local actor and thus the most promising instrument for counterbalancing the Soviet Union.[9] Even when internal opposition to the shah's rule became more apparent, Kissinger did not depart from his insistence that a powerful Iran served Washington's interests. Instead, he continued to maintain "that the Shah, should he survive a sufficient number of years, will have a key, if not the controlling, role among the regional powers in helping to assure stability in the Persian Gulf area."[10]

Supporting a preponderant power in Southwest Asia did have a downside, however, particularly given the importance of the Persian Gulf's energy resources, the extent of the shah's ambitions, and the contentious relationship between Iran and its Arab neighbors. For instance, U.S. intelligence reports explicitly highlighted Tehran's objective of improving its position at Washington's expense. Despite relying on the United States for military aid, the shah hoped to reduce, if not eliminate, the American military presence in the Gulf and the Indian Ocean, thus creating his own sphere of influence. This included removing the United States' forward-stationed naval forces from Bahrain, where they were headquartered.[11] For policymakers in Washington, however, the risk of containment failure outweighed the risk of access denial, and Iranian regional primacy was critical to managing the former, even if it increased the latter.

Regional Upheaval on Carter's Watch

Although Washington's enthusiasm for its informal alliance with Tehran peaked during the Richard Nixon and Gerald Ford administrations, the close partnership between the United States and Iran remained intact when President Carter came into office. In fact, key members of the new administration did not really differ from their predecessors when it came to U.S. strategy in Southwest Asia. According to National Security Advisor Zbigniew Brzezinski, Iran was a "major strategic asset" and the centerpiece "of a protected tier shielding the crucial oil-rich region of the Persian Gulf from possible Soviet intrusion." Likewise, Carter's first secretary of state, Cyrus Vance, recalled that Tehran's "military strength ensured Western access to gulf oil and served as a barrier to Soviet expansion."[12] Two critical developments in 1979 upended the United States' existing approach to the region, however, and heightened fears of external intervention. First, the Iranian revolution at the beginning of the year removed the shah from power and created an Islamic regime under the control of Supreme Leader Ayatollah Ruhollah Khomeini. As a result, the United States lost a local ally against the Soviet Union. Second, the Soviet invasion of Afghanistan at the end of the year brought Moscow's forces closer to the Persian Gulf. Not only did the invasion demonstrate its willingness to use force against its neighbors, but it also raised the possibility of further attacks against a fragile Pakistan and a weakened Iran.

Shortly after Moscow launched its assault against Afghanistan, Brzezinski wrote to Carter and expressed his concerns about the "regional crisis" that was unfolding. "Both Iran and Afghanistan are in turmoil," he noted, "and Pakistan is both unstable internally and extremely apprehensive externally." Moreover, if the Soviet Union successfully occupied Afghanistan and Pakistan fell into its orbit as well, "the age-long dream of Moscow to have direct access to the Indian Ocean will have been fulfilled." Brzezinski also pointed out that the growing threat to U.S. interests in the region could be traced directly back to the revolution in Iran, which "led to the collapse of the balance of power in Southwest Asia" and set the stage for a "Soviet presence right down on the edge of the Arabian and Oman Gulfs." In the end, without a capable Tehran on Washington's side, "there will be no firm bulwark in Southwest Asia against the Soviet drive to the Indian Ocean."[13] There was skepticism, however, at least on the part of the U.S. intelligence community, that Moscow was really embarking on "the preplanned first step in the implementation of a grand design for the rapid establishment of hegemonic control over all of Southwest Asia," or that its invasion of Afghanistan was "a dress rehearsal for an impending gala performance in Iran."[14] Yet there was little doubt that Iran was a far bigger prize, that an increased Soviet military presence nearby could enhance Moscow's influence throughout the region, and that local unrest provided a window of opportunity for aggression that might be too tempting for the Kremlin to pass up.[15]

Without a partner capable of safeguarding its interests, Washington had to respond to these developments on its own. The most visible step taken by the administration was the announcement of the Carter Doctrine during the January 1980 State of the Union address. As the president explained to the American people, "The Soviet effort to dominate Afghanistan has brought Soviet military forces to within 300 miles of the Indian Ocean and close to the Straits of Hormuz, a waterway through which most of the world's oil must flow." The enormous economic and strategic importance of this area meant that Washington could not stand idly by. "An attempt by any outside force to gain control of the Persian Gulf region will be regarded as an assault on the vital interests of the United States of America," Carter warned, "and such an assault will be repelled by any means necessary, including military force."[16] To back up this threat, Washington activated a new military organization—the Rapid Deployment Joint Task Force—that was intended to provide a quick-response capability for contingencies outside Europe or East Asia. It also pursued other measures to make power projection into the Persian Gulf easier, such as deploying a second carrier strike group to the Indian Ocean, prepositioning stockpiles of war-related materiel throughout the area, and expanding military access agreements with local nations.[17] These steps, Carter claimed, provided the United States with the "air and naval superiority to act instantly" if a threat emerged, which would allow it to keep open the Strait and ensure the continued flow of oil.[18]

In addition to bolstering its defensive capabilities in the vicinity of the Persian Gulf and enhancing its ability to send additional forces there if necessary, the Carter administration reexamined its policies toward Iran and its longtime rival, Iraq. Some officials in Washington initially held out hope of repairing ties with Tehran so that it could resume its role as a barrier to Soviet expansion. Nevertheless, relations between these former allies went from bad to worse as Iranian moderates were marginalized, conservative elements hostile to the United States consolidated their power, and the

American embassy staff was taken hostage. By contrast, ties between the United States and Iraq began to improve, despite a rocky history.

Baghdad had broken off diplomatic relations with Washington during the Six-Day War in 1967. It was also a widely recognized supporter of international terrorist groups, a vocal opponent of the Israeli–Palestinian peace process, and a major recipient of Soviet military equipment.[19] Yet it was still one of the most important nations in the region thanks to its large oil reserves, significant production capacity, and growing military strength. In fact, from the very start of the Carter administration, U.S. policymakers were building the case for a closer connection. "Barring major geopolitical disturbances," one proposal explained, "Iraq will emerge as a major regional power in the Gulf area over the next 5–10 years, and it is in our interests to be in a position to encourage them to adopt more moderate positions and reduce their dependence on the Soviet Union."[20] Iraq's importance only increased in the aftermath of Iran's revolution.[21] Moreover, the Soviet invasion of Afghanistan made Baghdad wary of its patron's intentions, which provided an opportunity for the United States. "Informal arrangements for sharing information with Iraq on matters of mutual concern are currently being explored," noted a State Department report. Should those arrangements come to fruition, they would "have a beneficial impact on our bilateral relationship."[22] Along with considering new information exchanges, Washington attempted to reestablish diplomatic ties with Baghdad and even approved the export of American-manufactured turbine engines for Iraqi frigates, despite opposition from Congress as well as the Israeli government (the decision was suspended after the initial shipment, however).[23] In a memo advocating the sale, Brzezinski argued that the loss of Iran made it "highly desirable to maintain correct relations with the Iraq regime for the moment."[24] As he later declared in a public interview, "We see no fundamental incompatibility of interests between the United States and Iraq. . . . We do not feel that American–Iraqi relations need to be frozen in antagonism."[25] Although these measures yielded few tangible benefits, they do suggest that U.S. policymakers were beginning to consider the possibility that Iraq could become a useful partner against an expansionist Soviet Union or an ideological Iran, whichever one proved to be the bigger threat.

U.S. officials had to deal with another setback to their Southwest Asia policy in 1980. In September of that year, Iraqi forces invaded Iran. The rivalry between Baghdad and Tehran had only intensified following Khomeini's ascension. Revolutionary regimes often adopt an increasingly hostile stance toward their perceived enemies both at home and abroad, particularly as they grapple with the dual imperatives of consolidating their power and exporting their ideology. The Islamic Republic was no different, and Iraq was one of its biggest external targets.[26] Not only had Iran been calling for the overthrow of President Saddam Hussein and the ruling Baath Party, but it was also providing encouragement and material support to Shiite opposition groups inside Iraq. Under pressure from Tehran's new leaders yet sensing a window of opportunity at the same time, Baghdad launched an offensive to gain control over the disputed Shatt al-Arab waterway, annex a portion of the Khuzestan region, and perhaps even topple the Khomeini regime.[27] This represented a novel problem for the United States, which had been focused on the threat of external intervention but now had to contend with a show-down between the region's two strongest military powers.[28]

From the outset, Washington opposed the conflict for a number of reasons, including the fear that Saudi Arabia might be attacked as part of any Iranian retaliation, the uncertain impact of the war on the hostage crisis, and, perhaps most important of all, the prospect that an Iranian defeat might open the door to a Soviet invasion of the region from its new base in Afghanistan. Despite these concerns, the U.S. reaction to the war was muted, which is not surprising given that the Carter administration was in the midst of a reelection campaign and was also preoccupied with the fate of the American captives in Tehran. Officially, Washington adopted a policy of strict neutrality, called for both sides to implement a cease-fire, and took steps to prevent the war from spreading to other Arab states, particularly after receiving reports that Iraq wanted to use Saudi territory to launch attacks against Iran. For instance, to ameliorate Riyadh's fear that it might become the target of Iranian reprisals, the United States deployed Airborne Warning and Control System aircraft to bolster the kingdom's air defenses and encouraged the Saudi government to refrain from any direct involvement in the war.[29]

There were suspicions in some quarters that the United States wanted to weaken Iran and that it might have even instigated the war by providing Iraq with a "green light." According to one assessment, although the United States claimed that it opposed the invasion, "its real attitude was very different."[30] To some extent, this view is understandable. After all, Baghdad was in a position to stop Tehran from reclaiming its status as the strongest actor in the region. Given Washington's deteriorating relations with the Islamic Republic, that might have seemed like the best possible outcome. Yet U.S. officials were still preoccupied with the risk of containment failure during the fall of 1980 and did not want to see Tehran suffer a total defeat that would leave the region far more vulnerable to external intervention.[31] As Deputy Secretary of State Warren Christopher announced shortly after the conflict began, the United States "would be strongly opposed to any dismemberment of Iran" and hoped the contest would remain a "limited war."[32]

Whether intentionally or not, U.S. neutrality actually benefited Iraq, at least at the outset. Saddam's forces quickly drove several dozen miles into Iranian territory before settling into defensive positions. In part, this initial success was the result of their initiative. But it also reflected a major shift in the military balance. Once the inferior power, Baghdad had been engaged in a major arms buildup while its rival was busy weakening its own armed forces.[33] Displaying little strategic foresight, the new regime in Tehran had purged officers across its military branches and created a parallel organ-ization, the Revolutionary Guards, which was neither well trained nor well integrated with Iran's existing units. Moreover, its American-manufactured equipment no longer had a steady stream of supplies.[34] According to a U.S. intelligence report that was issued more than a year before the conflict broke out, Iran's military was "undermanned, poorly led, undisciplined, and ineffective."[35] For instance, its air force—which had been a major source of advantage given Tehran's access to advanced U.S. platforms like the Grum-man F-14 Tomcat—was in especially bad shape. Another report predicted, therefore, that Iran "probably could not defeat Iraq in a major air war, and its capability will probably continue to decline in the months ahead."[36] The information that U.S. policymakers received once the war was under way painted an even bleaker picture of Tehran's prospects. One intelligence up-date issued shortly after Iraqi forces crossed the border indicated that Iran "has virtually no capability to sustain military operations at a high level of intensity." Therefore, it "would not be able to provide organized resistance against a major Iraqi ground offensive for more than a few days."[37] This meant that any serious efforts by the United States to impose the cease-fire it ostensibly wanted would have helped Iran alone by offsetting its military weakness.

While the local distribution of power was in flux, Washington was starting to reassess the challenges that it faced. In general, the risk of containment failure still overshadowed other concerns during the final months of the Carter administration. Yet the risk of access denial could not be ignored. From the very start, the Iran–Iraq War raised the possibility of diminished oil supplies, something that was already on the minds of policymakers given the sharp increase in prices that had occurred after the Iranian revolution. Carter attempted to calm these fears, arguing that the global economy could weather a temporary halt in exports from Iran and Iraq due to the surplus production capacity of other OPEC members as well as conservation efforts on the part of consumer nations. He also reaffirmed the enduring importance of maintaining access to the area. "Of course," he noted, "a total suspension of oil exports from the other nations who ship through the Persian Gulf region would create a serious threat to the world's oil supplies and consequently a threat to the economic health of all nations." It was essential, therefore, that freedom of navigation not be obstructed.[38] Yet the most immediate threat to oil exports now came from local actors, not outside powers.

These concerns did not lead to any significant change in U.S. policy. With the Iran–Iraq War devolving into a stalemate and a new administration taking over in Washington, the United States refrained from any direct involvement in the conflict. Rather, it opted "to keep hands off and let the two sides batter each other."[39] Yet it would soon abandon this approach and become more engaged, for two reasons. First, the risk of containment failure was beginning to wane. As the costs of controlling Afghanistan mounted, the possibility that

Moscow might launch an attack on the region seemed remote. Second, the risk of access denial continued to increase. Because Iraq failed to score a major victory over its rival, U.S. policymakers began to fear that Iran's superior resources would carry the day. Under these conditions, the United States was determined to prevent Tehran from reestablishing local primacy, which meant working with Baghdad to preserve local parity.

The Reagan Administration's Balance-of-Power Play

Just like its predecessor, the Reagan administration's approach to Southwest Asia was shaped by the enduring demands of containment and the growing risks to access. According to a National Security Decision Directive (NSDD) signed by the president, which outlined Washington's strategy for the region, the United States had two overarching interests in the Persian Gulf: "to prevent the Soviet Union from attaining a position of hegemony" and "to maintain continued access for the US and its principal allies to Gulf oil."[40] In fact, the latter objective was arguably even more important than it had been several years earlier. "The United States has a large stake in the continued flow of oil from the Persian Gulf in spite of the fact that US oil imports from the Gulf are small," one intelligence report explained, because Western Europe and Japan depended heavily on the region's petroleum. "Denial of all or most of the source of supply for a substantial period of time would create a worldwide oil shortfall much greater than that in 1973 or 1979. The United States could not insulate itself from the disruption of the world oil market."[41] As another NSDD declared in no uncertain terms, the United States would "undertake whatever measures may be necessary to keep the Strait of Hormuz open to international shipping." Because an interruption in oil supplies could have a crippling impact on the global economy, "we must assure our readiness to deal promptly with actions aimed at disrupting that traffic."[42]

This apparent continuity masked an important change. Whereas the Carter administration had focused almost exclusively on the prospect that the Soviet Union might intervene in the region and threaten oil supplies, the Reagan administration eventually concluded that the possibility of a local actor dominating the area and withholding its resources was much more worrisome. Rhetorically, policymakers continued to cite the danger from outside powers as the most significant challenge the United States faced in Southwest Asia. In reality, though, the likelihood that Moscow might try to seize territory along or near the Persian Gulf steadily declined as the occupation of Afghanistan took a heavy toll and, later, as the Cold War wound down.

Shortly after Soviet troops marched into Central Asia, fears that Afghanistan might not be Moscow's only target were high, while hopes that the Afghan people would be able to mount a serious resistance against the Red

Army seemed far-fetched. For instance, Brzezinski argued that despite the inherent challenges of pacifying an indigenous population—challenges that the United States had experienced firsthand in Southeast Asia—U.S. officials "should not be too sanguine about Afghanistan becoming a Soviet Vietnam." Unlike the Vietcong, Brzezinski observed, Afghan fighters had no external sanctuary, no serious outside support, and no effective military leadership.[43] Before long the situation began to change, however.

Pakistan quickly became a base of operations for the *mujahedin*, which gave them the ability to mobilize and organize in safety. Nations such as Saudi Arabia and the United States also started to provide insurgents with the money, weapons, and training that they needed to impose heavy costs on their occupiers. After more than two years of hard fighting, it became increasingly apparent that the Kremlin had miscalculated badly when it expected to defeat any opposition forces in short order. By this point, U.S. intelligence reports were consistently taking a dim view of the Soviet Union's prospects for success. Although Moscow had deployed nearly a hundred thousand soldiers to Afghanistan by 1982, analysts concluded that it would need to double its commitment of troops to stabilize the country—a commitment that the Kremlin appeared unwilling to make. Nor did it seem likely that Moscow would escalate the conflict by invading Pakistan to deny insurgents their sanctuary and cut off their supply lines, which would only expand the military campaign and create new headaches.[44] "Protracted stalemate," therefore, was judged to be the most plausible outcome, at least in the near term.[45]

This had important implications for the broader threat of Soviet expansion. As one senior State Department official testified before Congress in 1983, the "Soviet commitment of military assets to Afghanistan and Eastern Europe limits Moscow's ability to expend resources elsewhere."[46] That included Southwest Asia, which was a relatively low priority for the Kremlin in comparison to other regions, notwithstanding Washington's lingering fears that the Soviets might grab territory near the Gulf or gain a foothold along the Indian Ocean. In 1985, for example, a comprehensive intelligence assessment of Soviet military power and its ability to wage war in multiple theaters concluded that although a move against Southwest Asia could not be ruled out, the campaign in Afghanistan "will weigh heavily on Moscow's future capacity to conduct military operations in the Persian Gulf region."[47]

In sum, while the risk of containment failure in Southwest Asia had not completely receded, the Soviet occupation of Afghanistan reduced the chances of a military thrust against Iran or Pakistan and therefore the likelihood that the Carter Doctrine would need to be put into action. As a result, the United States began to look at the Iran–Iraq War through a different lens. Although the conflict was initially considered a threat to U.S. interests because it might erode the barriers to Soviet military intervention, shortly after Reagan entered office it was viewed in a more positive light, mainly because it prevented the emergence (or reemergence) of a preponderant local power that could deny access to the area.

As early as November 1981, for instance, a U.S. intelligence assessment observed that while Iran and Iraq were focused on fighting one another, neither could establish a leadership position in the Gulf. The war also had other benefits for Washington according to the report. For instance, it convinced moderate Arab nations that they were safest if they stood with the United States, which could defend them from any Iranian retaliation; it encouraged Baghdad to moderate its behavior, because Saddam Hussein needed the support of his neighbors to fund the war; it distracted Iran from exporting its revolutionary ideology, since it was preoccupied with protecting its own territory; and it led to the creation of the Gulf Cooperation Council (GCC), which suggested that moderate Arab nations were now prepared to take a more active role in regional politics. If Iran managed to win the conflict, these gains would be erased and the region would be destabilized. "A clear Iranian victory would be unsettling to the Gulf region—Iraq's role as a counterbalance to Iran would be seriously eroded making the other states of the area more vulnerable to Iranian pressures." Consequently, the Gulf Arab nations "probably view their interests as best served by the continuation of the stalemated war at its present low level of fighting," an outlook that the United States shared.[48] A State Department report painted a similar picture of the situation and expressed more serious concerns about any outcome that might "foreshadow Iranian hegemony over the entire Gulf." In particular, if Tehran gained control over Iraqi petroleum reserves, it could compel its neighbors to raise prices, which would upset global oil markets. Not surprisingly, therefore, the report argued that the chief U.S. objective in the region was preserving "stable, friendly governments in the GCC countries to protect continued access to their oil and unimpeded access to the Persian Gulf."[49]

In short, the declining risk of containment failure in Southwest Asia suggested that a conflict between the two strongest powers there actually worked to the United States' advantage. Nevertheless, Washington was unable to sit back and let both sides exhaust one another. After Iraq's initial success on the battlefield, its forces lost momentum and the war reached an impasse. Although Baghdad still had "the upper hand on the ground," there was "rough parity in the air," and Tehran enjoyed "naval supremacy in the Persian Gulf." Moreover, the advantages that Iraq had on paper were not nearly as great in practice. This was attributed to a variety of factors, including "military ineptitude, particularly at the general staff planning level," along with "a conscious decision to minimize casualties," which dictated a cautious advance that allowed Iranian forces to retreat, regroup, and establish well-defended positions.[50]

Iraq's inability to win was not a major concern from Washington's perspective; policymakers repeatedly noted that a major Iraqi victory was not actually in the interests of the United States. Over the next several years, however, it was unclear whether Baghdad would even manage to achieve a draw. As the conflict dragged on and turned into a grinding war of attrition, Iran's edge in latent power loomed larger and larger, and U.S. policymakers grew more and more fearful that it would be the one to pull off a victory. A 1982 intelligence report, for instance, predicted that Iran would eventually "emerge the victor from its war with Iraq, although fighting likely will continue for some time."[51] Another report the following year highlighted improvements in Iraq's military performance at the tactical level, yet concluded that Baghdad was still "trapped in a stalemated war that saps its financial reserves, restricts economic growth, wastes manpower resources, and limits its political options."[52] By 1986, the intelligence community was forecasting that Iraq would "suffer additional military setbacks and probably lose the war over the long term." It also cautioned that the "impact of an Iranian victory on the Gulf would be profound."[53]

Ultimately, while the distribution of power between Iran and Iraq ebbed and flowed during the 1980s, neither side seemed likely to achieve a major breakthrough on the battlefield. Iraq's low morale and conservative tactics undermined its advantage in military hardware. Meanwhile, Iran was able to use its much greater manpower, along with new tactics such as human wave attacks, to compensate for its lack of military proficiency and wear down its rival. It also exploited its position along the Strait of Hormuz to cut off Iraqi oil exports while getting its own oil to market, which enhanced its relative power and raised fears of Iraqi attacks on Iranian shipping that would cause further disruptions to commercial traffic in the Strait. As a result, the United States was faced with a choice: it could stand aside and accept the possibility that Iran might win the war, or it could take a more active role in the conflict by siding with Baghdad to help it remain an effective counterweight to Tehran. Given their preference for regional parity to mitigate the risk of access denial, U.S. policymakers opted for the latter course of action. As Undersecretary of State for Political Affairs Lawrence Eagleburger explained to a senior Iraqi diplomat, an Iranian victory "would constitute a major strategic defeat for the U.S."[54] In his colleague's pithy formulation, "the best outcome for the United States is one in which neither protagonist emerges as victor or vanquished."[55]

This change in policy was relatively subtle in its execution, explicit in its intent, and consistent with balance-of-power logic. According to an internal paper written at the request of Eagleburger, "the Iranian strategy of bringing about the Iraqi regime's political collapse through military attrition coupled with financial strangulation seems to be slowly having an effect." The paper therefore assessed the potential elements of a "tilt toward Iraq" that might forestall an Iranian victory. Notably, the report observed that the U.S. policy of "strict neutrality" had already been abandoned since the middle of 1982, when Iranian forces went on the offensive. "The steps we have taken toward the conflict since then have progressively favored Iraq." In short, the United States had already engaged in a "qualified tilt" toward Baghdad, one that "balances our interest in seeing that Iraq is not defeated with our interest in avoiding an escalation which could draw us directly into the conflict."[56]

This qualified tilt included a number of different elements, such as meetings between senior U.S. and Iraqi officials, which had both political and symbolic value. For instance, in late 1983, the administration's special envoy to the Middle East, former secretary of defense Donald Rumsfeld, traveled to Baghdad in a highly visible effort to improve relations between the United States and Iraq. It was also a public demonstration of U.S. support, one that observers in Tehran could hardly miss. Meeting with Foreign Minister and Deputy Prime Minister Tariq Aziz, Rumsfeld discussed the ongoing Iran–Iraq War and declared that the United States "had no interest in an Iranian victory." Rather, it "would not want Iran's influence expanded at the expense of Iraq." In another meeting, Rumsfeld told Saddam Hussein that Washington's "understanding of the importance of balance in the world and the region was similar to Iraq's" and that the United States did not want the outcome of the war in the Gulf "to be one which weakened Iraq's role or enhanced [the] interests and ambitions of Iran."[57] According to the U.S. interests section in Baghdad, the Rumsfeld visit was a great success and "elevated US–Iraqi relations to a new level."[58] The following year, Aziz visited Washington and met with Secretary of State George Shultz, who told his counterpart that both sides were in broad agreement when it came to the Iran–Iraq War and the policies they should adopt.[59]

Another key component of this tilt—one that had a more direct bearing on the course of the conflict—was "Operation Staunch." This was Washington's attempt to cut off the flow of arms to Iran by discouraging third parties from selling weapons to the Islamic Republic. According to a directive from the State Department to embassies throughout the world, this effort was a natural outgrowth of U.S. policy toward the region since the war began. "From the outset," the guidance noted, the United States "has sought an end to hostilities between Iran and Iraq." As long as the conflict persisted, however, "the U.S. believed it was in the interest of the West to discourage the emergence of either as dominant in the region." Given that Iran had demonstrated its "superior military capacity" as the war went on, it was "imperative for all who are able to do so to diminish Iran's ability, as well as its incentive, to prolong the war and use violence to spread its influence abroad."[60] Ultimately, because Iraq was on the defensive and Iran no longer seemed in danger of being defeated, the decision to forgo arms sales to both sides but to allow and even encourage others to sell weapons to Baghdad was a logical way to avoid direct intervention while "maintaining a strategic balance between the belligerents," which was the chief goal of the United States.[61]

Along with these diplomatic initiatives, Washington took other steps to improve relations with Baghdad and indirectly support its efforts on the battlefield. For example, it removed Iraq from its list of nations that sponsor terrorism, a move that preceded the restoration of formal diplomatic relations between the two countries in 1984; it provided Iraq with approximately $2 billion in agricultural credits, helping Baghdad meet its need for imported foodstuffs; it sold a number of dual-use items to Iraq, such as heavy trucks and helicopters; and it provided Saddam's military with tactical intelligence, including airborne- and satellite-based imagery.[62] The United States continued to refrain from weapons sales to Iraq, however. While other measures could be justified publicly or hidden from view, the transfer of arms would have clearly violated Washington's stated policy of neutrality. It was also considered unnecessary because Baghdad had better equipment than Tehran and many other weapons suppliers.[63] The strategy of tilting toward Iraq did face challenges, however, particularly when President Reagan allowed members of the NSC and the U.S. intelligence community to secretly transfer arms to Iran in the hope of securing the release of American hostages being held by its proxies in Lebanon. Nevertheless, Washington's support for Baghdad arguably reached a high point after the Iran-Contra affair, as the Iran–Iraq War neared its conclusion. Specifically, the decision to reflag and escort Kuwaiti oil tankers in 1987 has been described as "a de facto military alliance between the United States and Iraq." Not only did the reflagging effort protect one of Baghdad's chief financial backers and enable Saddam to escalate his attacks on Iranian shipping, but the United States also conducted a significant military campaign against Iranian naval forces in 1988 after the frigate USS *Samuel B. Roberts* struck a mine and sustained heavy damage during convoy operations in the Gulf.[64]

Consistent with a balance-of-power perspective, Washington's willingness to support Iraq only increased as Baghdad's performance on the battlefield deteriorated and concerns about a possible Iranian victory grew.[65] For instance, according to a memo written in the summer of 1986 by Richard Murphy, the assistant secretary of state for Near East and South Asian affairs, "General concern in Washington over Iraq's ability to sustain its defenses has substantially risen over the past three weeks." Although there were "differences of assessment" when it came to recent developments in the region, there was little ambiguity as to how the conflict was now progressing. "The trends in the war . . . underscore our long-held view that the longer the war continues, the greater the risk of an Iraqi defeat, whatever its form may take." He therefore recommended "a review of possible steps the [U.S. government] might take to bolster the Iraqi will to resist, both psychologically and militarily."[66]

Interestingly, the view that the United States should prioritize helping Iraq was not universally held within the Reagan administration. In fact, there were some officials who believed that the United States should considering abandoning its efforts to limit arms supplies to Iran—not in the hope of freeing American hostages in Lebanon but rather to remove any chance of an

Iranian defeat, lay the foundation for improved ties between Washington and Tehran, and preserve the option of once again employing Iran as a bulwark against Soviet expansion. "Preventing the disintegration of Iran and preserving it as an independent strategic buffer which separates the Soviet Union from the Persian Gulf" was the number one American interest in the region, according to a draft NSDD written in 1985. As the cover letter accompanying the draft noted, this was a "provocative" document. In essence, it called for the United States to emphasize steps that might "block Soviet advances in the short-term" while working more closely with Iran "to restore the U.S. position which existed under the Shah over the longer-term."[67] In sum, for a handful of policymakers, the risk of containment failure still outweighed the risk of access denial. The principals did not share this perspective, however. Secretary of Defense Caspar Weinberger, for example, apparently thought that the draft NSDD was "almost too absurd to comment on." "Under no circumstances," he argued, "should we now ease our restrictions on arms sales to Iran." Shultz concurred. "The steady decline of Iran's military capability is in our interest, and we should not facilitate the supply of weapons from Western Europe that would revive that military capacity."[68] Instead, the main source of disagreement among the highest-ranking members of the Reagan administration was just how far the United States should tilt toward Iraq if it were on the verge of a serious setback, with Weinberger advocating an "overt tilt" in these circumstances while Shultz was "more cautious."[69]

Ultimately, as the Soviet threat to the region declined, the Iran–Iraq War progressed, and the prospect of renewed Iranian primacy in the Persian Gulf became more plausible, officials in Washington realized that the chief danger to U.S. interests in Southwest Asia was internal rather than external. They concluded, therefore, that the United States' main objective was no longer containing Soviet expansion but instead stopping any local actor from controlling the entire area. Summarizing American policy toward the Gulf region during his tenure at the State Department, Shultz later wrote that although "the United States basically adhered to the policy of not supplying arms to either side, our support for Iraq increased in rough proportion to Iran's military successes: plain and simple, the United States was engaged in a limited form of balance-of-power policy." Given developments in the region over the previous half decade, "a tilt toward Iraq was warranted to prevent Iranian dominance of the Persian Gulf and the countries around it."[70] On the basis of this objective, Washington's strategy was a success. U.S. support helped Iraq avoid a total collapse during long bouts of stalemate and attrition and therefore preserved a barrier to Iranian hegemony.

By 1988, Iran's naval forces had been decimated, its urban populations had been terrorized by Iraqi missile attacks, and Baghdad had managed to launch a series of ground offensives, all of which exhausted Tehran and compelled it to finally accept a cease-fire. For U.S. officials who were afraid that Iraq was on the verge of defeat just a few years earlier, this was a surprising turn-around, even if the result of the war was basically a draw. Moreover, U.S.–Iraq relations appeared to be on the upswing in the aftermath of the conflict. According to a State Department briefing paper, Iraq's behavior toward its neighbors as well as the United States had become much more moderate, a shift that seemed "permanent and deepening." Because it needed the United States to support its recovery and because it faced an enduring threat from Iran, Baghdad was unlikely to create serious problems in the area any time soon. One of the lingering sources of tension in the region—territorial disputes between Iraq and Kuwait—also seemed to be under wraps for the time being. Iraq now enjoyed closer ties with its smaller neighbor, the report explained, "and is no longer trying to encroach on Kuwaiti territory, as it did in the early 1970s."[71] These predictions would prove to be faulty, however, as Baghdad soon posed a major threat to the other Arab nations of the Gulf.

Bush and Balance of Power by Force

The end of Reagan's second term and the election of his vice president, George H. W. Bush, resulted in few significant changes when it came to U.S. policy toward Southwest Asia, at least for the first eighteen months of the Bush presidency. Despite the considerable attention it had received over the preceding decade, the region was not a high priority for the new administration when it first came into office. After all, with the Iran–Iraq War finally over, the chief threat to U.S. interests in the Persian Gulf had receded and the main impetus for closer ties between Washington and Baghdad had declined. The Cold War was also nearing its conclusion. Although there might have been lingering doubts in some quarters about the sincerity of Soviet general secretary Mikhail Gorbachev's reforms, policymakers in Washington did not seriously worry about the Kremlin invading a peripheral region like Southwest Asia, especially after it had just brought its bloody and unpopular war in Afghanistan to a close. Finally, the Bush administration was quickly consumed by events elsewhere, from the Tiananmen Square Massacre in China, to the U.S. military intervention in Panama, to the political transformation that was occurring throughout Eastern Europe. As National Security Advisor Brent Scowcroft recalled, U.S. officials "were not preoccupied with Saddam Hussein."[72] In October 1989, however, after a lengthy interagency review process, the administration finally issued National Security Directive (NSD) 26, which outlined U.S. interests in Southwest Asia and provided the framework for U.S. policy toward the nations of the Gulf.

"Access to Persian Gulf oil and the security of key friendly states in the area are vital to U.S. national security," the document began. NSD 26 specifically called for preserving good relations with Iraq. The administration's hope, which ultimately proved to be misplaced, was that continued engagement with Baghdad would encourage Saddam's regime to play a more constructive role in regional politics. Engagement, it seemed, was also the only viable option for dealing with a number of worrisome issues, such as Iraq's poor human rights record, its demonstrated willingness to use chemical weapons, its apparent desire to build nuclear weapons, and its potential to obstruct the Arab–Israeli peace process. "Normal relations between the United States and Iraq would serve our longer-term interests and promote stability in both the Gulf and the Middle East," the document continued. "The United States Government should propose economic and political incentives for Iraq to moderate its behavior and to increase our influence with Iraq."[73]

The decision to pursue a strategy of engagement was a topic of debate within the administration, both before and after NSD 26 was issued. On the one hand, many policymakers believed that Iraq had considerable potential as a strategic ally because it could help to block any future Iranian expansion. It could also be a lucrative economic partner because it was beginning to rebuild after a long and destructive war. On the other hand, it was still an ambitious and unpredictable nation with a long record of violent behavior. Nevertheless, proponents of engagement had started making their case early on and eventually prevailed. According to a transition paper written on the day of Bush's inauguration, Iraq had "come through its war with Iran with great military and political power, and is aiming higher." Although it had adopted more reasonable positions on many issues in recent years, its intentions were "still evolving" and the durability of its turn toward moderation remained unclear. Yet taking a chance on improving U.S.–Iraq relations seemed like a good bet, especially since Iran could make another bid for regional dominance one day. "We may find ourselves opposed to Iraqi ambitions if they include hegemony in the Gulf," the paper's authors argued, "but we are in tune overall with Iraq's quest for stability, which focuses on containing Iran."[74]

Notably, although there was little doubt that Iraq had the potential to be a spoiler in the region, a danger to its neighbors, and an antagonist of the United States, the likelihood that Washington and Baghdad would come to blows seemed remote. After nearly a decade of conflict, many observers assumed that Iraq would be absorbed with the process of recovery. William Webster, for example, who served as director of central intelligence at the close of the Reagan administration and stayed in that position when Bush entered office, recalled that Iraq was not considered a serious threat at the time. Instead, the U.S. intelligence community assessed that it had "a very worn-out" military with "wounds to lick and heal." Although Saddam's ambitions clearly included being "the bully in the neighborhood," the prevailing view within the U.S. government was that the Iraqis would "take a pause while they regrouped and got back in order."[75] Despite winning its war with Iran, the heavy toll that Iraq had suffered seemed to ensure that it would not pursue primacy anytime soon, let alone achieve local dominance. Its latent resources and penchant for aggression were still a concern, however. All in all, it was a "significant regional military power with troubling technological potential yet attractive commercial possibilities."[76]

As the Bush administration weighed these competing incentives and concerns in Southwest Asia, it was ultimately guided by balance-of-power logic. Not unlike Reagan and his chief advisors, senior U.S. officials continued to view local parity as the preferred situation and continued to think of Iraq as a bulwark against Iran. In fact, Bush's approach to the region mirrored the one adopted during Reagan's time in office.[77] This approach was laid out explicitly in a paper prepared by the State Department's policy planning staff. American interests in the area were straightforward, it argued. "We want continuing (Western) access to multiple sources of oil through multiple points of export (e.g., through the Strait of Hormuz, Red Sea and Mediterranean) as the best means of reducing the chances that a hostile regional or extraregional state might gain preponderant control or influence over production and pricing decisions." Looking back, the paper recalled that Washington's pre-1979 strategy for the region entailed supporting Iranian primacy, which made sense at the time given Iran's large size and military strength, as well as "mutually shared perceptions about the nature of the Soviet threat, about the need to preserve the political status quo in the Gulf and about the importance of Israel's security." Looking forward, however, no local nation was willing and able to serve as a "friendly, regional hegemon" that could help Washington protect its interests (not to mention that it no longer needed a local hegemon to fend off an expansionist outside power). Thus, the policy planning staff recommended that the United States preserve parity in Southwest Asia so that no local actor dominated the area. This represented a direct continuation of the strategy that was pursued throughout the 1980s. When it came to the region's strongest nations, namely Iran and Iraq, Washington still wanted "a rough balance of power between the two."[78]

In principle, this strategy made sense. In practice, however, it overestimated the effectiveness of engagement and underestimated Iraq's willingness to start another war so soon after the last one. Despite the administration's early hope that Iraq would moderate its behavior, as well as its expectation that Baghdad would not engage in overly provocative or aggressive actions until it had recovered more fully, Iraqi–American relations experienced a sharp downturn in 1990. This deterioration can be traced back to a number of developments, including Saddam's increasingly hostile rhetoric toward Israel and his ongoing efforts to procure technologies useful for building nuclear weapons. Meanwhile, growing tensions between Arab nations also became a source of concern, in particular Iraq's worsening relationship with Kuwait. Baghdad had long coveted the tiny Gulf kingdom along its border, which required the assistance of British troops to rebuff an

Iraqi claim in 1961. For the most part, however, this dispute had been dormant while the threat from Iran loomed over the entire region. Now it was taking center stage once again. In the aftermath of the war, Iraq began to accuse Kuwait of stealing its oil and ignoring OPEC production limits to fill its coffers. Whether or not the accusations were true, Kuwait did not do itself any favors by demanding that Iraq repay loans it had received during the conflict, which fueled a sense of aggrievement in Baghdad that it had shielded the area from the Iranian threat at great cost but had received little in the way of gratitude. For its part, Washington monitored the unfolding situation, pressed Iraq to pursue a diplomatic solution, but refrained from any direct involvement. In other words, it hoped that the problem would simply go away.

This was a miscalculation. Tensions in the Gulf increased sharply during the summer of 1990. Beginning in July, Iraqi forces began to mobilize in large numbers along the Kuwaiti border. Most observers inside and outside the region assumed this was merely an act of saber rattling, including close U.S. allies such as Egypt, which reassured Washington that a war was unlikely. On August 2, however, the dispute between Iraq and Kuwait came to a head. Iraqi units entered the country and quickly overran its meager defenses, throwing the region into crisis once again. This time, however, outside actors were far less willing to sit back and watch than they had been a decade earlier, particularly the United States. Initially, policymakers in Washington were caught off guard by the invasion. Their first reaction, therefore, was to debate the stakes of the crisis as well as how far they should go to assist Kuwait. They soon reached a consensus, however, and implemented their response: condemning the action publicly; imposing unilateral economic sanctions against Iraq; mobilizing support at the United Nations for multilateral economic sanctions; and deploying U.S. military forces to Saudi Arabia in defense of the desert kingdom, which would have been an extremely valuable and extremely vulnerable target if Saddam had continued his advance. As President Bush declared shortly after he learned of the invasion, Baghdad's aggrandizement "will not stand."[79]

From the very start of the crisis, U.S. officials were doubtful that diplomatic pressure and economic coercion would be sufficient to end Iraq's occupation of Kuwait. They recognized, therefore, that a larger conflict might be on the horizon. In fact, President Bush came to the realization that war was the likely outcome almost immediately, and most of his chief advisors reached a similar conclusion soon afterward.[80] There was no guarantee that sanctions would impose sufficient pain or work fast enough to change Saddam's behavior, especially before the world's outrage began to wane, and the longer his forces remained entrenched in Kuwait, the more difficult it would be to throw them out. U.S. officials also agreed that a return to the territorial status quo ante was the only acceptable outcome, which meant that American military intervention might be necessary. In other words, Washington was unwilling to accept any resolution that did not completely restore Kuwait's sovereignty and believed that the use of force on a large scale was justified to achieve that aim. To the extent that policymakers were reticent to use force, it was not due to their expectation that sanctions would actually succeed or to any doubts about the merits of military action. Rather, officials were constrained by domestic and international opinion, neither of which was enthusiastic about a conflict over Kuwait. They also had to overcome the logistical challenges of conducting a campaign in a distant region, which required nearly six months of preparation to build up adequate forces in theater.

Why were the stakes so high for the United States? Although a number of factors were at play, arguably the most important consideration was the need to prevent Iraq from achieving local primacy, even if that meant going to war. The decisions to condemn the Iraqi invasion, reverse the occupation of Kuwait, and severely weaken Saddam's military power can all be explained by the judgment that a hegemonic power shift was taking place in the region, one that would put Iraq in a position to dominate the entire Persian Gulf, alter oil prices on a whim, and restrict the flow of resources to world markets unless it were stopped.[81]

Shortly after receiving news of the invasion, President Bush was briefed on the potential consequences of Baghdad's assault. The annexation of Kuwait, he was told, would give Iraq control of approximately 20 percent of the world's proven oil reserves. Moreover, if Iraq were to follow up its victory by sending forces into Saudi Arabia, that total could double. The president was "horrified." According to journalist Bob Woodward's account, Bush warned his advisors that possession of only 20 percent of global oil reserves would enable Saddam "to manipulate world prices and hold the United States and its allies at his mercy."[82] In Scowcroft's view, the Iraqi invasion posed a clear challenge to American national security interests as defined by the Carter Doctrine, even though the threat to the Gulf was coming from within rather than from without.[83] As he later recalled, if Iraq gained control over Kuwait it might be in a position to dominate OPEC, which would enable it to coerce other nations into cutting production and raising prices. That would represent "a tremendous danger to the United States and to the industrialised [sic] world."[84]

These fears were only heightened by CIA reports emphasizing the Iraqi threat to Saudi Arabia. While the loss of Kuwait would augment Iraq's economic power, expand its influence, and potentially enhance its military strength by providing the resources necessary to purchase more arms and equipment, the loss of Saudi Arabia would fundamentally alter the entire region. Riyadh was a close U.S. ally, it possessed some of the world's largest proven oil reserves, and it was a crucial "swing" producer that could offset supply disruptions and keep prices stable. Yet it appeared to be Iraq's next target. Administration officials were told that the Iraqi army would face only modest opposition if it moved against Saudi Arabia. Saddam also appeared to be pouring additional troops into Kuwait and massing forces near the Saudi border.[85] This had a galvanizing effect on U.S. policymakers. "Our first objective," the president declared to his advisors only days after the fall of Kuwait, "is to keep Saddam out of Saudi Arabia."[86] According to Richard Haass, who was the NSC staff member responsible for Near East Asia at the time, Iraq did not even need to expand beyond Kuwait to become the preponderant economic and military power in the region, although U.S. policymakers could not rule out the possibility. "If you had an Iraq that had conquered Kuwait," he recalled, "I didn't think the Saudis would be a terribly independent player any more." In short, Iraq was on the verge of gaining formal or informal control over a huge portion of the Gulf's energy reserves. "I thought, either way, it was unacceptable. So did Brent and the President. Very quickly, we all came out on the same page."[87]

As the crisis continued over the next several months and the administration sought to enhance public support for the continuing deployment of American troops to Saudi Arabia (and for deploying enough forces to not only defend a U.S. ally but also to launch an offensive campaign against Iraq), officials resorted to a variety of justifications. For instance, they highlighted the importance of creating a "new world order" where cross-border aggression was no longer acceptable, territorial aggrandizement would be punished, and great powers would cooperate with one another in peripheral regions rather than compete through local proxies. Policymakers also called attention to the plight of American hostages, who were being held at the U.S. embassy in Kuwait City and used by Saddam as a bargaining chip. Finally, they publicized the depredations of Iraqi occupying forces and the suffering of Kuwaiti citizens. According to Secretary of State James Baker, these were all acceptable rationales for opposing Iraq. Yet they obscured the "vital national interests at stake" during the crisis, namely, access to the Persian Gulf and its resources. "We had to make sure we could maintain a secure supply of energy. Our swift response in early August had deterred Saddam from invading Saudi Arabia. But if we allowed him to remain in Kuwait, an emboldened Saddam . . . would easily be able to influence worldwide oil pricing decisions. Higher crude prices would almost certainly follow, which in turn would likely create not only a global economic downturn but also a recession in the fragile U.S. economy."[88]

By January 1991, the deployment of American forces was essentially complete, the Iraqi army was still entrenched, and economic sanctions were expected to take months, if not years, to have their full effect, assuming they worked at all. Under these conditions, U.S. officials determined that war was not only necessary to end the occupation of Kuwait, but it was actually the best way to resolve the crisis. Maintaining 500,000 U.S. troops in Saudi Arabia while the international community waited for Iraq to withdraw was economically, diplomatically, and strategically unsustainable. Eventually, patience would wear thin in Washington, as well as in allied capitals. When it came to Kuwait's future, time seemed to be on Iraq's side. Moreover, even if he withdrew his forces, there was no guarantee that Saddam would not attack his neighbors again. This possibility was hardly trivial now that he had demonstrated his hegemonic ambitions. Yet the United States could not maintain a huge military presence in the Gulf indefinitely, nor could it bring its troops home only to redeploy them every time the Iraqi army was mobilized in a provocative manner. For U.S. officials, therefore, a diplomatic resolution would only create more problems in the future because Baghdad would remain the most powerful actor in the region and a persistent threat to the area.[89]

Despite these concerns, domestic political considerations—including the need to marshal enough support in Congress to pass a resolution explicitly authorizing the president to use force—convinced Bush to make one last effort to avoid a war. In January, the president sent Baker to Geneva, where he met with Saddam's emissary, Tariq Aziz, and gave the Iraqis a final chance to pull their forces back. Yet Saddam refused to budge. It is worth noting, though, that U.S. officials hoped the Geneva meeting would not actually succeed. They even feared that Aziz would offer some type of half measure, such as a partial withdrawal of Iraqi forces, which might be seen by audiences as a major concession and thus undermine the case for war at home and abroad. Nevertheless, the gamble was considered a necessary one. Although the president and his chief advisors were determined to restore Kuwait's sovereignty and degrade Saddam's military power, they preferred to have public backing for the coming campaign.[90] Much to their relief, the Geneva meeting did indeed fail, Congress narrowly authorized the use of force, and Operation Desert Storm commenced soon afterward. The results of these diplomatic and military efforts "were impressive and then some by any measure." The United States had assembled an unprecedented international coalition, freed a defenseless nation, demonstrated to the world that conquest did not pay, and suffered an astonishingly small number of casualties. Even more important, though, it managed to prevent Iraq from achieving regional primacy.[91]

The 1991 Gulf War was a watershed event. With the United States securing Soviet cooperation to oppose Iraq's invasion of Kuwait and then demonstrating its unparalleled military advantage by swiftly defeating one of the world's largest armies, the conflict marked the transition from a bipolar Cold War era to a unipolar post–Cold War world. It was also the culmination of Washington's balance-of-power approach to the region. U.S. policy toward Southwest Asia underwent a significant shift between 1979 and 1982, a period during which the fall of the shah upended Washington's strategy for containing the Soviet Union, Moscow's invasion of Afghanistan raised fears that it might send its forces all the way to the Persian Gulf, the outbreak of the Iran–Iraq War forced the United States to weigh the dangers of internal versus external threats to the region, and Iraq's declining fortunes in that conflict suggested that Iran might be able to restore its primacy. As these events transpired, U.S. policymakers had to determine what risks worried them most and how best to secure their interests. Eventually, the ambiguities that surrounded U.S. risk assessments faded away and the options available to the United States narrowed. Specifically, with the risk of containment failure receding and the risk of access denial on the rise, the United States focused on preventing any local actor from achieving a dominant position in the region. Moreover, given its preference for regional parity, Washington focused on the direction of the power shift that was taking place as it decided on a strategy. That meant accommodating Iraq when it was a counterweight to Iran and opposing it when Baghdad occupied Kuwait, threatened Saudi Arabia, and was on the verge of achieving local primacy.

Conclusion

The Past and Future of Rising Regional Powers

The rise and decline of the world's strongest nations is one of the most important topics in the study of international politics—and for good reason. An emerging great power can challenge the reigning global order by demanding status and benefits that it did not previously enjoy; it can provoke or initiate a major conflict against established great powers; and, if it wins, it can reshape the norms, rules, and institutions that govern the entire system. Today, for example, China's growing economy, increasingly capable military, and more assertive foreign policy have contributed to heightened tensions with the United States, which could have catastrophic implications if the two sides find themselves fighting a war.[1] Yet the rise and decline of minor powers in the periphery can have significant consequences as well, even though these consequences are sometimes overlooked. An emerging regional power can undermine and perhaps even overturn the status quo in its own neighborhood, whether it is trying to achieve parity with a dominant nation in decline or is making a bid for local primacy instead. When these events occur, great powers often pay close attention and might even intervene if they conclude that the changes taking place will help or harm them in some way. This is especially true for leading states such as Great Britain during the nineteenth century and the United States since 1945. With their extensive interests and diverse responsibilities, both functionally and geographically, leading states have been particularly sensitive to local power shifts. Thanks to their considerable wealth and military reach, they have also enjoyed a singular ability to influence how these changes unfold, whether they choose to become involved or decide to remain on the sidelines. The goal of this book, therefore, has been to explore how leading states have responded to RRPs in the past and to explain why they have accommodated some but opposed others. This chapter briefly summarizes the arguments and evidence, highlights several implications for international relations theory, and considers what my framework would suggest about U.S. relations with two contemporary regional powers: India and Iran.

Arguments and Evidence Revisited

Over the past two centuries, leading states have responded to RRPs in very different ways, from conducting military interventions that halt their rise to forming alliances that hasten their ascent. What accounts for this variation? To answer this question, the previous chapters developed and tested a new theory, one that emphasizes the interaction between the type of regional order that a leading state prefers and the type of power shift that it believes is taking place.

The first step in the theory entails figuring out whether a leading state favors regional parity, whether it favors regional primacy, or whether it is impartial between these alternative orders. I argue that a leading state's preferences can be traced back to its assessment of certain risks, in particular the risk of access denial and the risk of containment failure. If both are low, a leading state is unlikely to have a strong preference between parity and primacy because its chief interest will be preserving local stability, and either form of order can prevent regional conflicts. If a leading state is worried mainly that a local actor might withhold indigenous resources or restrict the presence of outside powers in its neighborhood, however, then it should have a preference for regional parity because a single dominant actor will heighten the risk of access denial. Finally, if a leading state is concerned about the prospect of external intervention, then it should have a preference for regional primacy instead because a preponderant power can best deter or repel threats from outside actors and therefore will mitigate the risk of containment failure.

The second step in the theory involves determining how an emerging regional power will alter the local status quo, presuming that outside actors do not stand in its way, and whether the expected consequences of its rise are compatible with a leading state's preferences. In other words, is an RRP on track to reinforce or establish the type of order that a leading state prefers, or is it on target to undermine or overturn that order? To estimate the outcome of a power shift, I argue that policymakers in a leading state will look at certain characteristics of the changing distribution of power. Specifically, a leading state that is impartial between parity and primacy should focus on the scope of the power shift that is taking place—that is, whether an RRP can create a durable regional order, irrespective of the type of order it is trying to create. In this case, a leading state should accommodate an RRP when a complete shift is under way because an emerging power is able to achieve equilibrium or dominate the area. It should oppose an RRP when an incomplete shift occurs, however, because an emerging power fails to do so. By contrast, a leading state that prefers regional parity should focus on the direction of the power shift that is taking place—that is, whether an RRP is weakening a local hegemon or is attempting to become one, regardless of whether it succeeds. In this situation, it should accommodate an RRP when a counterhegemonic shift is under way because an emerging power is challenging a preponderant power without trying to supplant it. It should oppose an RRP when a hegemonic shift is occurring, however, because an emerging power is making a bid for local dominance. Finally, a leading state that prefers regional primacy should focus on both the direction and scope of the power shift and should opt for accommodation only when that power shift is hegemonic and complete. Under these conditions, an RRP is likely to emerge as the dominant local actor and the only viable ally in the area.

I examined these arguments through five detailed case studies that assessed how Great Britain and the United States responded to emerging powers in multiple regions across nearly two centuries. Collectively, the cases in this book demonstrated variation on the independent variable (the leading state's preferred regional order), the intervening variable (the type of power shift that was taking place), and the dependent variable (the leading state's decision to accommodate or oppose an RRP). Individually, every case included a number of opportunities to explore the decision-making process within the leading state, as policymakers wrestled with how to manage an RRP on repeated occasions over an extended period of time.

Most of these cases offer strong support for the theory. In the 1830s, Great Britain opposed Egypt's attempt to dominate the Middle East and continued to support the declining Ottoman Empire, which was an informal but important security partner in the region. Although Mehmet Ali had a stronger military than the sultan, he was also more likely to threaten British access to the area. Meanwhile, key policymakers in London were convinced that the Porte could resume its place as a barrier to Russian expansion so long as it engaged in modest reforms. In other words, while their chief concern was avoiding containment failure, they believed that the hegemonic power shift that was taking place was incomplete. Thus, there was no need to accommodate an ambitious rising power and abandon an old ally. Later, during the American Civil War, Great Britain seriously considered intervening on behalf of the Confederacy, particularly as the conflict grew increasingly deadly and destructive. Yet it refused to become directly involved until the South proved that it could establish a durable balance of power, which it never managed to do. In short, while British policymakers did not face a serious risk of access denial or containment failure, they were concerned about restoring local stability and therefore would act only if a complete power shift clearly took place. Great Britain did accommodate Japan at the close of the nineteenth century and the start of the twentieth century, however, because improving ties with an emerging power seemed like the best way to avoid containment failure in the Far East. Although British policy-makers had previously relied on China as a barrier to Russian expansion, its decisive defeat in the 1894–1895 Sino-Japanese War took that option off the table. Moreover, China's weakness only became more apparent as the European powers began to carve it into spheres of interest over the next several years. In this case, the power shift that took place was both hege-monic and complete. As a result, there was little doubt that Japan was the dominant local actor and the best bet to help counterbalance Russia.

As for the United States, it confronted a number of regional power shifts during the Cold War, for instance, in South Asia and Southwest Asia. In the early 1960s, India seemed poised to become a local hegemon and appeared to be the only possible bulwark against Chinese expansion. Nevertheless, its failure to achieve a major victory over Pakistan during the Second Kashmir War in 1965 demonstrated that a hegemonic and complete power shift had not yet taken place. Rather, the conflict seemed to weaken both sides and heighten the risk of containment failure, leading Washington to give up its efforts at making New Delhi an ally. Then, in 1971, India and Pakistan went to war again. This time the situation was different. Not only was the United States concerned with maintaining regional stability rather than containing Communist China, but India also looked as if it might defeat its rival once and for all. Anticipating that a complete power shift was about to occur, Washington took steps to restrain New Delhi. This decision contradicts my theory. Even in this case, though, the dynamics I highlight were still at play, albeit not in the way that the framework predicts. Specifically, U.S. policymakers opposed India because they feared that a complete power shift in South Asia would actually trigger instability in other regions, par-ticularly the Middle East. Finally, U.S. strategy in the Persian Gulf between 1979 and 1991 lends support to the argument that concerns about access denial will lead to balance-of-power policies. During the Iran–Iraq War, the United States viewed Baghdad as a counterweight to Tehran, the once and perhaps future hegemon in the region, and therefore provided it with eco-nomic and military support to maintain local parity. That changed in 1990, however, when Iraq annexed Kuwait and appeared ready to assault Saudi Arabia. To stop it from achieving local primacy, the United States launched a massive military campaign to restore Kuwait's sovereignty and erode Iraq's military power.

Implications for International Relations Theory

These arguments have a number of theoretical implications. In general, the framework described above does not fit neatly into the balance-of-power re-alism or preponderance-of-power realism camps outlined in the introduc-tion. Rather, it borrows insights from both and offers a way to bridge the gap between them by presenting a more complex, layered, and regionally differentiated picture of the international system, one that incorporates alternate distributions of power and integrates different geographic levels of analysis. For instance, at the global level, the international system can be characterized by rough equality among multiple great powers or the dominance of just one. At the local level, regional subsystems populated by minor powers can be characterized by parity or primacy as well. Moreover, interactions across these levels can have a significant impact on both of them. Great powers, for example, can shape the trajectory of minor powers that are on the rise or in decline and therefore can influence the type of order that prevails in peripheral regions. Meanwhile, minor powers can directly impact the economic and security interests of great powers; they can draw them into local conflicts even when their material interests are negligible; and, in some cases, they can eventually become great powers themselves. By examining how leading states have responded to emerging regional powers, this book focused on one specific area where great power politics and regional power politics collide.[2]

Although it accommodates many of the core insights from balance-of-power realism and preponderance-of-power realism, my arguments depart from these approaches in several ways and highlight other limitations of existing theories. For instance, many balance-of-power realists—especially "defensive" realists—place a heavy emphasis on perceived intentions when it comes to explaining great power strategies. While intentions undoubtedly matter, especially for the development of policy on a day-to-day basis, the cases in this book show that the basic distinction between benign and malign intentions is not always useful. Great Britain, for example, opposed Egypt's rise in the 1830s, despite Mehmet Ali's insistence that he wanted to be its ally rather than its adversary, yet it accommodated Japan decades later, despite suspicions that Tokyo's aims might not be in alignment with London's. In these cases, intentions were subordinated to other considerations, namely, how the distribution of power was changing in a peripheral region and what those changes meant for a leading state's interests there. Going one step further, these and other cases provide support for a related point: although defensive realism often portrays great powers as inherently risk-averse and determined to preserve the status quo, sometimes strategic competitions with their rivals can make them much more risk-acceptant and much more willing to tolerate revisionism, especially in the periphery.[3]

For their part, preponderance-of-power realists note that leading states in decline often need help to counterbalance their rivals and cannot always maintain international order on their own. Thus, they have strong incentives to accommodate regional powers, especially those that are capable of playing a leading role within their own neighborhoods. This is the traditional explanation for a number of important foreign policy decisions that usually fall under the rubric of retrenchment, such as Great Britain's alliance with

Japan in 1902, as well as the United States' increasingly close relationship with Iran during the 1970s and its rapprochement with China at the same time.[4] Yet this argument overlooks the broader context of great power relations with regional powers. Due to their inherent resource limitations, their extensive economic and strategic interests, and the logistical challenges of defending those interests by force, leading states often rely on local actors in distant areas, even when they are not in the midst of a sharp decline. For instance, Great Britain counted on the Ottoman Empire as a bulwark against Russian expansion in the Middle East throughout the first half of the nineteenth century, when its relative power was near its peak, and relied on China during the latter part of the century, before its position was in jeopardy. Moreover, the United States hoped that India would become a barrier to Chinese expansion in South Asia during the 1960s, before the increasingly costly war in Vietnam, the escalating nuclear arms race, and the deteriorating conventional military balance in Europe all made it seem as though the Soviet Union was on the ascent. It also planned to use Iraq as a barrier to Iranian hegemony in the Gulf, even when the Cold War was winding down and the unipolar moment was on the horizon. In sum, forging closer ties with local actors is not necessarily a sign of pulling back. Rather, it is a well-established (although not always successful) way for leading states to manage challenges that they cannot easily handle on their own, even when they are at the height of their power and influence.

In addition, both schools of realism present an overly narrow perspective on how great powers in general and leading states in particular assess risks outside their home regions. Balance-of-power realism, for instance, tends to assume that leading states want to prevent the emergence of potential challengers and therefore prefer parity almost everywhere. Preponderance-of-power realism usually assumes that they prefer primacy in most places instead, which can enhance stability and enable open commerce. Yet these arguments overlook the breadth of a leading state's interests abroad and the competing incentives that these interests can generate. On the one hand, their economic and military power often depends on access to other regions and the resources that are located there, which can be threatened when local actors attempt to take over these areas. On the other hand, strategic competitions with rival great powers can create demands for capable allies, and the strongest nations are often the best possible partners. In other words, leading states need to consider the prospect of access denial and the possibility of containment failure—risks that have opposing implications yet can also go hand in hand.

Finally, the theory and cases examined in the book point to an issue that cuts across different versions of realism, namely, how officials assess national power. To date, international relations theorists have noted that power comes in a variety of forms, including economic power versus military power, latent power versus mobilized power, state power versus national power, and land power versus naval power, to name only a few.[5] Although the importance of these distinctions is largely self-evident, policymakers do not always give equal weight to each one. For example, during the 1830s, Great Britain downplayed Egypt's military strength, placed greater emphasis on the Ottoman Empire's resources, and encouraged the Porte to implement institutional reforms that would allow it to mobilize those resources more effectively. Then, in the early 1860s, officials in London assumed that the Confederacy's fighting skill and its apparent determination to achieve independence at any cost would compensate for the Union's resource advantages. Later, Great Britain believed that China's geographic size, large population, and quantitative military edge would carry the day in a conflict with Japan, at least until Tokyo's victory in 1895 highlighted just how superior its armed forces really were when it came to organization, training, and technology. A similar dynamic was at play in the 1960s, when U.S. policymakers viewed India as a natural candidate for regional hegemony, yet changed their minds after its troubled performance on the battlefield against a weaker rival. Finally, during the Iran–Iraq War, it was never clear whether Iran's resource advantages would turn the tide in its favor, which made it difficult for U.S. officials to forecast how the war would unfold. All of these examples suggest that understanding when and why observers choose to focus on certain types of power rather than others is an important area for future analysis.

Predicting U.S. Strategies toward Rising Regional Powers

Although the significance of regional power shifts over the past two centuries has often been overlooked, this issue is a difficult one to ignore today. There is little doubt that the distribution of power is now highly dynamic, not just at the global level but at local levels as well. For instance, even as debates over the character, extent, and, in some cases, the very existence of U.S. relative decline continue to play out among academics and pundits, there is a growing consensus in many quarters that unipolarity is under duress, even if the era of American primacy has not yet drawn to a close.[6] This is due not only to the rise of China and the resurgence of Russia, but also to ambitious and capable regional powers such as India and Iran. In fact, the United States has devoted an enormous amount of time and energy toward both nations in recent years, with policymakers in Washington betting on the idea that India will become an important partner and working to prevent Iran from becoming a more dangerous rival. What does my argument suggest about the future trajectory of U.S. relations with each RRP?

To start, it is clear that India is an emerging regional power with the potential to become a great power one day, although it does confront a number of domestic and international challenges that could constrain its rise.[7] Cooperation between Washington and New Delhi has also improved considerably over the past decade, especially in the security realm. This marks a significant departure from the mutual mistrust that once prevailed on both sides, which stemmed in large part from India's nonalignment during the Cold War and its development of nuclear weapons during the post–Cold War era. In fact, the two nations are closer now than they have been since their brief entente during the early 1960s. This changing relationship can be explained by a number of factors, arguably the most important of which is a shared concern over the consequences of China's rise.[8] As a result, even though few believe that a formal alliance is possible, most observers expect U.S.–India ties to become progressively closer over time, while many policymakers have invested heavily to make this happen. As Prime Minister Modi and President Obama wrote not long ago in a joint editorial, "our partnership is robust, reliable and enduring, and it is expanding."[9]

Applying my theory to the future relationship between these two powers requires making some assumptions about U.S. interests and how they could evolve. Moreover, history suggests that Washington's interests in South Asia could vary considerably depending on the circumstances. During the 1960s, for example, it was focused primarily on containing Chinese expansion, although this goal became much less important following the Sino-Soviet split. Then, during the late 1970s and early 1980s, it was preoccupied with countering Soviet efforts to extend its influence along the edges of the Persian Gulf. Finally, throughout the 1990s and into the 2000s, the United States was most worried about Pakistan's development of nuclear weapons, its support for terrorist groups, and the possible nexus between the two. Therefore, it was determined to preserve stability in the region and prevent local conflicts that could lead to nuclear theft or nuclear use—concerns that are unlikely to go away.[10] Looking forward, however, the key factor that will shape U.S. policy toward the area is almost certainly the rise of China, not unlike the situation more than fifty years ago.

Between its economic growth and its military modernization, China's rise has been a remarkable development.[11] The durability of that rise is not a foregone conclusion, however. As Avery Goldstein has argued, the idea that China's economic growth will proceed smoothly and without interruption is "a heroic assumption" thanks to a number of very serious economic, environmental, demographic, social, and political challenges that plague the People's Republic.[12] Likewise, one report by the National Intelligence Council explained that "The pace of China's economic growth almost certainly will slow, or even recede, even with additional reforms to address mounting social pressures arising from growing income disparities, a fraying social safety net, poor business regulation, hunger for foreign energy, enduring corruption, and environmental devastation. Any of these problems might be soluble in isolation, but the country could be hit by a 'perfect storm' if many of them demand attention at the same time."[13] Indeed, not only is China experiencing lower annual growth rates than it once did, but a slump in its stock market during the summer of 2015 raised concerns that a serious economic decline might come sooner than most anticipated—and that it might be deeper than most assumed.[14]

If Beijing's economic growth continues, however, then there is a strong likelihood that Washington will become more preoccupied with the risk of containment failure, particularly if China follows the example of past great powers and uses its increasing strength to challenge the status quo, not just in its own region but in others as well. Notably, Beijing is already taking steps to enhance its presence and its influence in India's neighborhood, for instance, by adopting new military missions such as counterpiracy and sealane security; by deploying expeditionary forces into the Indian Ocean with greater frequency; and by financing ports, roads, railways, pipelines, and other local infrastructure projects. To some extent, these moves are understandable. After all, China depends on uninterrupted shipping through the Indian Ocean to sustain its export-led and resource-hungry economy. Therefore, it has become increasingly concerned about the security of the region and increasingly reticent to outsource that security to other powers. Sending military forces to the area improves its ability to defend its interests, while underwriting infrastructure projects could enable it to create alternative transportation routes.[15] In New Delhi, however, these developments have raised concerns about the threat of Chinese expansion and provoked a variety of countermeasures.[16] Moreover, escalating tensions with China could drive India and the United States even closer together.

Alternatively, if the pace of China's economic growth slows substantially, if its foreign policy becomes increasingly inward focused, and if the risk of containment failure starts to diminish, then the United States might place a much higher value on avoiding access denial in the Indian Ocean region— and might become less willing to enable India's continued rise. There are, for example, factions in New Delhi that not only see India as the dominant power in South Asia but that also consider the area stretching from the east coast of Africa, to the Middle East, to the Indonesian archipelago as its rightful sphere of interest. According to one analysis, "in the expansive view of many Indians, India's security perimeter should extend from the Strait of Malacca to the Strait of Hormuz and from the coast of Africa to the western shores of Australia."[17] In fact, some strategists and commentators have invoked America's Monroe Doctrine as a precedent for extending India's influence over the region.[18] Although the United States is not nearly as dependent on seaborne commerce traveling through the Indian Ocean as nations like China, it does require unfettered access to the area as it shifts military forces between the Persian Gulf and Northeast Asia, which are likely to remain the most important geographic theaters for U.S. defense planners.[19]

What about U.S. relations with Iran? Unlike India, Iran is not on track to become a great power, despite having significant resources, including the world's fourth-largest crude oil reserves and second-largest natural gas reserves.[20] Moreover, its status as a rising regional power can even be questioned. For instance, its economy has been weakened by international sanctions; its conventional military forces suffer from a number of deficiencies that would make territorial conquest extremely difficult; and it is surrounded by rivals such as Israel, Saudi Arabia, and the United Arab Emirates, all of which field sophisticated forces of their own.[21] Nevertheless, international sanctions are due to be lifted as part of a nuclear deal, which will give Iran more financial resources and allow it to purchase more advanced weapons from abroad; it continues to support irregular military forces in a number of nations, including Lebanon and Yemen; and it no longer has to fear its traditional counterweight in the region now that Iraq is far too weak to block Iranian expansion.[22] Tehran has also been building an arsenal of ballistic missiles, which it could use to coerce its neighbors or inhibit the United States from coming to their defense, as well as fielding capabilities that could enable it to impede maritime traffic through the Strait of Hormuz, which remains "the world's most important oil chokepoint."[23] Finally, should Iran acquire nuclear weapons despite efforts by the international community to stop it, there is little doubt that the strategic dynamics within the region would be disrupted. For instance, Tehran might become more willing to place demands on its neighbors or engage in acts of aggression. Even if it does not grow bolder but continues its pattern of supporting proxy forces, local nations might think twice before they stand against it.[24]

Whereas U.S. interests in South Asia have fluctuated over the past several decades, they have remained relatively constant in the Persian Gulf. Given the area's abundant energy resources and Washington's commitment to preserving freedom of the global commons, U.S. policymakers have been determined to prevent any actor from withholding those resources or placing serious limits on the presence of outside powers. This emphasis on the risk of access denial seems unlikely to subside, notwithstanding other interests such as ongoing counterterrorism efforts or changes in global energy markets that have put the United States on the path to self-sufficiency when it comes to oil and gas. Consequently, Washington will almost certainly continue to ensure that Iran does not dominate the region, for instance, by maintaining a significant military presence in the Gulf and arming U.S. security partners. That could change if it were to abdicate its responsibility for ensuring the free flow of resources or if the emergence of a significant external threat made a local hegemon more acceptable. Neither of these possibilities seems very plausible today, however.

The rise of regional powers has received increased attention in recent years, particularly as debates over the apparent decline of the United States and the future structure of the international system have continued to play out among academics, analysts, and policymakers. Yet this issue has long been an important one, particularly for leading states, which have had to respond when new powers emerge and manage the consequences when local power shifts take place. This book has tried to place these interactions in a broader theoretical and historical context as a first step toward better understanding the relationship between great powers and regional powers, a topic that is likely to become even more consequential in the years ahead.

Notes

The following abbreviations are used in the notes:

BD	*British Documents on the Origins of the War, 1898–1914*
BDFA	*British Documents on Foreign Affairs: Reports and Papers from the Foreign Office Confidential Print*
CIA FOIA	Central Intelligence Agency Freedom of Information Act Electronic Reading Room
DDRS	Declassified Documents Reference System
DNSA	Digital National Security Archive
FRUS	*Foreign Relations of the United States*
HPD	Hansard's Parliamentary Debates
NARA	U.S. National Archives and Records Administration
PP	Palmerston Papers
WP	Wellington Papers

Introduction

1. The White House, Office of the Press Secretary, "Remarks by President Obama in Address to the People of India," January 27, 2015, https://www.whitehouse.gov/the-press-office/2015/01/27/remarks-president-obama-address-people-india; and "Statements by President Obama and Prime Minister Modi of the Republic of India," January 25, 2015, http://www.whitehouse.gov/the-press-office/2015/01/25/statements-president-obama-and-prime-minister-modi-republic-india.

2. The White House, Office of the Press Secretary, "Remarks of President Barack Obama to the People of Israel," March 21, 2013, http://www.whitehouse.gov/the-press-office/2013/03/21/remarks-president-barack-obama-people-israel.

3. The White House, Office of the Press Secretary, "Remarks by the President on the Iran Nuclear Deal," August 5, 2015, https://www.whitehouse.gov/the-press-office/2015/08/05/remarks-president-iran-nuclear-deal.

4. Although this specific question has not received much attention, there is a growing body of work on topics such as the significance of geographic regions, why some have fewer institutions or more wars than others, whether conflict-prone areas can become more peaceful, and

how second-tier powers interact with stronger ones. See, for example, Barry Buzan and Ole Wæver, *Regions and Powers: The Structure of International Security* (New York: Cambridge University Press, 2003); Peter J. Katzenstein, *A World of Regions: Asia and Europe in the American Imperium* (Ithaca, NY: Cornell University Press, 2005); Benjamin Miller, *States, Nations, and the Great Powers: The Sources of Regional War and Peace* (New York: Cambridge University Press, 2007); and Kristen P. Williams, Steven E. Lobell, and Neal G. Jesse, eds., *Beyond Great Powers and Hegemons: Why Secondary States Support, Follow, or Challenge* (Stanford, CA: Stanford University Press, 2012).

5. I use terms such as "the periphery" and "peripheral regions" in reference to geographic areas that are not home to any great powers. On the response of leading states to peer competitors located in Europe, which has been "the core" of the international system since the early modern period, see A. F. K. Organski and Jacek Kugler, *The War Ledger* (Chicago: University of Chicago Press, 1980); Robert Gilpin, *War and Change in World Politics* (New York: Cambridge University Press, 1981); Karen A. Rasler and William R. Thompson, *The Great Powers and Global Struggle, 1490–1990* (Lexington: University of Kentucky Press, 1994); John J. Mearsheimer, *The Tragedy of Great Power Politics* (New York: W. W. Norton, 2001); and Daniel Kliman, *Fateful Transitions: How Democracies Manage Rising Powers, from the Eve of World War I to China's Ascendance* (Philadelphia: University of Pennsylvania Press, 2015).

6. There are three principal reasons why I focus on periods of conflict. First, peaceful changes in the distribution of power are not always noticeable to outside observers. Second, violent changes can provide third parties with important information about the relative strength of the combatants. Third, a regional war often puts external powers on the spot, forcing them to reassess their policies toward the area and the main actors located there.

7. Fareed Zakaria, *The Post-American World* (New York: W. W. Norton, 2009); Joseph S. Nye Jr., *The Future of Power* (New York: Public Affairs, 2011); and Charles A. Kupchan, *No One's World: The West, the Rising Rest, and the Coming Global Turn* (New York: Oxford University Press, 2012).

8. National Intelligence Council, *Global Trends 2030: Alternative Worlds* (Washington, DC: Government Printing Office, 2012).

9. Whereas a power *transition* occurs when a rising actor overtakes a declining one, a power *shift* includes any significant change in the distribution of capabilities between competitors. On this distinction, see Frank Whelon Wayman, "Power Shifts and the Onset of War," in *Parity and War: Evaluations and Extensions of the War Ledger*, ed. Jacek Kugler and Douglas Lemke (Ann Arbor: University of Michigan Press, 1996), 145–146.

10. Kenneth N. Waltz, *Theory of International Politics* (New York: McGraw-Hill, 1979), 72. While realists tend not to focus on regional powers they have focused on peripheral regions, although usually as the location of costly and unsuccessful great power interventions. See, for example, Jack Snyder, *Myths of Empire: Domestic Politics and International Ambition* (Ithaca, NY: Cornell University Press, 1991); Charles A. Kupchan, *The Vulnerability of Empire* (Ithaca, NY: Cornell University Press, 1994); and Jeffrey W. Taliaferro, *Balancing Risks: Great Power Intervention in the Periphery* (Ithaca, NY: Cornell University Press, 2004).

11. This is a more realistic possibility in a multipolar international system than a bipolar or unipolar system because the disparity in strength between regional powers and great powers is smaller. See Randall L. Schweller, "Managing the Rise of Great Powers: History and Theory," in *Engaging China: Managing a Rising Power*, ed. Alastair Iain Johnston and Robert Ross (New York: Routledge, 1999), 6.

12. Jack S. Levy and William R. Thompson, "Hegemonic Threats and Great-Power Balancing in Europe, 1495–1999," *Security Studies* 14, no. 1 (January–March 2005), 5.

13. Robert Chase, Emily Hill, and Paul Kennedy, "Introduction," in *The Pivotal States: A New Framework for U.S. Policy in the Developing World*, ed. Robert Chase, Emily Hill, and Paul Kennedy (New York: W. W. Norton, 1999), 1–11.

14. See, for example, Vesna Danilovic, *When the Stakes Are High: Deterrence and Conflict among Major Powers* (Ann Arbor: University of Michigan Press, 2002).

15. One of the few scholars to consider the question addressed in this book is Ian Lustick, who has examined why a great power has not emerged from the Middle East despite several potential candidates over the past two centuries. According to Lustick, each of these candidates faced a daunting structural constraint: an international system already populated by great power

gatekeepers, some of which were unwilling to let aspiring peers join their ranks. Yet this study looks at only one part of the world; it accounts only for cases of great power opposition to emerging regional powers; and it does not identify the reasons why great powers have resisted RRPs. See Ian S. Lustick, "The Absence of Middle Eastern Great Powers: Political 'Backwardness' in Historical Perspective," *International Organization* 51, no. 4 (Autumn 1997).

16. Balance-of-power realism includes classical realism as well as offensive and defensive structural realism. Preponderance-of-power realism includes long-cycle, power-transition, and hegemonic stability theories. On this distinction, see Randall L. Schweller and William C. Wohlforth, "Power Test: Evaluating Realism in Response to the End of the Cold War," *Security Studies* 9, no. 3 (Spring 2000); and especially Jack S. Levy, "Interstate War and Peace," in *Handbook of International Relations*, 2nd ed., ed. Walter Carlsnaes, Thomas Risse, and Beth A. Simmons (Los Angeles: Sage, 2013), 583–584. Two theories in the preponderance-of-power school have notable parallels with the issues raised in this book, although they each have a very different empirical focus. First, long-cycle theory emphasizes the relationship between established global powers and emerging regional powers. Because it attempts to explain the causes and consequences of system-altering wars, however, it looks only at emerging powers in one particular region, namely, Europe. Second, the "multiple hierarchies" extension of power transition theory argues that the international system includes many regional subsystems outside Europe and explores the sources of local stability and the origins of local conflicts. Yet it does not explain great power intervention within these subsystems. On the former, see Rasler and Thompson, *Great Powers and Global Struggle*. On the latter, see Douglas Lemke and Suzanne Werner, "Power Parity, Commitment to Change, and War," *International Studies Quarterly* 40, no. 2 (June 1996); and Douglas Lemke, *Regions of War and Peace* (New York: Cambridge University Press, 2002).

17. Stephen M. Walt, *The Origins of Alliances* (Ithaca, NY: Cornell University Press, 1987); and Charles L. Glaser, *Rational Theory of International Politics: The Logic of Competition and Cooperation* (Princeton, NJ: Princeton University Press, 2010). On the security dilemma, see Robert Jervis, "Cooperation under the Security Dilemma," *World Politics* 30, no. 2 (January 1978), 167–214; and Charles L. Glaser, "The Security Dilemma Revisited," *World Politics* 50, no. 1 (October 1997), 171–201.

18. See, for example, David M. Edelstein, "Managing Uncertainty: Beliefs about Intentions and the Rise of Great Powers," *Security Studies* 12, no. 1 (Autumn 2002).

19. On the challenge of accurately gauging another state's near-term intentions as well as its underlying motives, see Jervis, "Cooperation under the Security Dilemma," 168; Mearsheimer, *Tragedy of Great Power Politics*, 31; Evan Braden Montgomery, "Breaking Out of the Security Dilemma: Realism, Reassurance, and the Problem of Uncertainty," *International Security* 31, no. 2 (Fall 2006); and Sebastian Rosato, "The Inscrutable Intentions of Great Powers," *International Security* 39, no. 3 (Winter 2014/15).

20. Alex Weisiger, *Logics of War: Explanations for Limited and Unlimited Conflicts* (Ithaca, NY: Cornell University Press, 2013), 17.

21. Gilpin, *War and Change in World Politics*, 191–193, quote at 191. See also Paul K. MacDonald and Joseph M. Parent, "Graceful Decline: The Surprising Success of Great Power Retrenchment," *International Security* 35, no. 4 (Spring 2011); and Kyle Haynes, "Decline and Devolution: The Sources of Strategic Military Retrenchment," *International Studies Quarterly* 59, no. 3 (September 2015).

22. On the application of realist theories to regional orders, see T. V. Paul, "Regional Transformation in International Relations," in *International Relations Theory and Regional Transformations*, ed. T. V. Paul (New York: Cambridge University Press, 2012), 7–12.

23. Mearsheimer, *Tragedy of Great Power Politics*, 41–42. According to Colin Elman, the United States is the one exception to this rule. Due to its unique geopolitical position as the only potential great power in an isolated region, established great powers allowed it to dominate North America, either because they were more preoccupied with nearby threats (in the case of continental European powers) or because they counted on it as a future ally against a continental rival (in the case of Great Britain). See Colin Elman, "Extending Offensive Realism: The Louisiana Purchase and America's Rise to Regional Hegemony," *American Political Science Review* 98, no. 4 (November 2004). As I discuss in chapter 3, however, London was actually willing to see North

America transformed into a balance-of-power subsystem during the Civil War, an outcome that certainly would have undermined Washington's value as an ally.

24. Lemke, *Regions of War and Peace*, chap. 3.

25. See, for example, Graham E. Fuller and John Arquilla, "The Intractable Problem of Regional Powers," *Orbis* 40, no. 4 (Fall 1996), 613.

26. Schweller, "Managing the Rise of Great Powers," 7–8. *Internal balancing* refers to arms buildups, whereas *external balancing* refers to the formation of alliances and alignments. See Waltz, *Theory of International Politics*, 118.

27. See, for example, the discussion in George Modelski, "The International Relations of Internal War," in *International Aspects of Civil Strife*, ed. James N. Rosenau (Princeton, NJ: Princeton University Press, 1964), 23–24.

28. This means the specific measures that a leading state adopts toward RRPs could be influenced by factors that fall outside the bounds of my theory, such as resources constraints, domestic political considerations, or individual personalities.

29. On the technique of process tracing and the importance of causal mechanisms in qualitative analysis, see Alexander L. George and Timothy J. McKeown, "Case Studies and Theories of Organizational Decision-Making," in *Advances in Information Processing in Organizations*, ed. R. F. Coulam and R. A. Smith (Greenwich, CT: JAI Press, 1985), 2:21–58; Alexander L. George and Andrew Bennett, *Case Studies and Theory Development in the Social Sciences* (Cambridge, MA: MIT Press, 2005); and David Waldner, "Transforming Inferences into Explanations: Lessons from the Study of Mass Extinctions," in *Theory and Evidence in Comparative Politics and International Relations*, ed. Richard Ned Lebow and Mark Irving Lichback (New York: Palgrave MacMillan, 2007), 145–175.

30. On the importance of policymakers' perceptions, see Geoffrey Blainey, *The Causes of War*, 3rd ed. (New York: Free Press, 1998); and William Curti Wohlforth, *The Elusive Balance: Power and Perceptions during the Cold War* (Ithaca, NY: Cornell University Press, 1993). Examining perceptions also helps to resolve issues such as what constitutes a region and whether nations are in fact regional powers rather than great powers. To a significant degree, both issues are in the eye of the beholder. Geographic regions, for example, are artificial constructs with subjective, uncertain, and shifting boundaries, while some regional powers might actually meet the great power threshold according to certain metrics, even though senior officials in other nations did not see them that way at the time.

1. How Leading States Respond to Rising Regional Powers

1. Leading states have not always outstripped their rivals in every measure of strength. Thus, the phenomenon of global leadership is not identical to the structural condition of unipolarity, in which a single nation exceeds potential competitors in every major dimension of power, although the two have gone together during the post–Cold War era. See William C. Wohlforth, "The Stability of a Unipolar World," *International Security* 24, no. 1 (Summer 1999); Stephen G. Brooks and William C. Wohlforth, *World out of Balance: International Relations and the Challenge of American Primacy* (Princeton, NJ: Princeton University Press, 2008), 29–31; and G. John Ikenberry, Michael Mastanduno, and William C. Wohlforth, "Introduction: Unipolarity, State Behavior, and Systemic Consequences," in *International Relations Theory and the Consequences of Unipolarity*, ed. G. John Ikenberry, Michael Mastanduno, and William C. Wohlforth (New York: Cambridge University Press, 2011), 2–5.

2. On the characteristics of leading states and their role in international politics, especially over the past two centuries, see Gilpin, *War and Change in World Politics*; Rasler and Thompson, *Great Powers and Global Struggle*; George Modelski and William R. Thompson, *Leading Sectors and World Powers: The Coevolution of Global Economics and Politics* (Columbia: University of South Carolina Press, 1996); G. John Ikenberry, *After Victory: Institutions, Strategic Restraint, and the Rebuilding of Order after Major Wars* (Princeton, NJ: Princeton University Press, 2001); and G. John Ikenberry, *Liberal Leviathan: The Origins, Crisis, and Transformation of the American World Order*

(Princeton, NJ: Princeton University Press, 2011); and the essays in G. John Ikenberry, ed., *Power, Order, and Change in World Politics* (Cambridge: Cambridge University Press, 2014). In addition, David A. Lake's work on hierarchy and authority provides an important window into understanding how leading states influence the international system. See Lake, *Entangling Relations: American Foreign Policy in Its Century* (Princeton, NJ: Princeton University Press, 1999); and Lake, *Hierarchy in International Relations* (Ithaca, NY: Cornell University Press, 2009).

3. Throughout this book, I use the terms *balance of power* and *preponderance of power* interchangeably with *parity* and *primacy*.

4. Ikenberry, *After Victory*, 22.

5. Ibid., 22–25. Ikenberry also identifies rule-based constitutionalism (or rule by consent) as a third type of international order, although this has mostly been limited to the post-1945 period. For other discussions of international order, see John A. Hall and T. V. Paul, "Introduction," in *International Order and the Future of World Politics*, ed. T. V. Paul and John A. Hall (New York: Cambridge University Press, 1999), 2–7; and Randall L. Schweller, "The Problem of International Order Revisited," *International Security* 26, no. 1 (Summer 2001), especially 169–173.

6. Lemke, *Regions of War and Peace*. Although balance-of-power realists generally dispute the notion that a single nation can dominate other great powers, they do acknowledge that regional preponderance is more likely than global primacy. See, for example, Robert Jervis, *System Effects: Complexity in Political and Social Life* (Princeton, NJ: Princeton University Press, 1997), 133. For a detailed assessment of preponderance-of-power systems and how frequently they have formed in the past, see the essays in Stuart J. Kaufman, Richard Little, and William C. Wohlforth, eds., *The Balance of Power in World History* (New York: Palgrave Macmillan, 2007).

7. William R. Thompson, "The Regional Subsystem: A Conceptual Explication and a Propositional Inventory," *International Studies Quarterly* 17, no. 1 (March 1973); Arthur A. Stein and Steven F. Lobell, "Geostructuralism and International Politics: The End of the Cold War and the Regionalization of International Society," in *Regional Orders: Building Security in a New World*, ed. David A. Lake and Patrick M. Morgan (University Park: Pennsylvania State University Press, 1997), 101–122; Jack S. Levy, "Balances and Balancing: Concepts, Propositions, and Research Design," in *Realism and the Balancing of Power: A New Debate*, ed. John A. Vasquez and Colin Elman (Englewood Cliffs, NJ: Prentice-Hall, 2002), 140–141; and Benjamin Miller, "The International System and Regional Balance in the Middle East," in *Balance of Power: Theory and Practice in the 21st Century*, ed. T. V. Paul, James Wirtz, and Michel Fortmann (Stanford, CA: Stanford University Press, 2004), 240–243.

8. On the potential economic and security interests of great powers in peripheral regions, see Michael C. Desch, "The Keys that Lock Up the World: Identifying American Interests in the Periphery," *International Security* 14, no. 1 (Summer 1989); and Gil Merom, "Realist Hypotheses on Regional Peace," *Journal of Strategic Studies* 26, no. 1 (March 2003). In general, whether leading states have meaningful interests in peripheral regions and the extent to which they should defend those interests have been controversial topics. See, for example, Stephen M. Walt, "The Case for Finite Containment: Analyzing U.S. Grand Strategy," *International Security* 14, no. 1 (Summer 1989); Steven R. David, "Why the Third World Matters," *International Security* 14, no. 1 (Summer 1989); and Steven Van Evera, "Why Europe Matters, Why the Third World Doesn't: American Grand Strategy after the Cold War," *Journal of Strategic Studies* 13, no. 2 (June 1990).

9. Desch, "The Keys that Lock up the World," 99.

10. In other words, just as balance-of-power realists maintain that parity is a barrier to conflict while preponderance-of-power realists argue that primacy is a deterrent to war, policymakers in a leading state might conclude that both types of order can preserve local stability.

11. Specifically, there has been a growing focus on antiaccess/area denial threats, that is, military strategies and capabilities that could prevent the United States (or any other extraregional actor) from deploying its forces into a distant theater and employing them effectively once they arrive. See, for example, Andrew F. Krepinevich Jr., "The Pentagon's Wasting Assets: The Eroding Foundations of American Power," *Foreign Affairs* 88, no. 4 (July/August 2009); and Evan Braden Montgomery, "Contested Primacy in the Western Pacific: China's Rise and the Future of U.S. Power Projection," *International Security* 38, no. 4 (Spring 2014). To date, assessments of access threats have emphasized the possibility of military attacks or political restrictions that

could prevent the United States from using its overseas bases, although the underlying issue is a much broader one. See Christopher J. Bowie, *The Anti-Access Threat to Theater Air Bases* (Washington, DC: Center for Strategic and Budgetary Assessments, 2002); Kent Calder, *Embattled Garrisons: Comparative Base Politics and American Globalism* (Princeton, NJ: Princeton University Press, 2008); Alexander Cooley, *Base Politics: Democratic Change and the U.S. Military Overseas* (Ithaca, NY: Cornell University Press, 2008); and Stacie L. Pettyjohn and Jennifer Kavanagh, *Access Granted: Political Challenges to America's Overseas Military Presence, 1945–2013* (Santa Monica, CA: RAND, forthcoming).

12. See Zbigniew Brzezinski, *The Grand Chessboard: American Primacy and Its Geostrategic Imperatives* (New York: Basic Books, 1998), 41; and Jakub J. Grygiel, *Great Powers and Geopolitical Change* (Baltimore: Johns Hopkins University Press, 2006), x.

13. Colin S. Gray, *War, Peace, and Victory: Strategy and Statecraft for the Next Century* (New York: Simon & Schuster, 1991), 57. On the maritime–continental distinction and its implications, see also Robert S. Ross, "The Geography of the Peace: East Asia in the Twenty-First Century," *International Security* 23, no. 4 (Spring 1999), 94–104; and Evan Braden Montgomery, "Competitive Strategies against Continental Powers: The Geopolitics of Sino-Indian-American Relations," *Journal of Strategic Studies* 36, no. 1 (February 2013), 78–81.

14. On the logistical challenges of power projection, see Mearsheimer, *Tragedy of Great Power Politics*, chap. 4; and James R. Holmes, "Schelling Goes to Sea: Managing Perceptions in China's 'Contested Zone'," *Defence Studies* 9, no. 2 (June 2009). More generally, Kenneth Boulding developed the "loss of strength gradient" concept to capture the difficulty of generating combat capability over significant distances. Kenneth E. Boulding, *Conflict and Defense: A General Theory* (New York: Harper & Row, 1962).

15. Sir Halford J. Mackinder, "The Round World and the Winning of the Peace," *Foreign Affairs* 21, no. 4 (July 1943), 601.

16. Jack S. Levy and William R. Thompson, "Balancing on Land and at Sea: Do States Ally against the Leading Global Power?" *International Security* 35, no. 1 (Summer 2010), 22. Leading states might require allies with strong naval capabilities as well, depending on their available military resources, the specific demands on those resources, and the geographic characteristics of strategically important regions.

17. For an overview of the British experience, see Paul M. Kennedy, *The Rise and Fall of British Naval Mastery* (New York: Humanity Books, 1976). On the American experience, see the description in Colin S. Gray, "Strategy in the Nuclear Age," in *The Making of Strategy: Rulers, States, and War*, ed. Williamson Murray, MacGregor Knox, and Alvin Bernstein (New York: Cambridge University Press, 1994), 579–613.

18. William R. Thompson, "Why Rivalries Matter and What Great Power Rivalries Can Tell Us about World Politics," in *Great Power Rivalries*, ed. William R. Thompson (Columbia: University of South Carolina Press, 1999), 16; and William R. Thompson, "Principal Rivalries," *Journal of Conflict Resolution* 39, no. 2 (June 1995), 209. These areas are sometimes referred to as "shatterbelts." See Saul Bernard Cohen, *Geopolitics of the World System* (Landham, MD: Roman & Littlefield, 2003).

19. For its part, a dominant local power should have strong incentives to cooperate with a leading state if its neighborhood is in danger, especially because maritime powers are generally much less threatening than continental powers. This is due to their geographic isolation as well as their emphasis on naval forces, which makes them less likely to seize and hold territory abroad. See Walt, *Origins of Alliances*, 23–24; and Levy and Thompson, "Balancing on Land and at Sea," 13–15.

20. Overviews of this literature include Jacek Kugler and A. F. K. Organski, "The Power Transition: A Retrospective and Prospective Evaluation," in *Handbook of War Studies*, ed. Manus I. Midlarsky (Boston: Unwin Hyman, 1989), 171–194; and Jonathan M. DiCicco and Jack S. Levy, "Power Shifts and Problem Shifts: The Evolution of the Power Transition Research Program," *Journal of Conflict Resolution* 43, no. 6 (December 1999).

21. See, respectively, A. F. K. Organski, *World Politics* (New York: Alfred A. Knopf, 1958); and Dale C. Copeland, *The Origins of Major War* (Ithaca, NY: Cornell University Press, 2000).

22. On the speed of power shifts and their potential impact on the likelihood of war, see Organski, *World Politics*; A. F. K. Organski and Jacek Kugler, *The War Ledger* (Chicago: University of Chicago Press, 1980), 62; Ronald L. Tammen et al., *Power Transitions: Strategies for the 21st Century* (New York: Chatham House, 2000), 30–31; and David P. Rapkin and William R. Thompson, *Transition Scenarios: China and the United States in the Twenty-First Century* (Chicago: University of Chicago Press, 2013), 50.

23. The claim that rapid shifts increase the probability of conflict between great powers has also received relatively little support. See Woosang Kim, "Power Transitions and Great Power War from Westphalia to Waterloo," *World Politics* 45, no. 1 (October 1992), 170–171; and Woosang Kim and James D. Morrow, "When Do Power Shifts Lead to War?" *American Journal of Political Science* 36, no. 4 (November 1992), 907.

24. Thus, an incomplete power shift could increase the odds of bargaining failure and renewed fighting due to mutual optimism regarding the outcome of a potential war. On this pathway to conflict, see Blainey, *Causes of War*, 114; and Branislav L. Slantchev and Ahmer Tarar, "Mutual Optimism as a Rationalist Explanation of War," *American Journal of Political Science* 55, no. 1 (January 2011).

25. There is, of course, the potential for an endogeneity problem, insofar as the leading state can influence the scope of a regional power shift by helping to strengthen one side or weaken another. Although this concern is a reasonable one, I argue that when a leading state assesses the scope of a power shift, it generally focuses on the likely outcome and implications of a local conflict absent external involvement (even though this assessment will be used to determine whether and how it should intervene). If an RRP needs considerable outside assistance to establish or sustain a new order, then that order will be inherently fragile and might not survive if its patrons withdraw their support. For a leading state, then, the scope of the power shift is determined primarily by factors internal to the region and exogenous to external influence, in particular an RRP's latent resources, economic strength, and military prowess.

26. See, for example, NSC 155/1, "United States Objectives and Policies with Respect to the Near East," July 14, 1953, in *FRUS, 1952–1954*, vol. 9, part 1: *The Near and Middle East* (Washington, DC: Government Printing Office, 1986), 399–400.

27. NSC 5428, "United States Objectives and Policies with Respect to the Near East," July 23, 1954, ibid., 533; National Security Council Planning Board, "Draft: Report on Deterrence of Major Armed Conflict between Israel and Egypt or Other Arab States," October 17, 1955, in *FRUS, 1955–1957*, vol. 14: *Arab–Israeli Dispute, 1955* (Washington, DC: Government Printing Office, 1989), 594–595; and Message from the Director of Central Intelligence, January 29, 1956, in *FRUS, 1955–1957*, vol. 15: *Arab–Israeli Dispute, January 1–July 26, 1956* (Washington, DC: Government Printing Office, 1989), 92–94.

28. Memorandum of Conversation (MemCon), February 10, 1956, in *FRUS, 1955–1957*, 15:163–166; and Memorandum from Herbert Hoover Jr. to John Foster Dulles, March 1, 1956, ibid., 260–261.

29. MemCon, "Israel," December 28, 1956, in *FRUS, 1955–1957*, vol. 16: *Suez Crisis, July 26–December 31, 1956* (Washington, DC: Government Printing Office, 1990), 1342–1343; and MemCon, "Israeli Withdrawal," February 17, 1957, in *FRUS, 1955–1957*, vol. 17: *Arab–Israeli Dispute, 1957* (Washington, DC: Government Printing Office, 1990), 194.

30. Special National Intelligence Estimate (SNIE) 30-3-67, "The Short-Term Arab–Israeli Military Balance," August 10, 1967, in *FRUS, 1964–1968*, vol. 19: *Arab–Israeli Crisis and War, 1967* (Washington, DC: Government Printing Office, 2004), 771.

31. Memorandum from Bundy to Johnson, "Bundy's Return to Ford, and Related Subjects," June 26, 1967, ibid., 566. Although U.S.–Israeli relations had become closer during John F. Kennedy's administration, most historians identify the Six-Day War as a key turning point. See Douglas Little, "The Making of a Special Relationship: The United States and Israel, 1957–1968," *International Journal of Middle East Studies* 25, no. 4 (November 1993); and William B. Quandt, *Peace Process: American Diplomacy and the Arab–Israeli Conflict since 1967*, 3rd ed. (Washington, DC: Brookings, 2005), 45.

32. On the power shift that was taking place in northern Europe at the time, see Francis J. Bowman, "Dutch Diplomacy and the Baltic Grain Trade," *Pacific Historical Review* 5, no. 4

(December 1936), 341; and Henry L. Schoolcraft, "England and Denmark, 1660–1667," *English Historical Review* 25, no. 99 (July 1910), 461–462. While the Netherlands did not view Denmark's control over the Sound as a major threat (because the two nations had close ties and the latter was no longer strong enough to use its leverage coercively), England had a very different view (because the Danes had closed the Sound to English ships during the first Anglo-Dutch War). See Menna Prestwich, "Diplomacy and Trade in the Protectorate," *Journal of Modern History* 22, no. 2 (June 1950), 112–113; and Michael Roberts, "Cromwell and the Baltic," *English Historical Review* 76, no. 300 (July 1961): 414–415.

33. W. F. Reddaway, "The Scandinavian North (1559–1660)," in *The Cambridge Modern History,* vol. 5: *The Thirty Years' War,* ed. A. W. Ward, G. W. Prothero, and Stanley Leathes (Cambridge: Cambridge University Press, 1906), 562; and Michael Roberts, *The Swedish Imperial Experience, 1560–1718* (Cambridge: Cambridge University Press, 1979), 8, 40.

34. Bowman, "Dutch Diplomacy and the Baltic Grain Trade," 345–348; and J. R. Jones, "The Dutch Navy and National Survival in the Seventeenth Century," *International History Review* 10, no. 1 (February 1988), 24.

35. Roberts, "Cromwell and the Baltic," 415, 436–438; Prestwich, "Diplomacy and Trade in the Protectorate," 114; Enid M. G. Routh, "The Attempts to Establish a Balance of Power in Europe during the Second Half of the Seventeenth Century (1648–1702)," *Transactions of the Royal Historical Society* 18 (1904), 41; and Roger Hainsworth, *The Swordsmen in Power: War and Politics under the English Republic, 1649–1660* (Stroud, England: Sutton Publishing, 1997), 206.

36. E. H. Kossmann, "The Dutch Republic," in *The New Cambridge Modern History,* vol. 5: *The Ascendancy of France, 1648–88,* ed. F. L. Carsten (Cambridge: Cambridge University Press, 1961), 275–300; and Mary Elizabeth Ailes, "Ships, Sailors, and Mediators: England's Naval Aid to Sweden, 1658–1659," *Historian* 67, no. 2 (Summer 2005).

37. Reddaway, "Scandinavian North," 588.

38. The difference between a counterhegemonic power shift and a hegemonic but incomplete power shift is subtle but important. In the former case, an RRP is attempting to establish parity at the expense of a local hegemon in decline, but it does not appear to have the capabilities or the ambition to overtake that local hegemon and become the preponderant power in the region. In the latter case, an RRP is clearly trying to become a local hegemon, possesses the necessary resources to make a plausible bid for dominance, and even gains a relative advantage over its nearest rival. Nevertheless, it is unable to translate that advantage into uncontested primacy.

39. For a discussion, see Fareed Zakaria, "Realism and Domestic Politics: A Review Essay," *International Security* 17, no. 1 (Summer 1992); and Fareed Zakaria, *From Wealth to Power: The Unusual Origins of America's World Role* (Princeton, NJ: Princeton University Press, 1998).

40. On entrapment, see Thomas Christensen and Jack Snyder, "Chain Gangs and Passed Bucks: Predicting Alliance Patterns in Multipolarity," *International Organization* 44, no. 2 (Spring 1990); and Glenn H. Snyder, *Alliance Politics* (Ithaca, NY: Cornell University Press, 1997), 181. On bandwagoning, see Walt, *Origins of Alliances*; and Randall Schweller, "Bandwagoning for Profit: Bringing the Revisionist State Back In," *International Security* 19, no. 1 (Summer 2004).

2. Egypt's Bid for Mastery of the Middle East, 1831–1841

1. Paul W. Schroeder, "Did the Vienna Settlement Rest on a Balance of Power?" *American Historical Review* 97, no. 3 (June 1992).

2. R. B. Mowat, "The Near East and France, 1829–1847," in *The Cambridge History of British Foreign Policy, 1783–1919,* ed. Sir A. W. Ward and G. P. Gooch, vol. 2, *1815–1866* (Cambridge: Cambridge University Press, 1923), 161; and William L. Langer, *Political and Social Upheaval, 1832–1852* (New York: Harper & Row, 1969), 285.

3. Sir Charles Webster, *The Foreign Policy of Palmerston, 1830–1841: Britain, the Liberal Movement and the Eastern Question* (New York: Humanities Press, 1969), 2:769.

4. R. W. Seton-Watson, *Britain in Europe, 1789–1914* (Cambridge: Cambridge University Press, 1937), 196 (emphasis in original).

5. M. S. Anderson, "Great Britain and the Russo-Turkish War of 1768–74," *English Historical Review* 69, no. 270 (January 1954), 39.

6. On British economic and strategic relations with the Ottomans in the eighteenth century, see W. Miller, "Europe and the Ottoman Power before the Nineteenth Century," *English Historical Review* 16, no. 63 (July 1901); M. S. Anderson, "Great Britain and the Russian Fleet, 1769–70," *Slavonic and East European Review* 31, no. 76 (December 1952); and Allan Cunningham, "The Oczakov Debate," *Middle Eastern Studies* 1, no. 3 (April 1965).

7. M. S. Anderson, "The Great Powers and the Annexation of the Crimea, 1783–4," *Slavonic and East European Review* 37, no. 88 (December 1958).

8. G. D. Clayton, *Britain and the Eastern Question: Missolonghi to Gallipoli* (London: University of London Press, 1971), 23, 33; Paull C. Webb, "Sea Power in the Ochakov Affair of 1791," *International History Review* 2, no. 1 (January 1980); David Fromkin, "The Great Game in Asia," *Foreign Affairs* 58, no. 4 (Spring 1980), 936; and Edward Ingram, *In Defence of British India: Great Britain and the Middle East, 1775–1842* (London: Frank Cass, 1984), 33.

9. H. W. V. Temperley, *England and the Near East: The Crimea* (London: Archon Books, 1936), 43; and John Ehrman, *The Younger Pitt: The Reluctant Transition* (Stanford, CA: Stanford University Press, 1983), 28.

10. Temperley, *England and the Near East*, 44.

11. On the origins and implications of the Treaty of the Dardanelles, see ibid., 45–48; Clayton, *Britain and the Eastern Question*, 34–35; and M. S. Anderson, *The Eastern Question, 1774–1923: A Study in International Relations* (London: St. Martin's Press, 1966), 44.

12. Anderson, *Eastern Question*, 58.

13. Kenneth Bourne, *The Foreign Policy of Victorian England, 1830–1902* (London: Oxford University Press, 1970), 19.

14. India did not formally become a British colony until 1858, following the Sepoy Rebellion. Until that time, the British East India Company governed most of the subcontinent, either directly (through its own administrative and military personnel) or indirectly (through local rulers). Nevertheless, India was under the de facto control of the British government; oversight of the East India Company was the responsibility of the Board of Control and its president, who generally held cabinet rank. After 1858, a new cabinet position—secretary of state for India—replaced the Board of Control.

15. The strategic implications of Great Britain's continental empire, as well as the threat assessments of British policymakers, are reviewed in David Gillard, *The Struggle for Asia, 1828–1914: A Study in British and Russian Imperialism* (London: Methuen, 1977), chaps. 2–3. See also C. W. Crawley, "Anglo-Russian Relations, 1815–1840," *Cambridge Historical Journal* 3, no. 1 (1929); Edward Ingram, "Great Britain's Great Game: An Introduction," *International History Review* 2, no. 2 (April 1980); and M. A. Yapp, "British Perceptions of the Russian Threat to India," *Modern Asian Studies* 21, no. 4 (1987).

16. On the decline of the Ottoman Empire, see Bernard Lewis, *The Emergence of Modern Turkey*, 2nd ed. (New York: Oxford University Press, 1961), chaps. 2–4; Albert Hourani, *Arabic Thought in the Liberal Age, 1789–1939* (Cambridge: Cambridge University Press, 1962), chap. 3; and Albert Hourani, *A History of the Arab Peoples* (New York: Warner Books, 1991), chaps. 15–16.

17. Anderson, *Eastern Question*, 76.

18. For discussions of British diplomacy during the Greek War of Independence, see Clayton, *Britain and the Eastern Question*, 43, 53–54; H. W. V. Temperley, "The Foreign Policy of Canning, 1820–1827," in *Cambridge History of British Foreign Policy, 1783–1919*, 2:90–96; and Loyal Cowles, "The Failure to Restrain Russia: Canning, Nesselrode, and the Greek Question, 1825–1827," *International History Review* 12, no. 5 (November 1990).

19. Clayton, *Britain and the Eastern Question*, 57. See also Temperley, "Foreign Policy of Canning," 102.

20. Wellington to Aberdeen, October 4, 1829, WP1/1054/7. Documents from the Wellington Papers are available through the University of Southampton Special Collections Database, http://www.archives.soton.ac.uk/wellington/.

21. Wellington to Aberdeen, October 10–11, 1829, WP1/1054/21. Although Wellington admitted that the terms of the treaty were relatively lenient given the scope of Russia's victory,

Russia's earlier pledges to avoid extending its territory at the Ottoman Empire's expense caused the treaty to be viewed in a much harsher light. See Wellington to Baron Heytesbury, December 15, 1829, WP1/1065/33.

22. Quoted in Allan Cunningham, *Eastern Questions in the Nineteenth Century: Collected Essays*, ed. Edward Ingram (London: Frank Cass, 1993), 2:27–28.

23. Peter Hopkirk, *The Great Game: The Struggle for Empire in Central Asia* (New York: Kodansha Globe, 1994), 111.

24. Aberdeen to Heytesbury, October 31, 1829, reprinted in Bourne, *Foreign Policy of Victorian England*, 211.

25. Mowat, "Near East and France," 164. See also Anderson, *Eastern Question*, 56–57; Bourne, *Foreign Policy of Victorian England*, 27; and Webster, *Foreign Policy of Palmerston*, 1:274.

26. The latter campaign came at a great cost, however. Prompted in part by Egypt's success against the rebels, Great Britain, France, and Russia signed the Treaty of London in 1827, which obligated the European powers to impose a settlement on Greece and Turkey that would establish a degree of autonomy for the former and provide compensation to the latter. It also called for a joint fleet to enforce the treaty, impose a ceasefire on the warring parties, and blockade the southern peninsula of Greece. On October 20, 1827, the naval forces of the three European powers engaged and destroyed a combined Turkish-Egyptian fleet, which was in harbor at Navarino Bay. See Clayton, *Britain and the Eastern Question*, 50–54; and C. W. Crawley, "The Near East and the Ottoman Empire," in *The New Cambridge Modern History*, vol. IX, *War and Peace in an Age of Upheaval, 1793–1830*, ed. C. W. Crawley (Cambridge: Cambridge University Press, 1969), 548–549.

27. Overviews of Egypt's rise include Afaf Lutfi al-Sayyid Marsot, *Egypt in the Reign of Mehmet Ali* (Cambridge: Cambridge University Press, 1984), especially chap. 4; David B. Ralston, *Importing the European Army: The Introduction of European Military Techniques and Institutions into the Extra-European World, 1600–1914* (Chicago: University of Chicago Press, 1990), chap. 4; Khaled Fahmy, "The Era of Mehmet Ali Pasha, 1805–1848," in *The Cambridge History of Egypt*, ed. M. W. Daly, vol. 2, *Modern Egypt from 1517 to the End of the Twentieth Century* (Cambridge: Cambridge University Press, 1998), 139–179; and Efraim Karsh and Inari Karsh, *Empires of the Sand: The Struggle for Mastery in the Middle East, 1789–1923* (Cambridge, MA: Harvard University Press 1999), chap. 3.

28. Hassan Ahmed Ibrahim, "The Egyptian Empire, 1805–1885," in *Cambridge History of Egypt*, 2:198.

29. Quoted in Marsot, *Egypt in the Reign of Mehmet Ali*, 214.

30. John Posonby to Palmerston, May 14, 1833, PP/GC/PO/142. Documents from the Palmerston Papers are available through the University of Southampton Special Collections Database, http://www.archives.soton.ac.uk/palmerston/.

31. Anderson, *Eastern Question*, 79; and Bourne, *Palmerston: The Early Years, 1784–1841* (New York: Macmillan, 1982), 376–377.

32. Palmerston to Stratford Canning, February 20, 1832, PP/GC/CA/253.

33. Canning to Palmerston, October 26, 1832, PP/GC/CA/114.

34. Webster, *Foreign Policy of Palmerston*, 1:281–282; and Temperley, *England and the Near East*, 63.

35. Palmerston, HPD, House of Commons, March 17, 1834, vol. 22, cols. 320–321.

36. Cited in Langer, *Political and Social Upheaval*, 290.

37. Marsot, *Egypt in the Reign of Mehmet Ali*, 227–229; Fahmy, "Era of Mehmet Ali Pasha," 166–168; Langer, *Political and Social Upheaval*, 288–291; and Anderson, *Eastern Question*, 81–83.

38. Matthew Anderson, "Russia and the Eastern Question, 1821–41," in *Europe's Balance of Power, 1815–1848*, ed. Alan Sked (London: Macmillan, 1979); and Matthew Rendall, "Restraint or Self-Restraint: Nicholas I, the Treaty of Unkiar Skelessi, and the Vienna System, 1832–1841," *International History Review* 24, no. 1 (March 2002). It is important to note that although Great Britain and Russia had similar objectives with respect to Turkey—that is, preserving it as a buffer state—neither knew the other's preferences.

39. Shortly after the Russo-Turkish treaty was signed, there were widespread suspicions that its secret protocol actually granted Russia the ability to freely transit the Straits with its war-

ships during a conflict while excluding the warships of other nations. These fears were unfounded, however, and Palmerston was quickly notified of its actual terms by his ambassador at Constantinople. See Bourne, *Palmerston: The Early Years*, 382.

40. Gillard, *Struggle for Asia*, 43–44; Bourne, *Foreign Policy of Victorian England*, 28; Langer, *Political and Social Upheaval*, 291–293; and Anderson, *Eastern Question*, 84–86.

41. Anderson, *Eastern Question*, 84–85.

42. Clayton, *Britain and the Eastern Question*, 67.

43. Crawley, "Anglo-Russian Relations," 71.

44. This assumes that the Porte would have allowed Great Britain to pass through the Straits freely in the case of an Anglo-Russian war, which was not guaranteed. During any war between Russia and the Ottoman Empire, moreover, Unkiar Skelessi would effectively have been nullified. In that instance, the Porte could have invited British forces to enter the Straits and attack Russia in its defense. Hence, the real impact of the treaty was that it would secure Russia's Black Sea coast during a conflict between London and St. Petersburg that did not directly involve Constantinople—a scenario that was now much more likely given the improvement in relations between the two former rivals.

45. Anderson, *Eastern Question*, 85–90.

46. Quoted in Temperley, *England and the Near East*, 72.

47. Mowat, "Near East and France," 166.

48. Palmerston to William Temple, March 3, 1834, in Sir Henry Lytton Bulwer, *The Life of Henry John Temple, Viscount Palmerston, with Selections from His Diaries and Correspondence* (London: Richard Bentley, 1870), 2:179.

49. Palmerston to William Temple, December 3, 1833, ibid., 176.

50. Palmerston to Posonby, December 6, 1833, in R. L. Baker and Viscount Palmerston, "Palmerston on the Treaty of Unkiar Skelessi," *English Historical Review* 43, no. 169 (January 1928), quotes at 86, 88.

51. Palmerston to William Temple, October 8, 1833, in Bulwer, *Life of Henry John Temple*, 2:169.

52. Gillard, *Struggle for Asia*, 38; Bourne, *Palmerston: The Early Years*, 374; and Webster, *Foreign Policy of Palmerston*, 1:314.

53. Paul W. Schroeder, *The Transformation of European Politics, 1763–1848* (Oxford: Clarendon Press, 1994), 732.

54. Webster, *Foreign Policy of Palmerston*, 1:309.

55. Palmerston to William Temple, April 21, 1834, in Bulwer, *Life of Henry John Temple*, 2:183.

56. Palmerston to William Temple, March 30, 1829, in Bulwer, *Life of Henry John Temple*, 1:329. This assessment was not unreasonable at the time because the apparent magnitude of Russia's victory masked the difficulties that it faced in defeating a weaker Ottoman Empire. See Clayton, *Britain and the Eastern Question*, 55.

57. Quoted in Bourne, *Palmerston: The Early Years*, 375.

58. Webster, *Foreign Policy of Palmerston*, 1:87, 278–279; Langer, *Political and Social Upheaval*, 287–289; and Clayton, *Britain and the Eastern Question*, 63.

59. Quoted in M. Verete, "Palmerston and the Levant Crisis, 1832," *Journal of Modern History* 24, no. 2 (June 1952), 145.

60. Quoted ibid., 150.

61. Palmerston, HPD, House of Commons, July 11, 1833, vol. 19, cols. 579–580.

62. Schroeder, *Transformation of European Politics*, 732.

63. Grey to Palmerston, April 23, 1833; and Grey to Palmerston, September 18, 1833, reprinted in Webster, *Foreign Policy of Palmerston*, 2:832–834.

64. Temperley, *England and the Near East*, 93.

65. Quoted in Marsot, *Egypt in the Reign of Mehmet Ali*, 221–222. See also Anderson, *Eastern Question*, 78.

66. Palmerston to William Temple, October 7, 1833, reprinted in Bourne, *Foreign Policy of Victorian England*, 222.

67. Palmerston to Posonby, December 6, 1833, reprinted in Baker and Viscount Palmerston, "Palmerston on the Treaty of Unkiar Skelessi," 89.

68. Palmerston to Lamb, October 16, 1834, reprinted in Frederick Stanley Rodkey, "The Views of Palmerston and Metternich on the Eastern Question in 1834," *English Historical Review* 45, no. 180 (October 1930), 638.

69. Bourne, *Palmerston: The Early Years*, 383.

70. Temperley, *England and the Near East*, 72, 93.

71. Palmerston to Canning, May 24, 1833, PP/GC/CA/259.

72. Palmerston to William Temple, October 7, 1833, reprinted in Bourne, *Foreign Policy of Victorian England*, 221.

73. Palmerston to Patrick Campbell, September 29, 1834, PP/GC/CA/61.

74. Verete, "Palmerston and the Levant Crisis," 150.

75. See Palmerston to Henry Bulwer, September 22, 1838, in Bulwer, *Life of Henry John Temple*, 2:286.

76. On the foreign secretary's fears of alignment between Egypt and France, see Palmerston to Granville, November 22, 1839, ibid., 305; and Palmerston to Granville, November 15, 1840, ibid., 351. On his fears of alignment between Egypt and Russia, see Temperley, *England and the Near East*, 94.

77. Palmerston, HPD, House of Commons, July 11, 1833, vol. 19, col. 580.

78. Schroeder, *Transformation of European Politics*, 742.

79. Bourne, *Foreign Policy of Victorian England*, 38; Gillard, *Struggle for Asia*, 57; Langer, *Political and Social Upheaval*, 297–298; Clayton, *Britain and the Eastern Question*, 17, 77; Anderson, *Eastern Question*, 97; Temperley, *England and the Near East*, 94–96; Seton-Watson, *Britain in Europe*, 192–193; and Marsot, *Egypt in the Reign of Mehmet Ali*, 242. In fact, by 1838, the viceroy's forces actually reached the Persian Gulf. In response, Great Britain warned Egypt against conquering Bahrain and preemptively occupied (and subsequently leased) the port of Aden.

80. Quoted in Verete, "Palmerston and the Levant Crisis," 149.

81. Webster, *Foreign Policy of Palmerston*, 1:287.

82. Temperley, *England and the Near East*, 64.

83. Verete, "Palmerston and the Levant Crisis," 147–148; Bourne, *Palmerston: The Early Years*, 375–376; Webster, *Foreign Policy of Palmerston*, 1:257; Gillard, *Struggle for Asia*, 36; and Cunningham, *Eastern Questions in the Nineteenth Century*, 54.

84. Stanley Lane-Poole, *The Life of the Right Honourable Stratford Canning, Viscount Stratford de Redcliffe, from His Memoirs and Private and Official Papers* (London: Longmans, Green, 1888), 1:426.

85. Cunningham, *Eastern Questions in the Nineteenth Century*, 51.

86. Canning to Palmerston, March 7, 1832, in Lane-Poole, *Life of the Right Honourable Stratford Canning*, 2:76–77.

87. Cunningham, *Eastern Questions in the Nineteenth Century*, 57–65, quotes at 57 and 60.

88. Palmerston to Posonby, December 6, 1833, quoted in Webster, *Foreign Policy of Palmerston*, 2:540.

89. Cunningham, *Eastern Questions in the Nineteenth Century*, 67; and Vernon John Puryear, *International Economics and Diplomacy in the Near East: A Study of British Commercial Policy in the Levant, 1834–1853* (Hamden, CT: Archon Books, 1969), 13.

90. Palmerston to William Temple, March 21, 1833, in Bulwer, *Life of Henry John Temple*, 2:145; and Palmerston to William Temple, April 19, 1833, ibid., 154.

91. Webster, *Foreign Policy of Palmerston*, 2:606–607; and Anderson, *Eastern Question*, 92.

92. Palmerston to Granville, June 5, 1838, in Bulwer, *Life of Henry John Temple*, 2:266.

93. Quoted in Temperley, *England and the Near East*, 90.

94. Palmerston to Henry Fox, May 10, 1836, PP/GC/FO/159.

95. Palmerston to Granville, June 8, 1838, in Bulwer, *Life of Henry John Temple*, 2:267.

96. Palmerston to Fox, May 10, 1836.

97. Palmerston to Charles Vaughan, April 10, 1837, PP/GC/VA/102.

98. Palmerston to Vaughan, May 11, 1837, quoted in Frederick Stanley Rodkey, "Lord Palmerston and the Rejuvenation of Turkey, 1830–41," *Journal of Modern History* 1, no. 4 (December 1929), 587.

99. Palmerston to Posonby, September 13, 1838, in Bulwer, *Life of Henry John Temple* 2:281.

100. Rodkey, "Lord Palmerston and the Rejuvenation of Turkey"; Puryear, *International Economics and Diplomacy in the Near East*, 53–58, 93–97; Webster, *Foreign Policy of Palmerston*, 2:544–548; and Gillard, *Struggle for Asia*, 45.

101. Ralston, *Importing the European Army*, 84.

102. Puryear, *International Economics and Diplomacy in the Near East*, chap. 3; Webster, *Foreign Policy of Palmerston*, 2:548–557, 613; Seton-Watson, *Britain in Europe*, 194–195; and Marsot, *Egypt in the Reign of Mehmet Ali*, 238.

103. Palmerston to Bulwer, September 22, 1838, in Bulwer, *Life of Henry John Temple*, 2:287. See also Palmerston to Bulwer, September 13, 1838, ibid., 285.

104. Palmerston to Bulwer, September 22, 1838, ibid., 286.

105. Palmerston to Bulwer, September 1, 1839, ibid., 299.

106. Temperley, *England and the Near East*, 105–106.

107. Palmerston, HPD, House of Commons, May 4, 1840, vol. 53, col. 1181.

108. Palmerston to Posonby, September 13, 1838, in Bulwer, *Life of Henry John Temple*, 2:281–282.

109. Quoted in Webster, *Foreign Policy of Palmerston*, 2:692.

110. Ibid., 648; Bourne, *Palmerston: The Early Years*, 580–581; and Temperley, *England and the Near East*, 148.

111. Palmerston to Bulwer, October 3, 1840, in Bulwer, *Life of Henry John Temple*, 2:333.

112. Langer, *Political and Social Upheaval*, 301.

113. Harold N. Ingle, *Nesselrode and the Russian Rapprochement with Britain, 1836–1844* (Berkeley: University of California Press, 1976), 106–111. The quote is from Marquess of Clanricarde to Palmerston, June 8, 1839, ibid., 110.

114. Puryear, *International Economics and Diplomacy in the Near East*, 152–160. French opposition gave Russia an added incentive to abandon Unkiar Skelessi in favor of a multilateral arrangement, insofar as this shift in policy had the potential to drive a wedge between Great Britain (which supported the new arrangement) and France (which did not). See Webster, *Foreign Policy of Palmerston*, 2:646, 671–672; Bourne, *Palmerston: The Early Years*, 579; and Anderson, *Eastern Question*, 98.

115. Webster, *Foreign Policy of Palmerston*, 2:653, 665, 708; and Bourne, *Palmerston: The Early Years*, 582–584, 596.

116. Bourne, *Palmerston: The Early Years*, 589.

117. Melbourne to Palmerston, July 4, 1840, reprinted in Webster, *Foreign Policy of Palmerston*, 2:857.

118. Sir Herbert Maxwell, *The Life and Letters of George William Frederick, Fourth Earl of Clarendon* (London: Edward Arnold, 1913), 1:186–191.

119. Quoted in Temperley, *England and the Near East*, 114. This was a point that Palmerston repeatedly emphasized in his correspondence with Great Britain's ambassador in Paris. See Palmerston to Granville, November 3, 1840; Palmerston to Granville, November 15, 1840; and Palmerston to Granville, November 20, 1840, in Bulwer, *Life of Henry John Temple*, 2:350–352. On the French views of Mehmet Ali's ability to withstand a British assault, see Anderson, *Eastern Question*, 100–101, 105.

120. Frederick Stanley Rodkey, "Lord Palmerston and the Rejuvenation of Turkey, 1830–1841: Part II, 1839–1841," *Journal of Modern History* 2, no. 2 (June 1930).

121. Palmerston to Bulwer, September 1, 1839, in Bulwer, *Life of Henry John Temple*, 2:298.

122. Lewis, *Emergence of Modern Turkey*, 106–108, quote at 106; and Hourani, *History of the Arab Peoples*, 272.

123. Quoted in Webster, *Foreign Policy of Palmerston*, 2:657.

124. Ibid., 686–690; and Bourne, *Palmerston: The Early Years*, 592.

125. Palmerston to Melbourne, July 5, 1840, in Bulwer, *Life of Henry John Temple*, 2:359–360 (emphasis in original).

126. Anderson, *Eastern Question*, 101; and Langer, *Political and Social Upheaval*, 302–303.

3. The Confederacy's Quest for Intervention and Independence, 1861–1862

1. Brian Holden Reid, "Power, Sovereignty, and the Great Republic: Anglo-American Diplomatic Relations in the Era of the Civil War," *Diplomacy & Statecraft* 14, no. 2 (2003), 66.

2. These figures are from Joseph L. Harsh, *Confederate Tide Rising: Robert E. Lee and the Making of Southern Strategy, 1861–1862* (Kent, OH: Kent State Press, 1998), 11.

3. Ephraim Douglass Adams, *Great Britain and the American Civil War* (Gloucester, MA: Peter Smith, 1957), 2:34.

4. Howard Jones, *Blue & Gray Diplomacy: A History of Union and Confederate Foreign Relations* (Chapel Hill: University of North Carolina Press, 2010), 232.

5. Frank J. Merli, *The Alabama, British Neutrality, and the American Civil War*, ed. David M. Fahey (Bloomington: Indiana University Press, 2004), 20. The historical narrative in this chapter draws on the work of several Civil War historians, especially James McPherson. See James M. McPherson, *Battle Cry of Freedom: The Civil War Era* (New York: Oxford University Press, 1988); James M. McPherson, *Antietam: Crossroads of Freedom* (New York: Oxford University Press, 2002); James M. McPherson, "Presidential Address: No Peace without Victory, 1861–1865," *American Historical Review* 109, no. 1 (February 2004); and James M. McPherson, *The Mighty Scourge: Perspectives on the Civil War* (New York: Oxford University Press, 2007).

6. On the defense of Canada during the Civil War period, see especially Kenneth Bourne, *Britain and the Balance of Power in North America, 1815–1908* (Berkeley: University of California Press, 1967), chaps. 7–8.

7. See, for example, Amanda Foreman, *A World on Fire: Britain's Crucial Role in the American Civil War* (New York: Random House, 2010), chaps. 1–3; and John Boyko, *Blood and Daring: How Canada Fought the Civil War and Forged a Nation* (Toronto: Alfred A. Knopf Canada, 2013), chap. 2.

8. To deter intervention on the part of Great Britain or any other power, Seward did indeed hint that the United States might be willing to provoke a foreign conflict that, he assumed, would bind the nation together against a common enemy. Just before the start of the Civil War, Seward actually proposed this course of action to Lincoln in a memo, although the president ignored his advice. See Jones, *Blue & Gray Diplomacy*, 23–28. For the text of Seward's memo and Lincoln's response, see *Lincoln: Addresses and Letters*, ed. Charles W. Moores (New York: American Book Company, 1914), 158–161.

9. Palmerston to Lewis, August 26, 1861, PP/LE/230.

10. See, for example, Lewis to Palmerston, August 27, 1861, PP/GC/LE/143; and Lewis to Palmerston, September 3, 1861, PP/GC/LE/144.

11. Dean B. Mahin, *One War at a Time: The International Dimensions of the American Civil War* (Dulles, VA: Brassey's, 1999).

12. Sven Beckert, "Emancipation and Empire: Reconstructing the Worldwide Web of Cotton Production in the Age of the American Civil War," *American Historical Review* 109, no. 5 (December 2004).

13. McPherson, *Battle Cry of Freedom*, 380–386.

14. Disraeli to Sarah Brydges Willyams, June 13, 1862, published in Benjamin Disraeli, *Letters: 1860–1864* (Toronto: University of Toronto Press, 2009), 194.

15. Beckert, "Emancipation and Empire."

16. Norman Graebner, "European Intervention and the Crisis of 1862," *Journal of the Illinois State Historical Society* 69, no. 1 (February 1976), 36.

17. Jones, *Blue & Gray Diplomacy*, 2.

18. Palmerston, HPD, House of Commons, July 18, 1862, vol. 168, col. 570.

19. Russell, HPD, House of Lords, March 23, 1863, vol. 169, col. 1734.

20. The constraining impact of opportunity costs on the European powers is an important theme in Colin Elman's explanation for how the United States was able to become a regional hegemon. See Elman, "Extending Offensive Realism."

21. Palmerston to Russell, January 19, 1862, cited in George L. Bernstein, "Special Relationship and Appeasement: Liberal Policy towards America in the Age of Palmerston," *Historical Journal* 41, no. 3 (1998), 741. See also Bourne, *Britain and the Balance of Power*, 252–253.

22. John Morley, *The Life of William Ewart Gladstone*, vol. 2, *1859–1880* (Toronto: Macmillan, 1903), 93.

23. Russell, HPD, House of Lords, February 5, 1863, vol. 169, col. 42 (emphasis added).

24. Recognizing the Confederacy as a belligerent power provided Richmond with more international rights than it would have received if the conflict were labeled an insurrection. In Washington, this infuriated officials like Seward, who thought that the decision overestimated the South's capabilities and might be a precursor to recognizing its independence. McPherson, *Battle Cry of Freedom*, 387–388; and Walter Stahr, *Seward: Lincoln's Indispensable Man* (New York: Simon & Schuster, 2012), 293–294.

25. Russell, HPD, House of Commons, May 2, 1861, vol. 162, col. 1379; and Russell, HPD, House of Commons, May 28, 1861, vol. 163, col. 195.

26. Palmerston to Russell, October 18, 1861, cited in Evelyn Ashley, *The Life and Correspondence of Henry John Temple, Viscount Palmerston* (London: Richard Bentley & Sons, 1879), 2:411.

27. Palmerston, HPD, House of Commons, February 6, 1862, vol. 165, col. 72.

28. Editorial, *Times*, September 17, 1861.

29. Editorial, *Morning Post*, July 30, 1862.

30. Palmerston to Edward Ellice, May 5, 1861, cited in Ashley, *Life and Correspondence of Henry John Temple*, 2:405.

31. Palmerston, HPD, House of Commons, June 30, 1862, vol. 167, col. 1214.

32. Russell, HPD, House of Lords, February 6, 1862, vol. 165, col. 45.

33. McPherson, *Mighty Scourge*, 66. See also Graebner, "European Intervention and the Crisis of 1862."

34. John Earl Russell, *Recollections and Suggestions, 1813–1873* (Boston: Roberts Brothers, 1875), 227–228. See also Russell to Lord Lyons, Foreign Office, May 11, 1861, in *BDFA*, part I, series C (North America, 1837–1914), vol. 5, *The Civil War Years, 1859–1862*, ed. Kenneth Bourne (Bethesda: University Publications of America, 1986), 199.

35. Quoted in Jones, *Blue & Gray Diplomacy*, 157.

36. On the Confederate military victories that preceded the British debate over intervention, see McPherson, *Antietam*, chaps. 1–3; and Richard Slotkin, *The Long Road to Antietam: How the Civil War Became a Revolution* (New York: Liveright, 2012).

37. Russell, HPD, House of Lords, June 13, 1862, vol. 167, col. 536.

38. Slotkin, *Long Road to Antietam*, chap. 1.

39. Editorial, *Times*, July 3, 1862; and Editorial, *Times*, August 29, 1862.

40. McPherson, *Mighty Scourge*, 70.

41. *Morning Post*, June 30, 1862; *Morning Post*, July 26, 1862; and *Morning Post*, July 22, 1862.

42. Palmerston, HPD, House of Commons, July 18, 1862, vol. 168, cols. 571, 573.

43. McPherson, *Mighty Scourge*, 71.

44. Slotkin, *Long Road to Antietam*, 73–81.

45. *Morning Post*, September 16, 1862.

46. Palmerston to Russell, September 14, 1862; Russell to Palmerston, September 17, 1862; and Palmerston to Russell, September 23, 1862; all cited in Spencer Walpole, *The Life of Lord John Russell* (London: Longmans, Green, 1889), 2:349–350. In Russell's view, Great Britain should propose to mediate in concert with France and Russia, if the two other powers would agree. See A. P. Newton, "Anglo-American Relations during the Civil War, 1860–1865," in *The Cambridge History of British Foreign Policy, 1783–1919*, ed. A. W. Ward and G. P. Gooch, vol. 2, *1815–1866* (Cambridge: Cambridge University Press, 1923), 510.

47. Slotkin, *Long Road to Antietam*.

48. *Morning Post*, September 26, 1862.

49. Palmerston to Russell, September 23, 1862.

50. Palmerston to William Gladstone, September 24, 1862, in Philip Guedalla, ed., *Gladstone and Palmerston: Being the Correspondence of Lord Palmerston with Mister Gladstone, 1851–1865* (New York: Books for Libraries Press, 1928), 233.

51. Palmerston to Russell, September 23, 1862.

52. Palmerston to Russell, September 30, 1862, quoted in Kinley J. Brauer, "British Mediation and the American Civil War: A Reconsideration," *Journal of Southern History* 38, no. 1 (February 1972), 58.

53. Editorial, *Times*, October 2, 1862.

54. Palmerston to Russell, October 2, 1862, cited in Adams, *Great Britain and the American Civil War*, 2:43–44.

55. "Mr. Gladstone at Newcastle," *Morning Post*, October 9, 1862.

56. Russell, Memorandum, Foreign Office, October 13, 1862, in *BDFA*, part I, series C (North America, 1837–1914), vol. 6, *The Civil War Years, 1862–1865*, ed. Kenneth Bourne (Bethesda: University Publications of America, 1986), 95–96.

57. Palmerston to Russell, October 22, 1862, cited in Adams, *Great Britain and the American Civil War*, 2:54–55. Leading Conservative politicians also held views that were very similar to those of Palmerston. See Wilbur Devereux Jones, "The British Conservatives and the American Civil War," *American Historical Review* 58, no. 3 (April 1953), 527–543.

58. McPherson, *Battle Cry of Freedom*, 556; and McPherson, *Mighty Scourge*, 73–74.

59. On this argument see, for example, John M. Owen, *Liberal Peace, Liberal War: American Politics and International Security* (Ithaca, NY: Cornell University Press, 1997), 133–136. Also emphasizing the impact of the Emancipation Proclamation is Brent J. Steele, "Ontological Security and the Power of Self-Identity: British Neutrality and the American Civil War, *Review of International Studies* 31, no. 3 (July 2005).

60. Abraham Lincoln, "A Letter from President Lincoln," *New York Tribune*, August 22, 1862.

61. Douglas A. Lorimer, "The Role of Anti-Slavery Sentiment in English Reactions to the American Civil War," *Historical Journal* 19, no. 2 (June 1976), 407.

62. Russell to Stuart, Foreign Office, August 7, 1862, in *BDFA*, part I, series C, vol. 6, 74.

63. Jones, *Blue & Gray Diplomacy*, chap. 7; Merli, *The Alabama, British Neutrality, and the American Civil War*, 22–23; and Reid, "Power, Sovereignty, and the Great Republic," 65–66. Public and political sentiment in Great Britain gradually became more favorable to Lincoln's proclamation, however, particularly after he carried out his promise in January 1863. See McPherson, *Battle Cry of Freedom*, 567.

64. Russell, Memorandum, 95.

65. Russell to Lyons, Foreign Office, January 17, 1863, in *BDFA*, part I, series C, vol. 6, 138.

66. Lorimer, "Role of Anti-Slavery Sentiment," 408 (emphasis added).

67. Jones, *Blue & Gray Diplomacy*, 290.

68. Interestingly, popular and elite views regarding the likely outcome of the war did not change dramatically in the wake of Antietam. Rather, the consensus remained that a Union victory was not likely given the inherent difficulties of subduing the South. "Already the Northern States are gradually awakening to the fact that two nations are not like two pike," one paper observed following the battle, "and that it does not follow because one is somewhat larger than the other that the larger can swallow and digest the smaller." As the year drew to a close, even Palmerston continued to believe that the conflict would ultimately result "in the separation of the south from the north." From his perspective, however, the Union's success at Antietam would only encourage it to fight on, even if its prospects for success were dim over the long run. See Editorial, *Times*, October 10, 1862; and Palmerston to Lewis, December 31, 1862, PP/GC/LE/251.

69. Russell, HPD, House of Commons, March 23, 1863, vol. 169, cols. 1734–1735, 1740–1741.

70. W. L. Morton, "British North America and a Continent in Dissolution, 1861–1871," *History* 47, no. 160 (January 1962), 152.

4. Japan and the Creation of a New Order in East Asia, 1894–1902

1. G. F. Hudson, "The Far East," in *The New Cambridge Modern History*, ed. J. P. T. Bury, vol. 10, *The Zenith of European Power, 1830–70* (Cambridge: Cambridge University Press, 1960), 708.

2. A. J. P. Taylor, *The Struggle for Mastery in Europe, 1848–1918* (Oxford: Oxford University Press, 1971), 391.

3. J. A. S. Grenville, *Lord Salisbury and Foreign Policy: The Close of the Nineteenth Century* (London: Athlone Press, 1964), 4.

4. George Curzon, HPD, House of Commons, March 1, 1898, vol. 54, col. 333.

5. Gillard, *Struggle for Asia*, 104–105; J. M. K. Vyvyan, "Russia in Europe and Asia," in *The New Cambridge Modern History*, 10:384; and John P. LeDonne, *The Russian Empire and the World, 1700–1917: The Geopolitics of Expansion and Containment* (New York: Oxford University Press, 1997), 178–185.

6. Ian Nish, *The Origins of the Russo-Japanese War* (New York: Longman, 1985), 15–17; and J. N. Westwood, *Russia against Japan, 1904–1905: A New Look at the Russo-Japanese War* (Albany: State University of New York Press, 1986), 3–4.

7. Taylor, *Struggle for Mastery in Europe*, 347.

8. Grenville, *Lord Salisbury and Foreign Policy*, 131; Hudson, "Far East," 701; and Kenneth Young, *British Policy in China, 1895–1902* (Oxford: Clarendon Press, 1970), 2–7.

9. Bourne, *Foreign Policy of Victorian England*, 5.

10. Inouye Yuichi, "From Unequal Treaty to the Anglo-Japanese Alliance, 1867–1902," in *The History of the Anglo-Japanese Alliance*, ed. Ian Nish and Yoichi Kibata, vol. 1, *The Political-Diplomatic Dimension, 1600–1930* (New York: Palgrave Macmillan, 2000), 131–132; and Ian Nish, "Politics, Trade and Communications in East Asia: Thoughts on Anglo-Russian Relations, 1861–1907," *Modern Asian Studies* 21, no. 4 (1987), 669.

11. William L. Langer, *The Diplomacy of Imperialism, 1890–1902*, 2nd ed. (New York: Alfred A. Knopf, 1965), 170. See also Charles Nelson Spinks, "The Background to the Anglo-Japanese Alliance," *Pacific Historical Review* 8, no. 3 (September 1939), 318–319.

12. Gillard, *Struggle for Asia*, 120–130; Hopkirk, *Great Game*, 314–315; LeDonne, *Russian Empire and the World*, 130–136; and A. P. Thorton, "Rivalries in the Mediterranean, the Middle East and Egypt," in *The New Cambridge Modern History*, ed. F. H. Hinsley, vol. 11, *Material Progress and World-Wide Problems, 1870–98* (Cambridge: Cambridge University Press, 1962), 575–576.

13. C. J. Lowe, *The Reluctant Imperialists: British Foreign Policy, 1878–1902* (New York: Macmillan, 1967), 75.

14. Hopkirk, *Great Game*, 353.

15. Gillard, *Struggle for Asia*, 155.

16. Gordon Martel, *Imperial Diplomacy: Rosebery and the Failure of Foreign Policy* (Kingston: McGill-Queen's University Press, 1986), 77. Interestingly, this is precisely how some policymakers in other nations saw Great Britain's relationship with China. During the Sino-Japanese War, for example, Germany's chancellor surmised that London's principal interest in the conflict was "to keep China as far as possible unharmed as a buffer State to protect India against a Russian advance." The Chancellor, Prince von Hohenlohe, to the Emperor, March 19, 1895, in *German Diplomatic Documents, 1871–1914*, selected and translated by E. T. S. Dugdale, vol. 3, *The Growing Antagonism, 1898–1910* (New York: Harper & Brothers, 1930), 7.

17. Martel, *Imperial Diplomacy*, 216–218.

18. Hudson, "Far East," 685.

19. Susan Mann Jones and Philip A. Kuhn, "Dynastic Decline and the Roots of Rebellion," in *The Cambridge History of China*, ed. John K. Fairbank, vol. 10, *Late Ch'ing 1800–1911, Part 1* (Cambridge: Cambridge University Press, 1978), 107–162.

20. Hudson, "Far East," 690.

21. Paul Kennedy, *The Rise and Fall of the Great Powers: Economic Change and Military Conflict from 1500 to 2000* (New York: Random House, 1987), 206. From the perspective of the British government, however, Japan was only a regional power, albeit an increasingly capable and ambitious one, at least until its success during the Russo-Japanese War in 1904–1905. See B. J. C. McKercher and D. J. Moss, "Introduction," in *Shadow and Substance in British Foreign Policy, 1895–1939: Memorial Essays Honouring C. J. Lowe*, ed. B. J. C. McKercher and D. J. Moss (Edmonton: University of Alberta Press, 1984), 7.

22. For an overview of these developments, see W. G. Beasley, "Japan," in *The New Cambridge Modern History*, 11:464–486; and W. G. Beasley, *The Rise of Modern Japan: Political, Economic, and Social Change since 1850*, 3rd ed. (New York: St. Martin's Press, 2000).

23. Langer, *Diplomacy of Imperialism*, 175.

24. Beasley, *Rise of Modern Japan*, 142.

25. W. G. Beasley, *Japanese Imperialism, 1894–1945* (New York: Oxford University Press, 1987), 43.

26. Langer, *Diplomacy of Imperialism*, 170; Beasley, *Japanese Imperialism*, 43–45; C. P. Fitzgerald, "China," in *New Cambridge Modern History*, 11:451; and Akira Iriye, "Japan's Drive to Great-Power Status," in *The Cambridge History of Japan*, ed. Marius B. Jansen, vol. 5, *The Nineteenth Century* (Cambridge: Cambridge University Press, 1989), 751–756.

27. Beasley, *Japanese Imperialism*, 47–48.

28. On the course of the war, the peace negotiations that followed, and the subsequent European intervention, see ibid., chaps. 4–5; Langer, *Diplomacy of Imperialism*, chap. 6; and S. C. M. Paine, *The Sino-Japanese War of 1894–1895: Perceptions, Power, and Primacy* (New York: Cambridge University Press, 2003).

29. Ian H. Nish, *The Anglo-Japanese Alliance: The Diplomacy of Two Island Empires, 1894–1907* (London: Athlone Press, 1966), 26. Even some policymakers in Tokyo had not expected to achieve major territorial gains when the war began. See Gillard, *Struggle for Asia*, 162; and Beasley, *Japanese Imperialism*, 55.

30. Nish, *Origins of the Russo-Japanese War*, 24.

31. Sir Frank Lascelles to Kimberley, St. Petersburg, April 10, 1895, in *BDFA*, part 1, series E (Asia, 1860–1914), vol. 5, *Sino-Japanese War and Triple Intervention, 1894–1895*, ed. Ian Nish (Bethesda: University Publications of America, 1989), 211.

32. Martel, *Imperial Diplomacy*, 79; and John Douglas Powell, *The Life of John Wodehouse, First Earl of Kimberley* (PhD diss., Texas Tech University, 1986), 332–337.

33. Kimberley to Ralph Paget, Foreign Office, June 23, 1894, in *BDFA*, part 1, series E (Asia, 1860–1914), vol. 4, *Sino-Japanese War, 1894*, ed. Ian Nish (Bethesda: University Publications of America, 1989), 28.

34. Kimberley to Paget, Foreign Office, June 28, 1894, ibid., 30. See also Langer, *Diplomacy of Imperialism*, 173–174; and Martel, *Imperial Diplomacy*, 216.

35. Kimberley to the Marquis of Dufferin, Foreign Office, July 7, 1894, in *BDFA*, part 1, series E, vol. 4, 40; and Kimberley to Henry Howard, Foreign Office, July 16, 1894, ibid., 57–58.

36. See Bourne, *Foreign Policy of Victorian England*, 154; Langer, *Diplomacy of Imperialism*, 173–175; Martel, *Imperial Diplomacy*, 219; and especially T. G. Otte, *The China Question: Great Power Rivalry and British Isolation, 1894–1905* (Oxford: Oxford University Press, 2007), 39–44.

37. Kimberley to Paget, Foreign Office, July 7, 1894, in *BDFA*, part 1, series E, vol. 4, 40.

38. Nish, *Anglo-Japanese Alliance*, 2; and Michio Asakawa, "Anglo-Japanese Military Relations, 1800–1900," in *The History of Anglo-Japanese Relations, 1600–2000*, ed. Ian Gow and Yoichi Hirama with John Chapman, vol. 3, *The Military Dimension* (New York: Palgrave Macmillan, 2000), 13–34.

39. Ralston, *Importing the European Army*, chap. 5; and Barton C. Hacker, "The Weapons of the West: Military Technology and Modernization in 19th-Century China and Japan," *Technology and Culture* 18, no. 1 (June 1977).

40. On public opinion before and during the war, see Langer, *Diplomacy of Imperialism*, 174; Paine, *Sino-Japanese War of 1894–1895*, 138; and Samuel Henry Jeyes, *The Earl of Rosebery* (London: J. M. Dent, 1906), 160.

41. "China and Japan," *Times*, July 24, 1894.

42. "Japan Anxious for a Fight," *New York Times* [reprinted from *Naval and Military Record*], July 30, 1894.

43. George N. Curzon, "The War in the East," *Times*, August 9, 1894. China and France had fought one another for control of Tonkin (present-day northern Vietnam) in the mid-1880s.

44. Memorandum by Francis Bertie, Foreign Office, July 12, 1894, in *BDFA*, part 1, series E, vol. 4, 46; and O'Conor to Kimberley, Peking, July 28, 1894, ibid., 81.

45. Admiralty to Foreign Office, "Comparative Statement of the Chinese and Japanese Navies," July 16, 1894, ibid., 54; and Intelligence Division to Foreign Office, "Memorandum on the Relative Values of the Armies of China and Japan," July 16, 1894, ibid., 55–56.

46. Rosebery's Memorandum on the Eve of the Sino-Japanese War, July 30, 1894, reprinted in Bourne, *Foreign Policy of Victorian England*, 434. See also Otte, *China Question*, 15.

47. Martel, *Imperial Diplomacy*, 217. See also Otte, *China Question*, 36.

48. Langer, *Diplomacy of Imperialism*, 174; and Lowe, *Reluctant Imperialists*, 192.

49. See, for example, "The War in the East," *Times*, September 19, 1894; and "The Naval Battle off Korea," *Times*, September 20, 1894.

50. Kimberley to O'Conor, Foreign Office, September 23, 1894, in *BDFA*, part 1, series E, vol. 4, 276; and O'Conor to Kimberley, Chefoo, September 25, 1894, ibid., 299.

51. "1894," *Times*, December 31, 1894.

52. See, for example, "Forces of China and Japan," *New York Times*, July 23, 1894; "Japan a More Powerful Nation," *New York Times*, July 29, 1894; "Predicts Japan's Success," *New York Times*, July 31, 1894; and "Numbers Will Probably Win," *New York Times*, August 2, 1894.

53. "The Japanese Victories," *New York Times*, September 22, 1894; and "Japan and Europe," *New York Times*, October 7, 1894.

54. O'Conor to Kimberley, Peking, November 12, 1894, in *BDFA*, part 1, series E, vol. 4, 341–342.

55. O'Conor to Kimberley, Peking, January 7, 1895, in *BDFA*, part 1, series E, vol. 5, 1–2.

56. Quoted in Otte, *China Question*, 52.

57. "Peace in the East," *Times*, April 17, 1895.

58. Paine, *Sino-Japanese War of 1894–1895*, 183.

59. Langer, *Diplomacy of Imperialism*, 385.

60. "Europe, Japan, and China," *Times*, April 23, 1895.

61. Martel, *Imperial Diplomacy*, 221–222.

62. Rosebery's Memorandum on the Eve of the Sino-Japanese War, reprinted in Bourne, *Foreign Policy of Victorian England*, 434. See also Otte, *China Question*, 36–37; Martel, *Imperial Diplomacy*, 216–217; and Keith Neilson, *Britain and the Last Tsar: British Policy and Russia, 1894–1917* (Oxford: Clarendon Press, 1995), 148.

63. Quoted in Martel, *Imperial Diplomacy*, 218.

64. Otte, *China Question*, 46, also 72–73.

65. Kimberley to P. H. Le Poer Trench, Foreign Office, April 24, 1895, in *BDFA*, part 1, series E, vol. 5, 228; and Kimberley to Gerard Lowther, Foreign Office, April 29, 1895, ibid., 261.

66. Rosebery, quoted in Neilson, *Britain and the Last Tsar*, 159.

67. Kimberley's Cabinet Report to the Queen, April 23, 1895, reprinted in Bourne, *Foreign Policy of Victorian England*, 435. The Yangtze River and its major ports, in particular Shanghai, were the center of British economic activity in China during the nineteenth century.

68. Langer, *Diplomacy of Imperialism*, 179, 386; Otte, *China Question*, 62; Nish, *Anglo-Japanese Alliance*, 31–33; and Beasley, *Japanese Imperialism*, 60–65.

69. Kimberley to Lascelles, Foreign Office, April 10, 1895, in *BDFA*, part 1, series E, vol. 5, 183; and Kimberly to O'Conor, Foreign Office, April 25, 1895, ibid., 229.

70. Rosebery to Kimberley, Private, April 10, 1895, reprinted in Gordon Martel, "Documenting the Great Game: 'World Policy' and the 'Turbulent Frontier' in the 1890s," *International History Review* 2, no. 2 (April 1980), 305.

71. Martel, *Imperial Diplomacy*, especially 67–76, 160–161, 218, 242–245.

72. Kimberley to Rosebery, Private, April 10, 1895, reprinted in Martel, "Documenting the Great Game," 306–307; Kimberley's Cabinet Report to the Queen, reprinted in Bourne, *Foreign Policy of Victorian England*, 435; and Kimberley to Lascelles, Foreign Office, April 10, 1895, in *BDFA*, part 1, series E, vol. 5, 183. In addition to risking a breach in relations with Russia, Great Britain was willing to risk the possibility that China might collapse if London did not come to its aid. Given the potential humanitarian consequences of this scenario, policymakers fretted about it publicly and privately. See Lord Rosebery, "Foreign Policy and the Little Englanders," Speech at the Cutlers' Feat, Sheffield, October 25, 1894, in *Lord Rosebery's Speeches, 1874–1896* (London: Neville Beeman, 1896), 257–258; and Kimberley to Trench, Foreign Office, February 8, 1895, in *BDFA*, part 1, series E, vol. 5, 57.

73. See especially Otte, *China Question*, 40.

74. Martel, *Imperial Diplomacy*, 218–220; and Otte, *China Question*, 37, 72–73.

75. *The Diaries of Sir Ernest Satow, British Minister in Tokyo (1895–1900): A Diplomat Returns to Japan*, 2nd ed., edited and annotated by Ian Ruxton (Morrisville, NC: Lulu Press, 2010), entry for May 31, 1895, 2; entry for June 28, 1895, 5; and entry for September 20, 1895, 21.

Despite his repeated references to "an alliance" between Great Britain and Japan, Kimberley apparently did not envision the type of formal arrangement that would develop between the two powers seven years later. See Otte, *China Question*, 71; and Martel, *Imperial Diplomacy*, 217, 244.

76. Kimberley, HPD, House of Lords, May 17, 1898, vol. 57, cols. 1510–1511.

77. Rosebery to Wemyss Reid, December 30, 1897, quoted in The Marquess of Crewe, *Lord Rosebery* (London: John Murray, 1931), 2:554.

78. Bourne, *Foreign Policy of Victorian England*, 154; and Powell, *Life of John Wodehouse*, 353–356.

79. Fitzgerald, "China," 11:453.

80. Grenville, *Lord Salisbury and Foreign Policy*, 304–305.

81. Langer, *Diplomacy of Imperialism*, 390. See also Taylor, *Struggle for Mastery in Europe*, 357; Gillard, *Struggle for Asia*, 164; and Neilson, *Britain and the Last Tsar*, 178–181.

82. Taylor, *Struggle for Mastery in Europe*, 373. See also Gillard, *Struggle for Asia*, 157; Langer, *Diplomacy of Imperialism*, 404; and Nish, *Origins of the Russo-Japanese War*, 30–31.

83. F. C. Langdon, "Expansion in the Pacific and the Scramble for China," in *New Cambridge Modern History*, 11:660. The scramble for concessions was actually initiated by France, which reached agreements with the Chinese government in 1895 that delineated the border between China and French-controlled Tonkin, provided France with the right of first refusal to exploit mines in southern China, and allowed Paris to build railroads from its colony in Southeast Asia across the border into China.

84. O'Conor to Salisbury, St. Petersburg, January 28, 1898, in *BD*, ed. G. P. Gooch and Harold Temperley, vol. 1, *The End of British Isolation* (London: His Majesty's Stationary Office, 1927), 7.

85. Nish, *Origins of the Russo-Japanese War*, 43. See also Gillard, *Struggle for Asia*, 163–165; and Langer, *Diplomacy of Imperialism*, 473.

86. Westwood, *Russia against Japan*, 14; and G. Patrick March, *Eastern Destiny: Russia in Asia and the North Pacific* (Westport, CT: Praeger, 1996), chap. 17.

87. "Japan and the European Concert in China," *Times*, March 21, 1901.

88. Otte, *China Question*, 222.

89. T. G. Otte, "A Question of Leadership: Lord Salisbury, the Unionist Cabinet and Foreign Policy Making, 1895–1900," *Contemporary British History* 14, no. 4 (Winter 2000).

90. Grenville, *Lord Salisbury and Foreign Policy*, 134–135. This view was not unique to Salisbury. Lansdowne, for example, acknowledged that the British government "had never concealed from ourselves that Russia had special interests in Manchuria, and was likely, whatever happened, to retain a predominant interest in that province, owing to her geographical position." Lansdowne to Claude MacDonald, Foreign Office, January 7, 1902, in *BD*, ed. G. P. Gooch and Harold Temperley, vol. 2, *The Anglo-Japanese Alliance and the Franco-British Entente* (London: His Majesty's Stationary Office, 1927), 109.

91. *Diaries of Sir Ernest Satow*, entry for October 6, 1897, 205.

92. Gillard, *Struggle for Asia*, 158; and Langer, *Diplomacy of Imperialism*, 400, 476. In addition, Russia's growing interest in China was viewed as a potentially useful distraction, one that might limit St. Petersburg's ability to challenge the status quo in other theaters. See Lowe, *Reluctant Imperialists*, 230; and Young, *British Policy in China*, 25, 41.

93. Salisbury, HPD, House of Lords, May 17, 1898, vol. 57, col. 1515.

94. Quoted in Otte, *China Question*, 99.

95. Salisbury to Satow, October 3, 1895, in *The Correspondence of Sir Ernest Satow, British Minister in Japan, 1895–1900*, ed. Ian Ruxton (Morrisville, NC: Lulu Press, 2005), 1:6–7. See also the comments in *Diaries of Sir Ernest Satow*, entry for June 4, 1897, 184; and, more generally, Nish, *Anglo-Japanese Alliance*, 40–41; and Otte, *China Question*, 83–84.

96. *Diaries of Sir Ernest Satow*, entry for October 13, 1897, 209.

97. Salisbury to O'Conor, Foreign Office, March 22, 1898, in *BD*, 1:23; Salisbury to O'Conor, March 24, 1898, ibid., 24–25; and Salisbury to O'Conor, March 28, 1898, ibid., 27–29.

98. Balfour to MacDonald, Foreign Office, March 19, 1898, ibid., 21–22.

99. Salisbury, HPD, House of Lords, May 17, 1898, vol. 57, col. 1516.

100. Balfour, HPD, House of Commons, April 5, 1898, vol. 56, col. 225.

101. Ibid., col. 238.

102. William L. Langer, "The Origins of the Russo-Japanese War," in *Explorations in Crisis*, ed. Carl Schorske and Elizabeth Schorske (Cambridge, MA: Harvard University Press, 1969), 17.

103. Salisbury to O'Conor, Foreign Office, January 25, 1898, in *BD*, 1:8.

104. Despite the failure of these talks, the two sides reached a more limited arrangement the following year: St. Petersburg pledged not to seek any railway concessions in the Yangtze Valley, while London pledged not to seek any similar concessions north of the Great Wall. See Taylor, *Struggle for Mastery in Europe*, 391; and Otte, *China Question*, 167–176.

105. On the Chinese offer and Salisbury's response, see MacDonald to Salisbury, Peking, February 25, 1898, in *BD*, 1:18; and Salisbury to MacDonald, Foreign Office, February 25, 1898, ibid.

106. Salisbury, HPD, House of Lords, May 17, 1898, vol. 57, col. 1520. On the decision to acquire Wei-Hai-Wei, see Nish, *Anglo-Japanese Alliance*, 53–57; Grenville, *Lord Salisbury and Foreign Policy*, 143–146; and T. G. Otte, "Great Britain, Germany, and the Far-Eastern Crisis of 1897–8," *English Historical Review* 110, no. 439 (1995).

107. Memorandum by Bertie, September 13, 1900, in *BDFA*, part 1, series E (Asia, 1860–1914), vol. 25, *Suppression of Boxers and Negotiations for China Settlement, August 1900–October 1900*, ed. Ian Nish (Bethesda: University Publications of America, 1994), 37.

108. Memorandum by Salisbury, May 29, 1901, in *BD*, 2:68–69 (emphasis in original). As Bertie observed, moreover, even while Great Britain was tied down in South Africa, no coalition of powers had emerged to challenge it. Memorandum by Bertie, November 9, 1901, ibid., 76.

109. Salisbury's minute, Memorandum by Lansdowne, December 6, 1901, ibid., 80.

110. Memorandum by Lansdowne, November 11, 1901, ibid., 78. The two powers did manage to reach a limited agreement in 1900 to maintain the Open Door in China "as far as they can exercise influence." This vaguely worded compromise was designed so that neither side would be obligated to enforce freedom of trade throughout Russia's sphere of interest in northern China. Although some British officials touted the agreement as an important step toward a true alliance, Germany's subsequent announcement that its terms did not apply to Manchuria rendered it largely worthless. On the Anglo-German agreement and the repeated efforts to forge an Anglo-German alliance, see Taylor, *Struggle for Mastery in Europe*, 392–393; Lowe, *Reluctant Imperialists*, 233; Grenville, *Lord Salisbury and Foreign Policy*, chaps. 7, 14–15; R. B. Mowat, "Great Britain and Germany in the Early Twentieth Century," *English Historical Review* 46, no. 183 (July 1931); H. W. Koch, "The Anglo-German Alliance Negotiations: Missed Opportunity or Myth?" *History* 54, no. 182 (October 1969); and Paul M. Kennedy, "German World Policy and the Alliance Negotiations with England, 1897–1900," *Journal of Modern History* 45, no. 4 (December 1973).

111. Gillard, *Struggle for Asia*, 169; Nish, *Anglo-Japanese Alliance*, 92, 99; and Akira Iriye, *Japan and the Wider World: From the Mid-Nineteenth Century to the Present* (London: Longman, 1997), 16–17.

112. "Russia and Manchuria," *Times*, November 6, 1900.

113. Quoted in Otte, *China Question*, 246.

114. Lansdowne to MacDonald, Foreign Office, January 30, 1902, in *BD*, 2:114.

115. Lansdowne to J. B. Whitehead, Foreign Office, October 16, 1901, ibid., 97.

116. Otte, *China Question*, 292; and Grenville, *Lord Salisbury and Foreign Policy*, chap. 17. In addition to making one last attempt to enlist German support, which was partly responsible for the delay of several months between the initial Lansdowne–Hayashi dialogue and more formal alliance discussions, London made a final effort to reach an agreement with St. Petersburg in late 1901 that would have limited its expansion in China (by requiring Russia to respect British treaty rights there) as well as Persia (by providing the shah with a joint Anglo-Russian loan that would prevent Russia from funding him on its own and gaining a preponderant influence over Tehran). There was little hope that this effort would succeed, however. In fact, Lansdowne proposed the agreement expecting that it would fail but calculating that this failure would increase support for an alliance with Japan, both in the cabinet and among the British public. See Zara S. Steiner, "Great Britain and the Creation of the Anglo-Japanese Alliance," *Journal of Modern History* 31, no. 1 (March 1959).

117. Memorandum by Bertie, Foreign Office, March 11, 1901, in *BD*, 2:43. On these concerns, see Nish, *Anglo-Japanese Alliance*, 145, 154; Grenville, *Lord Salisbury and Foreign Policy*, 337; Otte, *China Question*, 286–287; and especially Langer, *Diplomacy of Imperialism*, 782–783.

118. Grenville, *Lord Salisbury and Foreign Policy*, 344. See also Nish, *Anglo-Japanese Alliance*, 181.

119. See, for example, Lansdowne to MacDonald, Foreign Office, December 12, 1901, in *BD*, 2:103.

120. Grenville, *Lord Salisbury and Foreign Policy*, 402–403.

121. See, for example, Aaron L. Friedberg, *The Weary Titan: Britain and the Experience of Relative Decline, 1895–1905* (Princeton, NJ: Princeton University Press, 1988), chap. 4.

122. Grenville, *Lord Salisbury and Foreign Policy*, 402–404; Otte, *China Question*, 292–294; Nish, *Anglo-Japanese Alliance*, 174–176; and Lowe, *Reluctant Imperialists*, 246–247.

123. Ian Nish, "The First Anglo-Japanese Alliance Treaty," Discussion Paper No. IS/02/432, London School of Economics and Political Science (April 2002), http://eprints.lse.ac.uk/6884 /1/Anglo-Japanese_Alliance.pdf.

124. The impact of relative decline on British security policy remains controversial. For arguments that this factor has been overstated, see Gordon Martel, "The Meaning of Power: Rethinking the Decline and Fall of Great Britain," *International History Review* 13, no. 4 (November 1991); Keith Neilson, " 'Greatly Exaggerated': The Myth of the Decline of Great Britain before 1914," *International History Review* 13, no. 4 (November 1991); and Phillips Payson O'Brien, "The Titan Refreshed: Imperial Overstretch and the British Navy before the First World War," *Past and Present*, no. 172 (August 2001).

5. India's Rise and the Struggle for South Asia, 1962–1971

1. For an overview of American policy toward South Asia from the end of the Second World War through the 1960s, see Gary R. Hess, "Global Expansion and Regional Balances: The Emerging Scholarship on United States Relations with India and Pakistan," *Pacific Historical Review* 56, no. 2 (May 1987); Dennis Kux, *India and the United States: Estranged Democracies, 1941–1991* (Washington, DC: National Defense University/Sage Press, 1993); and Robert J. McMahon, *The Cold War on the Periphery: The United States, India, and Pakistan* (New York: Columbia University Press, 1996).

2. McMahon, *Cold War on the Periphery*, 308. As one intelligence report explained, China's objectives included not only "the acquisition of Taiwan" but also "the communizing of Japan and India," which were key steps toward its ultimate goal of undercutting U.S. power, undermining U.S. influence, and achieving hegemony throughout Asia. SNIE 13-3-61, "Chinese Communist Capabilities and Intentions in the Far East," November 30, 1961, 5 (DNSA Doc. CH00007).

3. During this period, Rawalpindi was the temporary capital of Pakistan while Islamabad was under construction.

4. Frank Leith Jones, *Blowtorch: Robert Komer, Vietnam, and American Cold War Strategy* (Annapolis, MD: Naval Institute Press, 2013).

5. Memorandum from Komer to McGeorge Bundy, "A New Look at Pakistani Tie," January 6, 1962, in *FRUS, 1961–1963*, vol. 19, *South Asia* (Washington, DC: Government Printing Office, 1996), 179–181.

6. Ibid., 180.

7. Transcript of an interview with Robert Komer, Lyndon Johnson Presidential Oral History Project, January 30, 1970, http://web2.millercenter.org/lbj/oralhistory/komer_robert _1970_0130.pdf, 7–8.

8. MemCon, "Political Consultation," June 21, 1961, 3:15 pm, in *FRUS, 1961–1963*, vol. 22, *Northeast Asia* (Washington, DC: Government Printing Office, 1996), 692.

9. Bureau of Near Eastern and South Asian Affairs, "United States Relations with South Asia: Major Issues and Recommended Courses of Action," no date, in *FRUS, 1961–1963*, 19:183; and Memorandum of Discussion, "Discussion on Pakistan–U.S. Relations," May 13, 1962, ibid., 244–245.

10. Komer to Carl Kaysen, November 16, 1962, 1 (DDRS Doc. CK3100329136).

11. Telegram from the Department of State to the Embassy in Pakistan, October 27, 1962, in *FRUS, 1961–1963*, 19:356.

12. Telegram from the Department of State to the Embassy in India, November 25, 1962, ibid., 406–407.

13. Telegram from the Department of State to the Embassy in India, December 6, 1962, ibid., 422. Although settling the Kashmir issue would enable India to redistribute its forces to the border with China and better defend against an assault from the north, it would also have another benefit: improving India's image in the eyes of Congress and reducing the domestic political barriers to receiving increased aid. See Department of State, "Estimate of Renewed Sino-Indian Border Conflict in 1963," March 1963, 4 (DNSA Doc. CH00008).

14. Memorandum from Komer to Phillips Talbot, October 24, 1962, p. 1 (DDRS Doc. CK3100462104). On U.S. assistance to India, see David R. Devereux, "The Sino-Indian War of 1962 in Anglo-American Relations," *Journal of Contemporary History* 44, no. 1 (2009).

15. Department of State, Bureau of Intelligence and Research, "The Five-Fold Problem: The Implications of the Sino-Indian Conflict," November 17, 1962, 22–23 (DDRS Doc. CK3100488466).

16. MemCon, "Sino-Indian Dispute," December 20, 1962, in *FRUS, 1961–1963*, 19:456.

17. Record of the 508th Meeting of the National Security Council, January 22, 1963, in *FRUS, 1961–1963*, vol. 8, *National Security Policy* (Washington, DC: Government Printing Office, 1996), 460.

18. Memorandum for the Record, "President's Meeting on India," April 25, 1963, in *FRUS, 1961–1963*, 19:563–564, quote at 563. See also Summary Record of the 514th Meeting of the National Security Council, May 9, 1963, ibid., 583–588.

19. Memorandum from Rusk to Kennedy, "Air Defense for India," May 8, 1963, ibid., 580.

20. Instructions for Under Secretary George Ball's Mission to Pakistan, August 28, 1963, 2 (DDRS Doc. CK3100284527).

21. Memorandum from Komer to Johnson, February 26, 1964, in *FRUS, 1964–1968*, vol. 25, *South Asia* (Washington, DC: Government Printing Office, 1999), 45–46.

22. Transcript of an interview with Robert Komer, Lyndon Johnson Presidential Oral History Project, November 15, 1971, http://web2.millercenter.org/lbj/oralhistory/komer_robert _1971_1115.pdf, 4.

23. Johnson to Bowles, January 21, 1964, in *FRUS, 1964–1968*, 25:13; and Bundy to Bowles, March 9, 1964, ibid., 51.

24. MemCon, "Meeting on China Study," August 27, 1965, in *FRUS, 1964–1968*, vol. 30, *China* (Washington, DC: Government Printing Office, 2000), 201; and Joint Chiefs of Staff Memorandum 41-65, "Possible Responses to the ChiCom Nuclear Threat," January 16, 1965, ibid., 145.

25. In fact, most of these worrisome developments did occur eventually. Pakistan, for example, reached a border agreement with China in 1962, ceding territory to Beijing that was claimed by India, and closed most of the facilities used by the United States following the Second Kashmir War in 1965. For its part, India sought increased Soviet support, in particular military hardware, to modernize its forces after the Sino-Indian War.

26. Memorandum from Komer to Johnson, "Our Pakistan Affairs," April 22, 1965, 3 (DDRS Doc. CK3100500182).

27. See, for example, Memorandum for the Record, September 24, 1964, in *FRUS, 1964–1968*, 25:161.

28. Memo, Department of State, "What Do We Want in Pakistan?" July 16, 1965, 1 (DDRS Doc. CK3100161549).

29. MemCon, "President's Conversation with Ambassador McConaughy," July 15, 1964, in *FRUS, 1964–1968*, 25:138. Johnson also questioned the value of U.S. aid to India, although he determined that Washington was "set on that course and would see it through." Ibid.

30. Memo, Department of State, March 8, 1964, 1 (DDRS Doc. CK3100531341).

31. On the origins of the Second Kashmir War, see Sumit Ganguly, *Conflict Unending: India–Pakistan Tensions since 1947* (New York: Columbia University Press, 2001), chap. 2.

32. Johnson Telephone Conversation with Bundy, May 31, 1965, no. 7848, http://millercenter.org/scripps/archive/presidentialrecordings/johnson/1965/05_1965; and Editorial Note, in *FRUS, 1964–1968*, 25:339.

33. Transcript, Dean Rusk Oral History Interview III, January 2, 1970, tape 1–26, Lyndon B. Johnson Library, http://web2.millercenter.org/lbj/oralhistory/rusk_dean_1970_0102.pdf.

34. Memorandum for the Record, "Meeting with the President on Ball Mission to Pakistan," September 9, 1963, in *FRUS, 1961–1963*, 19:677.

35. NIE 31-64, "The Prospects for India," December 10, 1964, in *FRUS, 1964–1968*, 25:169.

36. Ganguly, *Conflict Unending*, 45.

37. Memorandum from Komer to Johnson, "Pak/Indian Roundup," September 7, 1965, in *FRUS, 1964–1968*, 25:368; and Memorandum from Komer to Johnson, "Pak/Indian Roundup," September 10, 1965, ibid., 383.

38. Memorandum from Rusk to Johnson, "India and Pakistan," September 9, 1965, ibid., 376–377.

39. Johnson Telephone Conversation with McNamara, September 12, 1965, Johnson Tapes, no. 8851, http://millercenter.org/scripps/archive/presidentialrecordings/johnson/1965/09_1965.

40. Kux, *Estranged Democracies*, 238. Likewise, Sumit Ganguly notes that the result of the war was "far from decisive." Ganguly, *Conflict Unending*, 72. According to U.S. intelligence estimates, however, the military balance between the two sides was more lopsided after the war ended than before it began. SNIE 31-32-65, "Indo-Pakistani Reactions to Certain US Courses of Action," December 7, 1965, in *FRUS, 1964–1968*, 25:489.

41. Memorandum from Bundy and Komer to Johnson, "India and Pakistan," October 5, 1965, in *FRUS, 1964–1968*, 25:446; and Memorandum from Komer to Johnson, November 16, 1965, ibid., 469 (emphasis in original).

42. See Johnson Telephone Conversation with McNamara, September 12, 1965; and SNIE 13-10-65, "Prospects of Chinese Communist Involvement in the Indo-Pakistan War," September 16, 1965, 1 (DDRS Doc. CK3100130731).

43. Washington continued to provide economic assistance to both sides along with a very modest amount of military assistance. In October 1970, however, it made an exception to its ban on lethal military aid to Pakistan, agreeing to provide Islamabad with several hundred armored personnel carriers, among other items.

44. On the origins of the war, see Ganguly, *Conflict Unending*, chap. 3; and Onkar Marwah, "India's Military Intervention in East Pakistan, 1971–1972," *Modern Asian Studies* 13, no. 4 (1979).

45. Sumit Ganguly, "Pakistan's Forgotten Genocide—A Review Essay," *International Security* 39, no. 2 (Fall 2014), 170.

46. Ganguly, *Conflict Unending*, 67–69.

47. Memorandum from Harold Saunders and Samuel Hoskinson to Kissinger, "Situation in Pakistan," March 1, 1971, in *FRUS, 1969–1976*, vol. 11, *South Asia Crisis, 1971* (Washington, DC: Government Printing Office, 2005), 4–5; and Minutes of Senior Review Group Meeting, "Pakistan," March 6, 1971, ibid., 10.

48. Minutes of Washington Special Actions Group Meeting, "Pakistan," March 26, 1971, ibid., 26.

49. Transcript of a Telephone Conversation between Nixon and Kissinger, March 30, 1971, ibid., 37; and Conversation among Nixon, Kissinger, and H. R. Haldeman, White House Tapes, April 12, 1971, cited ibid., 65.

50. Memorandum from Saunders to Kissinger, "Pakistan–A Personal Reflection on the Choice Before Us," April 19, 1971, ibid., 85; and MemCon, June 3, 1971, ibid., 166.

51. CIA Weekly Summary, "India-Pakistan: Danger of War Persists," November 12, 1971, 2 (DDRS Doc. CK3100331047).

52. Memorandum from Kissinger to Nixon, "Policy Options Toward Pakistan," April 28, 1971, in *FRUS, 1969–1976*, 11:94–98, quote at 96.

53. MemCon, June 3, 1971, ibid., 164.

54. MemCon, May 21, 1971, ibid., 130; and Minutes of Senior Review Group Meeting, "South Asia," July 23, 1971, ibid., 271. Specifically, Nixon and Kissinger decided that the United States

would cut off all economic aid to India if it conducted an overt military intervention in East Pakistan and communicated their position to the government in New Delhi. See Transcript of a Phone Conversation between Nixon and Kissinger, May 23, 1971, ibid., 140; Minutes of a Washington Special Actions Group Meeting, "South Asia," September 8, 1971, ibid., 404; and Minutes of a Washington Special Actions Group Meeting, "India and Pakistan," October 7, 1971, ibid., 442.

55. Minutes of a Washington Special Actions Group Meeting, "Pakistan," May 26, 1971, ibid., 155. In his memoirs, Kissinger argued that the United States had "every incentive to maintain Pakistan's goodwill. It was our crucial link to Peking; and Pakistan was one of China's closest allies." Henry Kissinger, *White House Years* (Boston: Little, Brown, 1979), 853.

56. Transcript of Telephone Conversation between Rogers and Kissinger, December 5, 1971, in *FRUS, 1969–1976*, 11:634.

57. Conversation between Nixon and Kissinger, December 8, 1971, in *FRUS, 1969–1976*, vol. E-7, *Documents on South Asia, 1969–1972*, Doc. 166. Documents from this volume are available at https://history.state.gov/historicaldocuments/frus1969-76ve07.

58. Transcript of a Telephone Conversation between Nixon and Kissinger, December 4, 1971, in *FRUS, 1969–1976*, 11:614.

59. Conversation among Nixon, Kissinger, and Attorney General Mitchell, December 8, 1971, in *FRUS, 1969–1976*, vol. E-7, Doc. 165.

60. Kissinger, *White House Years*, 848.

61. MemCon, July 7, 1971, in *FRUS, 1969–1976*, 11:230.

62. National Security Council Staff, "Contingency Planning on South Asia," July 12, 1971, ibid., 249–250. See also National Security Council Staff, "Contingency Paper–Indo-Pakistan Hostilities," August 17, 1971, ibid., 335.

63. MemCon, September 11, 1971, ibid., 408; and Minutes of a Washington Special Actions Group Meeting, "South Asia," November 24, 1971, ibid., 552.

64. CIA, "Implications of an Indian Victory over Pakistan," December 9, 1971, 1 (DDRS Doc. CK3100536783).

65. Memorandum for the Record, "NSC Meeting on the Middle East and South Asia," July 16, 1971, in *FRUS, 1969–1976*, 11:265. See also MemCon, July 30, 1971, ibid., 303–305; and Minutes of Washington Special Actions Group Meeting, "India and Pakistan," October 7, 1971, ibid., 441.

66. Ganguly, *Conflict Unending*, 51–52, 72.

67. Conversation among Nixon, Kissinger, and Ambassador to Pakistan Joseph Farland, July 28, 1971, in *FRUS, 1969–1976*, vol. E-7, Doc. 141.

68. Conversation among Nixon, Kissinger, and Rogers, November 24, 1971, ibid., Doc. 156.

69. Minutes of Washington Special Actions Group Meeting, "South Asia," December 1, 1971, in *FRUS, 1969–1976*, 11:586.

70. Kissinger, *White House Years*, 866.

71. Memorandum from John Irwin to Nixon, "Indo-Soviet Treaty of Peace, Friendship and Cooperation," August 9, 1971, in *FRUS, 1969–1976*, 11:314–315; MemCon, August 9, 1971, ibid., 316; and Memorandum from Kissinger to Nixon, "Indo-Soviet Friendship Treaty," August 24, 1971, ibid., 362–364.

72. Memorandum for the President's File, "Meeting between President Nixon, Prime Minister Indira Gandhi, Mr. Parmeshwar Narain Haksar and Dr. Henry A. Kissinger," November 4, 1971, ibid., 496.

73. Conversation among Nixon, Kissinger, and Haldeman, November 5, 1971, in *FRUS, 1969–1976*, vol. E-7, Doc. 150.

74. CIA Information Cable, "Indian Prime Minister Indira Gandhi's Briefing on the Indo-Pakistani War," December 7, 1971, in *FRUS, 1969–1976*, 11:687. As one former policymaker involved in the American deliberations notes, however, "Nixon and Kissinger were virtually alone in the U.S. government in interpreting the report as they did." In fact, "There is no evidence for Kissinger's claim that India had a definite war aim to dismember West Pakistan." Christopher Van Hollen, "The Tilt Policy Revisited: Nixon–Kissinger Geopolitics and South Asia," *Asian Survey* 20,

no. 4 (April 1980), 351–352. For a similar critique, see Raymond L. Garthoff, *Détente and Confrontation: American–Soviet Relations from Nixon to Reagan*, rev. ed. (Washington, DC: Brookings, 1994), 300–301.

75. Richard M. Nixon, *Third Annual Report to the Congress on United States Foreign Policy*, February 9, 1972, http://www.presidency.ucsb.edu/ws/index.php?pid=3736&st=pakistan&st1=#axzz1YuLGMuM6.

76. Minutes of Washington Special Actions Group Meeting, "South Asia," December 8, 1971, in *FRUS, 1969–1976*, 11:695.

77. Robert Dallek, *Nixon and Kissinger: Partners in Power* (New York: HarperCollins, 2007), 337.

78. Minutes of Washington Special Actions Group Meeting, "South Asia," December 8, 1971.

79. Conversation between Nixon and Kissinger, December 9, 1971, in *FRUS, 1969–1976*, vol. E-7, Doc. 168.

80. Transcript of a Telephone Conversation between Kissinger and Secretary of the Treasury John Connally, December 5, 1971 (DNSA Doc. KA07005). See also Transcript of a Telephone Conversation between Nixon and Kissinger, December 5, 1971, in *FRUS, 1969–1976*, 11:644.

81. MemCon between Nixon, Kissinger, and French President Georges Pompidou, December 13, 1971, quoted in Dennis Kux, *The United States and Pakistan, 1957–2000: Disenchanted Allies* (Baltimore: Johns Hopkins University Press, 2001), 203. The CIA was skeptical about this line of argument, however, and maintained that the Soviet Union would not encourage nations like Egypt to engage in more aggressive behavior even if India were able to defeat Pakistan. CIA, "Implications of an Indian Victory over Pakistan," 9–10.

6. The Emergence of Iraq and the Competition to Control the Gulf, 1979–1991

1. Gary Sick, "The United States in the Persian Gulf: From Twin Pillars to Dual Containment," in *The Middle East and the United States: A Historical and Political Assessment*, 3rd ed., ed. David W. Lesch (Boulder, CO: Westview, 2003), 291. See also Thomas L. McNaugher, *Arms and Oil: U.S. Military Strategy and the Persian Gulf* (Washington, DC: Brookings, 1985), chap. 1.

2. On Great Britain's historical role in the Persian Gulf, see Robert Johnson, "The Great Game and Power Projection," in *Imperial Crossroads: The Great Powers and the Persian Gulf*, ed. Jeffrey R. Macris and Saul Kelly (Annapolis, MD: Naval Institute Press, 2012), 31–48; and Saul Kelly, "The Gamekeeper versus the Mercenary Spirit: The Pax Britannica in the Gulf," ibid., 49–59.

3. Paper Prepared by the National Security Staff, "Persian Gulf," June 4, 1970, in *FRUS, 1969–1976*, vol. 24, *The Middle East Region and Arabian Peninsula, 1969–1972; Jordan, September 1970* (Washington, DC: U.S. Government Printing Office, 2008), 258.

4. On the Nixon Doctrine, see Henry Kissinger, *Diplomacy* (New York: Simon & Schuster, 1994), chap. 28; and Jeffrey Kimball, "The Nixon Doctrine: A Saga of Misunderstanding," *Presidential Studies Quarterly* 36, no. 1 (March 2006). The decision to rely on Iran and Saudi Arabia to protect the region was actually taken during the Johnson administration, shortly after Great Britain's intention to withdraw from the area became known, even though this strategy is often associated with the Nixon administration, which embraced and extended it. See Jeffrey Macris, "Why Didn't America Replace the British in the Persian Gulf?" in Macris and Kelly, *Imperial Crossroads*, 67–68.

5. McNaugher, *Arms and Oil*, 12. See also Sick, "United States in the Persian Gulf," 292.

6. Department of State, "Future U.S. Policy in the Persian Gulf," February 5, 1970, pp. 13–15 (DNSA Doc. PR00508). There was, moreover, an assumption that the Soviet Union would attempt to exploit Great Britain's withdrawal to extend its own influence in the region. See ibid., 9.

7. Sick, "United States in the Persian Gulf," 292; James A. Bill, *The Eagle and the Lion: The Tragedy of American–Iranian Relations* (New Haven, CT: Yale University Press, 1988), 197–203;

and Stephen McGlinchey, "Richard Nixon's Road to Tehran: The Making of the U.S.–Iran Arms Agreement of May 1972," *Diplomatic History* 37, no. 4 (September 2013).

8. Memorandum from Kissinger to Nixon, "The Persian Gulf," October 22, 1970, in *FRUS, 1969–1976*, vol. E-4, *Documents on Iran and Iraq, 1969–1972*, Doc. 91, https://history.state.gov /historicaldocuments/frus1969-76ve04/d91.

9. National Security Decision Memorandum 92, "U.S. Policy toward the Persian Gulf," November 7, 1970, in *FRUS, 1969–1976*, 24:286.

10. Quoted in Douglas Little, *American Orientalism: The United States and the Middle East since 1945* (Chapel Hill: University of North Carolina Press, 2008), 146.

11. NIE 34-1-75, "Iran," May 9, 1975, in *FRUS, 1969–1976*, vol. 27, *Iran; Iraq, 1973–1976* (Washington, DC: Government Printing Office, 2012), 348. The shah's ambitions to reduce or eliminate the U.S. naval presence in and around the Persian Gulf surfaced soon after Great Britain announced its impending withdrawal from the region. See Macris, "Why Didn't America Replace the British in the Persian Gulf?" 68–72.

12. Zbigniew Brzezinski, *Power and Principle: Memoirs of the National Security Advisor, 1977–1981* (New York: Farrar, Straus & Giroux, 1983), 356; and Cyrus Vance, *Hard Choices: Critical Years in America's Foreign Policy* (New York: Simon & Schuster, 1983), 314.

13. Brzezinski to Carter, "Reflections on Soviet Intervention in Afghanistan," December 26, 1979, 1–2 (DDRS Doc. CK3100098563).

14. CIA, "The Soviet Union and Southwest Asia," January 15, 1980, 1, 3 (DDRS Doc. CK3100685165).

15. Ibid.; and Paul Henze to Brzezinski, "Iran and the Soviets," April 11, 1980, 1 (DDRS Doc. CK3100469805).

16. Jimmy Carter, "The State of the Union Address Delivered before a Joint Session of Congress," January 23, 1980, *American Presidency Project*, http://www.presidency.ucsb.edu/ws /?pid=33079.

17. For an overview of these measures and their origins, see Thomas L. McNaugher, "Balancing Soviet Power in the Persian Gulf," *Brookings Review* 1, no. 4 (Summer 1983); Michael A. Palmer, *Guardians of the Gulf: A History of America's Expanding Role in the Persian Gulf, 1833–1992* (New York: Free Press, 1992), chap. 5; William E. Odom, "The Cold War Origins of the U.S. Central Command," *Journal of Cold War Studies* 8, no. 2 (Spring 2006); and Frank L. Jones, "In Brzezinski's Forge: Fashioning the Carter Doctrine's Military Instrument," in Macris and Kelly, *Imperial Crossroads*, 109–128.

18. Jimmy Carter, "Foreign Policy Radio Address to the Nation," October 19, 1980, http:// www.presidency.ucsb.edu/ws/index.php?pid=45327&st=hormuz&st1=#axzz1YuLGMuM6.

19. Relations between Iraq and the Soviet Union grew more distant after the early 1970s, however, due to the Baath Party's opposition to Iraqi communists and Baghdad's efforts to diversify its arms suppliers. See Marvine Howe, "Iraq Edging away from Soviet and Restoring Links with West," *New York Times*, February 3, 1980.

20. Memorandum from William Quandt and Gary Sick to Brzezinski, "Four-Year Goals in the Middle East," February 2, 1977, in *FRUS, 1977–1980*, vol. 18, *Middle East Region; Arabian Peninsula* (Washington, DC: Government Printing Office, 2015), 3–4. See also Memorandum from Brzezinski to Carter, "U.S. Relations with Libya and Iraq," February 24, 1977, ibid., 420–421. On the Carter administration's efforts to improve ties with Iraq before the Iranian revolution, see Hal Brands, "Before the Tilt: The Carter Administration Engages Saddam Hussein," *Diplomacy and Statecraft* 26, no. 1 (2015).

21. Minutes of a Special Coordination Committee Meeting, "Middle East Security Issues," May 11, 1979, in *FRUS, 1977–1980*, 18:76.

22. Memorandum from Peter Tarnoff to Brzezinski, "U.S. Relations with the Radical Arabs," January 16, 1980, quote at 7 (DDRS Doc. CK3100664598).

23. Richard Burt, "U.S. Officials Say Iraq Is Harboring Iranians Seeking to Oust Khomeini," *New York Times*, April 10, 1980; Jonathan C. Randal, "Iraq Rebuffs U.S. on Formal Links," *Washington Post*, May 12, 1980; Michael Getler, "Objections Overridden, Warship Turbines Will Be Sold to Iraq," *Washington Post*, August 2, 1980; Bernard Gwertzman, "U.S. May Let Iraq Buy Jets

Despite Terrorism Question," *New York Times*, August 6, 1980; and Lee Lescaze, "U.S. Stops Shipment of Turbines to Iraq," *Washington Post*, September 26, 1980. The Carter administration also considered but ultimately opposed the sale of five Boeing commercial jets to Iraq in the summer of 1980.

24. Brzezinski to Stu Eizenstat, "Naval Engine Sales to Iraq," March 14, 1980 (DDRS Doc. CK3100084963). See also William Odom to Brzezinski, "Eizenstat Memorandum on Iraq," March 13, 1980 (DDRS Doc. CK3100084962).

25. Brzezinski interview, April 14, 1980, quoted in Sandra Mackey, *The Reckoning: Iraq and the Legacy of Saddam Hussein* (New York: W. W. Norton, 2002), 339.

26. Stephen M. Walt, *Revolution and War* (Ithaca, NY: Cornell University Press, 1997).

27. On the origins and course of the war, see Efraim Karsh, "Military Power and Foreign Policy Goals: The Iran–Iraq War Revisited," *International Affairs* 64, no. 1 (Winter 1987/88); and Gary Sick, "Trial by Error: Reflections on the Iran–Iraq War," *Middle East Journal* 43, no. 2 (Spring 1989).

28. Palmer, *Guardians of the Gulf*, 109.

29. Brzezinski, *Power and Principle*, 452–454.

30. Amatzia Baram, "U.S. Input into Iraqi Decisionmaking, 1988–1990," in *The Middle East and the United States: A Historical and Political Reassessment*, ed. David W. Lesch (Boulder, CO: Westview Press, 1996), 325.

31. Hal Brands, "Saddam Hussein, the United States, and the Invasion of Iran: Was There a Green Light?" *Cold War History* 12, no. 2 (May 2012), 319–343; and Christian Emery, "United States Iran Policy 1979–1980: The Anatomy and Legacy of American Diplomacy," *Diplomacy & Statecraft* 24, no. 4 (2013), 619–639.

32. Quoted in Bernard Gwertzman, "U.S. Warns Iraq on Seizing Oil Region," *New York Times*, September 29, 1980. See also Internal State Department Memo, "U.S. Policy toward Iran," February 15, 1980 (DDRS Doc. CK3100112391).

33. Interagency Intelligence Memorandum 79-10026, "New Realities in the Middle East," December 1979, in *FRUS, 1977–1980*, 18:128.

34. Michael Getler, "Iraq Gets Key Regional Role as Iran's Military Deteriorates," *Washington Post*, April 11, 1980; and Drew Middleton, "Iran and Iraq Test Mettle," *New York Times*, September 23, 1980.

35. CIA, "Iran and the USSR after the Shah," August 17, 1979, 2 (DDRS Doc. CK3100219663).

36. CIA, "Iran: Decline in Air Force Capability," May 1, 1980, 6 (DDRS Doc. CK3100581867).

37. CIA, "Prospects for Escalation of Iran–Iraq Conflict," September 22, 1980, 2 (DDRS Doc. CK3100669141).

38. Jimmy Carter, "Situation in Iraq and Iran Remarks Concerning the Conflict," September, 24, 1980, http://www.presidency.ucsb.edu/ws/index.php?pid=45129&st=hormuz&st1=#axzz1YuLGMuM6.

39. Sick, "Trial by Error," 239.

40. NSDD 99, "United States Security Strategy for the Near East and South Asia," July 12, 1983, 1 (NARA Doc. 6879698).

41. SNIE 34/36.2-83, "Iran–Iraq War: Increased Threat to Persian Gulf Oil Exports," October 13, 1983, 4 (CIA FOIA Doc. 0001220927).

42. NSDD 114, "U.S. Policy toward the Iran–Iraq War," November 26, 1983 (DNSA Doc. PR01512).

43. Brzezinski to Carter, "Reflections on Soviet Intervention in Afghanistan," 2.

44. NIE 11/4-82, "The Soviet Challenge to U.S. Security Interests," August 10, 1982, 24–25 (NARA Doc. 7327152); and Defense Intelligence Agency, "Afghan Resistance," November 5, 1982 (DNSA Doc. AF01397).

45. SNIE 11/30-83, "Soviet Policy in the Middle East and South Asia under Andropov," February 8, 1983, 13 (NARA Doc. 7327022).

46. Statement of William A. Brown, Deputy Assistant Secretary of State for East Asian and Pacific Affairs, "The Soviet Role in Asia," October 19, 1983, reprinted in *Current Policy*, no. 521, 2 (DNSA Doc. AF01504).

47. NIE 11-19-85/D, "Soviet Strategy and Capabilities for Multitheater War," June 1985, 30 (NARA Doc. 7327313).

48. CIA, "Iran–Iraq War: Status, Impact, and Prospects," November 20, 1981, 2, 7 (CIA FOIA Doc. 0001267222). See also SNIE 36.2-83, "Prospects for Iraq," July 19, 1983 (CIA FOIA Doc. 0001220920).

49. Department of State, "Iran–Iraq War: U.S. Responses to Escalation Scenarios and Threats to Persian Gulf States," March 20, 1984, 11 (DDRS Doc. CK3100676774).

50. Department of State, "The Iran–Iraq Conflict: Status and Prospects," February 13, 1981, 1–3 (DNSA Doc. HN02021).

51. CIA, "Possible Outcomes and Implications of Iran–Iraq War," May 12, 1982, 1 (CIA FOIA Doc. 0000763742).

52. SNIE 36.2-83, "Prospects for Iraq," 7.

53. SNIE 34/36.2-86, "Is Iraq Losing the War?" April 1986, 1, 13 (CIA FOIA Doc. 0001078094).

54. Cable, Department of State, "Acting Secretary's September 7 Meeting with Iraqi Under Secretary Kittani," September 9, 1983 (DDRS Doc. CK3100641423).

55. Cable, Department of State, "Turkey's Assessment of Iran," June 21, 1984 (DDRS Doc. CK3100671398).

56. Memorandum from Nicholas Veliotes and Jonathan Howe to Eagleburger, "Iran–Iraq War: Analysis of Possible U.S. Shift from Position of Strict Neutrality," October 7, 1983, 2, 7–8 (DNSA Doc. IG00139).

57. Cable, Department of State, "Rumsfeld One-on-One Meeting with Iraqi Deputy Prime Minister and Foreign Minister Tariq Aziz," December 21, 1983 (DNSA Doc. IG00157); and Cable, Department of State, "Rumsfeld Mission: December 20 Meeting with Iraqi President Saddam Hussein," December 21, 1983 (DNSA Doc. IG00156).

58. Cable, Department of State, "Follow-up on Rumsfeld Visit to Baghdad," December 26, 1983 (DNSA Doc. IG00160). The Interests Section, which was based in the Belgian embassy, represented the United States in Baghdad after Iraq broke off diplomatic relations with Washington in 1967.

59. MemCon, "Secretary of State's Meeting with Iraqi Deputy Prime Minister Tariq Aziz," November 29, 1984 (DNSA Doc. IG00228).

60. Cable, Department of State, "Staunching Iran's Imports of Western Arms and Urging Restraint on Iraq," December 14, 1983 (DNSA Doc. IG00152).

61. Cable, Department of State, "Proposal to Provide Arms to Iraq," June 14, 1984 (DNSA Doc. IG00207).

62. Bruce W. Jentleson, *With Friends like These: Reagan, Bush, and Saddam, 1982–1990* (New York: W. W. Norton, 1994), chap. 1.

63. Department of State, "Iran–Iraq War," 12–13; SNIE 34/36.2-86, "Is Iraq Losing the War?" 4; and Department of State, "Emergency Assistance for the Middle East," January 21, 1987, 2 (DNSA Doc. IG00401).

64. Jentleson, *With Friends like These*, 61.

65. Put another way, Iran may have actually been the rising power at certain points during the conflict, but determining which side was rising or declining was difficult in the midst of a war that was often a stalemate and that appeared to change course several times. Whether the United States was assisting a rising Iraq or resisting a rising Iran, however, its actions were consistent with the argument developed in chapter 1: when they are most concerned about the risk of access denial, leading states should accommodate an RRP that is weakening a potential hegemon in the region and oppose an RRP that is trying to become one.

66. Murphy to Michael Armacost, "Iraq: Pre-Crisis Planning Group Meeting," July 23, 1986 (DNSA Doc. IG00346). Notably, more than two years earlier, Reagan had signed a directive ordering the secretaries of state and defense, along with the director of the CIA, to "prepare a plan of action designed to avert an Iraqi collapse." See NSDD 139, "Measures to Improve U.S. Posture and Readiness to Respond to Developments in the Iran–Iraq War," April 5, 1984 (DNSA Doc. PR01528).

67. Memorandum from Don Fortier and Howard Teicher to Robert McFarlane, "U.S. Policy toward Iran," June 11, 1985; and Draft NSDD, "U.S. Policy toward Iran," June 11, 1985 (DNSA Doc. IG00254).

68. Colin Powell to Fred Iklé and Richard Armitage, "Note for Undersecretary of Defense (Policy) and Assistant Secretary of Defense (International Security Affairs)," June 19, 1985 (DNSA Doc. IG00258); Memorandum from Weinberger to McFarlane, "U.S. Policy toward Iran," July 16, 1985 (DNSA Doc. IG00266); and Shultz to McFarlane, "U.S. Policy toward Iran: Comment on Draft NSDD," June 29, 1985 (DNSA Doc. IG00261).

69. Frank Carlucci to Robert Pearson, "Response on Waite and Status of Iran–Iraq War," January 20, 1987 (DNSA Doc. IG00396).

70. George P. Shultz, *Turmoil and Triumph: My Years as Secretary of State* (New York: Charles Scribner's Sons, 1993), 237.

71. Morton Abramowitz to Armacost, "Iraq's Foreign Policy: Deeper into the Mainstream," March 3, 1988 (DDRS Doc. IG00519).

72. Brent Scowcroft Interview, *PBS Frontline: The Gulf War*, oral history, http://www.pbs.org/wgbh/pages/frontline/gulf/oral/scowcroft/1.html.

73. NSD 26, "U.S. Policy toward the Persian Gulf," October 2, 1989 (DNSA Doc. PR01741).

74. Department of State, "Background Paper: Guidelines for U.S.–Iraq Policy" January 20, 1989, quotes at 1 and 4 (DNSA Doc. IG00761).

75. Interview with William H. Webster, Ronald Reagan Oral History Project, Miller Center, University of Virginia, August 21, 2002, http://millercenter.org/president/reagan/oralhistory/william-webster, 50.

76. Memorandum from Jim Noble to R. Stratford, "Today's Meeting on Iraq Policy," January 3, 1990, 2 (DNSA Doc. IG01187).

77. Scowcroft interview.

78. Policy Planning Staff, "Thinking about a Policy for Iraq," January 12, 1990 (DNSA Doc. IG01194).

79. Overviews of the Gulf War and the diplomacy that preceded it include Janice Gross Stein, "Deterrence and Compellence in the Gulf, 1990–91: A Failed or Impossible Task?" *International Security* 17, no. 2 (Autumn 1992); Lawrence Freedman and Efraim Karsh, *The Gulf Conflict, 1990–1991: Diplomacy and War in the New World* (Princeton, NJ: Princeton University Press, 1993); Richard Herrmann, "Coercive Diplomacy and the Crisis over Kuwait, 1990–1991," in *The Limits of Coercive Diplomacy*, 2nd ed., ed. Alexander L. George and William E. Simons (Boulder, CO: Westview Press, 1994), 229–264; and H. W. Brands, "George Bush and the Gulf War of 1991," *Presidential Studies Quarterly* 34, no. 1 (March 2004).

80. See, for example, Scowcroft interview; George Bush and Brent Scowcroft, *A World Transformed* (New York: Alfred A. Knopf, 1998), 353, 394; and Bob Woodward, *The Commanders* (New York: Simon & Schuster, 1991), 300.

81. Dennis Ross, *Statecraft and How to Restore America's Standing in the World* (New York: Farrar, Straus & Giroux, 2007), 75–76.

82. Woodward, *Commanders*, 226. See also Bush and Scowcroft, *World Transformed*, 341.

83. Woodward, *Commanders*, 230.

84. Scowcroft interview.

85. Woodward, *Commanders*, 237, 248, 258; and Bush and Scowcroft, *World Transformed*, 322–323.

86. Bush and Scowcroft, *World Transformed*, 328.

87. Richard Haass Interview, George H. W. Bush Oral History Project, Miller Center, University of Virginia, May 27, 2004, 56, http://millercenter.org/oralhistory/interview/richard-haass.

88. James A. Baker III with Thomas M. DeFrank, *The Politics of Diplomacy: Revolution, War & Peace, 1989–1992* (New York: G. P. Putnam's Sons, 1995), 336.

89. See, for example, Bob Woodward, *Shadow: Five Presidents and the Legacy of Watergate* (New York: Simon & Schuster, 1999), 185; and Richard B. Cheney Interview, George H. W. Bush Oral History Project, Miller Center, University of Virginia, May 16–17, 2000, 71, http://millercenter.org/oralhistory/interview/richard-cheney.

90. Evan Braden Montgomery, "Counterfeit Diplomacy and Mobilization in Democracies," *Security Studies* 22, no. 1 (January 2013), 58–64.

91. Richard N. Haass, *War of Necessity, War of Choice: A Memoir of Two Iraq Wars* (New York: Simon & Schuster, 2009), quote at 132.

Conclusion

1. On the possibility of a conflict between the United States and China, see Graham Allison, "The Thucydides Trap: Are the United States and China Headed for War?" *The Atlantic*, September 24, 2015.

2. For a thoughtful assessment of how existing theories have tried to address the interactions between great powers and regional powers, as well as the limitations of these efforts, see Jack S. Levy, "Power Transition Theory and the Rise of China," in *China's Ascent: Power, Security, and the Future of International Politics*, ed. Robert S. Ross and Zhu Feng (Ithaca, NY: Cornell University Press, 2008), 20.

3. On this "status quo bias" in defensive realism, see Mearsheimer, *Tragedy of Great Power Politics*, 20; and Randall Schweller, "Neorealism's Status-Quo Bias: What Security Dilemma," *Security Studies* 5, no. 3 (Spring 1996).

4. In a similar vein, William Wohlforth has suggested that the United States could extend the unipolar moment by "promoting" friendly regional powers to help counter an emerging peer competitor that challenges its dominance of the international system. Wohlforth, "Stability of a Unipolar World," 30.

5. For discussions of various types of power, see Copeland, *Origins of Major War*; Mearsheimer, *Tragedy of Great Power Politics*; Zakaria, *From Wealth to Power*; and Ashley J. Tellis et al., *Measuring National Power in the Postindustrial Age* (Santa Monica, CA: RAND, 2000). On the complexities of assessing military power in particular, see Allan R. Millet, Williamson Murray, and Kenneth H. Watman, "The Effectiveness of Military Organizations," *International Security* 11, no. 1 (Summer 1986), 37–71; Stephen Biddle, *Military Power: Explaining Victory and Defeat in Modern Battle* (Princeton, NJ: Princeton University Press, 2004); and Risa A. Brooks and Elizabeth Stanley, eds., *Creating Military Power: The Sources of Military Effectiveness* (Redwood City, CA: Stanford University Press, 2007).

6. On the debate over American decline see, for example, Robert A. Pape, "Empire Falls," *The National Interest* 99 (January/February 2009); Eric S. Edelman, *Understanding America's Contested Primacy* (Washington, DC: Center for Strategic and Budgetary Assessments, 2010); Michael Beckley, "China's Century? Why America's Edge Will Endure," *International Security* 36, no. 3 (Winter 2011/12); Christopher Layne, "This Time It's Real: The End of Unipolarity and the *Pax Americana*," *International Studies Quarterly* 56, no. 1 (March 2012); and Stephen G. Brooks, G. John Ikenberry, and William C. Wohlforth, "Don't Come Home, America: The Case against Retrenchment," *International Security* 37, no. 3 (Winter 2012/13). On the characteristics and implications of unipolarity, see Wohlforth, "The Stability of a Unipolar World"; Brooks and Wohlforth, *World Out of Balance*; and Nuno P. Monteiro, *Theory of Unipolar Politics* (New York: Cambridge University Press, 2014).

7. Stephen P. Cohen, *India: Emerging Power* (Washington, DC: Brookings, 2001); Stephen P. Cohen and Sunil Dasgupta, *Arming without Aiming: India's Military Modernization* (Washington, DC: Brookings, 2010); and T. V. Paul, "India's Role in Asia: A Rising Regional Power," in *International Relations of Asia*, ed. David Shambaugh and Michael Yahuda (Lanham, MD: Roman & Littlefield, 2014), 173–196.

8. Ashley J. Tellis, *Unity in Difference: Overcoming the U.S.–India Divide* (Washington, DC: Carnegie Endowment for International Peace, 2015).

9. Narendra Modi and Barack Obama, "A Renewed U.S.–India Partnership for the 21st Century," *Washington Post*, September 30, 2014.

10. Bruce Riedel, "Pakistan and Terror: The Eye of the Storm," *Annals of the American Academy of Political and Social Science*, no. 618 (July 2008); and Bruce Riedel, *Deadly Embrace: Pakistan, America, and the Future of the Global Jihad* (Washington, DC: Brookings, 2011).

11. For overviews of China's rise, including its economic development and military modernization, see David M. Lampton, *The Three Faces of Chinese Power: Might, Money, and Minds* (Berkeley: University of California Press, 2008); and C. Fred Bergsten et al., *China's Rise: Challenges and Opportunities* (Washington, DC: Peterson Institute for International Economics/Center for Strategic and International Studies, 2009).

12. Avery Goldstein, "Power Transitions, Institutions, and China's Rise in East Asia," *Journal of Strategic Studies* 30, nos. 4–5 (August–October 2007), 642.

13. National Intelligence Council, *Global Trends 2025: A Transformed World* (Washington, DC: Government Printing Office, 2008), 29–30.

14. Mark Magnier, Lingling Wei, and Ian Talley, "Chinese Economic Growth is Slowest in Decades," *Wall Street Journal*, January 19, 2015; and "The Causes and Consequences of China's Market Crash," *Economist*, August 24, 2015.

15. James R. Holmes and Toshi Yoshihara, "China's Naval Ambitions in the Indian Ocean," *Journal of Strategic Studies* 31, no. 3 (June 2008); Staff Report, "China's Navy Extends its Combat Reach to the Indian Ocean," *U.S.–China Economic and Security Review Commission* (March 14, 2014); and Office of Naval Intelligence, *The PLA Navy: New Capabilities and Missions for the 21st Century* (Suitland, MD: Office of Naval Intelligence, 2015).

16. See, for example, David Tweed, "Modi Touring Indian Ocean to Keep China's Submarines at Bay," *Bloomberg*, March 9, 2015; Sanjeev Miglani, "From Remote Outpost, India Looks to Check China's Indian Ocean Thrust," *Reuters*, July 14, 2015; David Tweed and N. C. Bipindra, "Submarine Killers: India's $61 Billion Warning to China," *Bloomberg*, July 28, 2015; and Manu Pubby, "As Sightings of Chinese Submarines Become Frequent, Navy Steps up Guard in Indian Ocean Region," *Economic Times*, August 8, 2015.

17. Donald L. Berlin, "India in the Indian Ocean," *Naval War College Review* 59, no. 2 (Spring 2006), 60.

18. James R. Holmes and Toshi Yoshihara, "China and the United States in the Indian Ocean: An Emerging Strategic Triangle?" *Naval War College Review* 61, no. 3 (Summer 2008), 57. See also James R. Holmes and Toshi Yoshihara, "Strongman, Constable, or Free-Rider? India's 'Monroe Doctrine' and Indian Naval Strategy," *Comparative Strategy* 28, no. 4 (September 2009).

19. Andrew S. Erickson, Walter C. Ladwig III, and Justin D. Mikolay, "Diego Garcia and the United States' Emerging Indian Ocean Strategy," *Asian Security* 6, no. 3 (September 2010), 218; and James Holmes and Toshi Yoshihara, "US Navy's Indian Ocean Folly?" *Diplomat*, January 4, 2011. On the growing economic and strategic importance of the Indian Ocean region, see Robert Kaplan, "Center Stage for the 21st Century: Power Plays in the Indian Ocean," *Foreign Affairs* 88, no. 2 (March/April 2009); and Michael J. Green and Andrew Shearer, "Defining U.S. Indian Ocean Strategy," *The Washington Quarterly* 35, no. 2 (Spring 2012).

20. U.S. Energy Information Agency, "Iran," updated June 19, 2015, http://www.eia.gov/beta/international/analysis_includes/countries_long/Iran/iran.pdf.

21. Rick Gladstone, "I.M.F. Study Details Perils of Iranian Economy," *New York Times*, February 12, 2014; and Department of Defense, *Unclassified Report on Military Power of Iran* (Washington, DC: Department of Defense, April 2010), 7.

22. Kambiz Foroohar and Ladene Nasseri, "Iran Wields Power from Syria to Gulf as Rise Alarms Sunni Rivals," *Bloomberg*, February 18, 2015; Samia Nakhoul, "Iran Expands Regional 'Empire' Ahead of Nuclear Deal," *Reuters*, March 23, 2015; "The Shia Crescendo," *Economist*, March 28, 2015; and Loveday Morris and Hugh Naylor, "Arab States Fear Nuclear Deal Will Give Iran a Bigger Regional Role," *Washington Post*, July 14, 2015.

23. Currently, Iran's ballistic missiles represent only a modest danger because they are not accurate enough to reliably strike point targets such as economic infrastructure and military bases, although their quality is improving. See Anthony H. Cordesman and Alexander Wilner, *The Gulf Military Balance in 2012* (Washington, DC: Center for Strategic and International Studies, 2012), 132; Department of Defense, *Annual Report on Military Power of Iran* (Washington, DC: Department of Defense, April 2012), 4; and Joshua R. Itzkowitz Shifrinson and Miranda Priebe, "A Crude Threat: The Limits of an Iranian Missile Campaign against Saudi Arabian Oil," *International Security* 36, no. 1 (Summer 2011). Iranian capabilities to close the Strait include land-based coastal defense cruise missile batteries, fast-attack craft armed with antiship missiles, a large inventory of sea mines that can be delivered by military or civilian vessels, and submarines. See Caitlin Talmadge, "Closing Time: Assessing the Iranian Threat to the Strait of Hormuz," *International Security* 33, no. 1 (Summer 2008); and Office of Naval Intelligence, *Iran's Naval Forces: From Guerilla Warfare to a Modern Naval Strategy* (Suitland, MD: Office of Naval Intelligence, 2009). The quotation is from U.S. Energy Information Agency, "World Oil Transit

Chokepoints," updated November 10, 2014, http://www.eia.gov/beta/international/analysis
_includes/special_topics/World_Oil_Transit_Chokepoints/wotc.pdf.

24. See, for example, James M. Lindsay and Ray Takeyh, "After Iran Gets the Bomb: Containment and Its Complications," *Foreign Affairs* 89, no. 2 (March/April 2010); and Eric S. Edelman, Andrew F. Krepinevich, and Evan Braden Montgomery, "The Dangers of a Nuclear Iran: The Limits of Containment," *Foreign Affairs* 90, no. 1 (January/February 2011).

Index

Note: Italic page numbers refer to figures and tables.